HELEN ANDELIN AND THE FASCINATING WOMANHOOD MOVEMENT

JULIE DEBRA NEUFFER

Helen Andelin
and the
Fascinating Womanhood Movement

THE UNIVERSITY OF UTAH PRESS
SALT LAKE CITY

The Defiance House Man colophon is a registered trademark of the
University of Utah Press. It is based on a four-foot-tall Ancient Puebloan
pictograph (late PIII) near Glen Canyon, Utah.

Library of Congress Cataloging-in-Publication Data

Neuffer, Julie Debra.
Helen Andelin and the fascinating womanhood movement/Julie Debra Neuffer.
    pages   cm
Includes bibliographical references and index.
ISBN 978-1-60781-327-9 (paperback)—ISBN 978-1-60781-328-6 (ebook)
1. Andelin, Helen B.
2. Andelin, Helen B. Fascinating womanhood.
3. Anti-feminism—United States—History—20th century.
4. Housewives—United States—Social conditions—20th century.
5. Homemakers—United States—Social conditions—20th century.
6. Sex role—United States—History—20th century.
7. Women—United States—Social conditions—20th century.
I. Title.
HQ1426.N475 2014
305.40973090'04—dc23
                    2014007967

Cover photograph: Helen Andelin and daughter Dixie. Author's Collection.

All photographs are from the author's collection, unless otherwise noted.

Printed and bound in the United States of America.

Contents

Photographs follow page 84

Preface

$\mathcal{I}$ first heard about Helen Andelin and her book, *Fascinating Womanhood*, when I was a teenager. In 1969 my mother, Alice Neuffer, was invited by a friend to attend a Fascinating Womanhood (FW) class at the local YMCA. She was so taken with Andelin's teachings that she decided to become an FW teacher herself. Mom proved to be a popular teacher and soon became an area director. Helen came to Phoenix in 1975 to promote her book. This was the first time I had ever seen her. My mother took me to the airport to get her autograph. Andelin, charismatic and pretty, made a huge impression on me and I have described this encounter on the first page of this book. Eventually, my mother had a falling out with Andelin over the use of her teaching materials and left the organization. But she was a true believer in FW and continued to live by its principles.

After I turned eighteen and left home, I didn't think about FW anymore. I graduated with a degree in history from Pacific Lutheran University in 1991. I went on to get a master's degree in religious studies from Gonzaga University, and a few years later I entered the PhD program at Washington State University. I planned to study American women's religious history, but my director, a women's historian, had little interest in religion. I began casting about for a suitable topic that she would support. At the time, I was working as a teaching assistant for Dr. LeRoy Ashby. Ashby, a twentieth-century American historian, taught a wonderful class in American pop culture. One day he held up a book, a marriage manual that he said was so popular during the 1960s and '70s that it had sold over three million copies. The book was *Fascinating Womanhood*. I was stunned. I had thought that FW was a local phenomenon, limited to the Mormon community in Arizona where I grew up and to California, where Andelin lived. The fact that I was hearing about it in a college classroom was both amazing and exciting. I knew I had found my subject.

I approached Dr. Ashby after class and excitedly told him that I had been *raised* as a Fascinating woman. He was a little taken aback by this confession, but listened intently as I explained why I thought FW would be perfect for me to study. I was familiar with the philosophy, I understood the women who adopted it, and I didn't think anyone had done any scholarship on it. I also believed that I could get Andelin, who was still living, to talk to me. Dr. Ashby agreed to direct my dissertation.

It was with great reluctance that Helen agreed to let me interview her. When I first called, she remembered my mother and wanted to know if I was a "friend" or an "enemy" of FW. I told her that I was neither. I was a historian and assured her I would tell her story without judgment. She said she would only agree to participate in the project if she could censor anything she didn't like. I explained that I couldn't do that. "Forget it," she said, and hung up the phone. A week later, Helen called back and said that she wanted to meet me in person. If she liked me, she said, she might allow a "very brief" interview, but nothing more. I agreed.

I flew to Missouri in 2001. Helen, now in her eighties, was no longer the fashionable beauty that I remembered. Instead she was a tiny, shrunken woman with hunched shoulders, wearing a wig that was much too large for her. She graciously invited me to stay with her at her cottage on the family farm. In the beginning, Helen was standoffish and unfriendly. She would not allow me to look at any of her papers or photographs unless she held them herself. I was not allowed to examine the back of any of her documents. Eventually, however, she got tired of holding the documents while I read them and handed me a folder of papers to look through on my own. When I set it down to open my briefcase, she immediately took it away and put it in the other room. "You had your chance," she said. Our first interview started out rocky. Helen had carefully rehearsed what she wanted to say and recited it for the tape recorder without stopping. When I interrupted her to ask a question, she became irritated and abruptly ended the interview. She was fearful that I was trying to "skew" the information and make her look bad. Questions, she said, were not allowed. Things went like that for a couple of days. On the evening of the third unproductive day,

Helen asked me if I wanted to watch a movie with her. She made a big bowl of popcorn and suggested we get into our pajamas. We did and sat on the couch together watching a movie that I can no longer recall. That was how we became friends. The next day Helen was cheerful. She took me into her tidy office and with a sweep of her arm she said, "This is yours, do what you want with it." Helen's son Paul, a local physician, loaned me his copy machine and I copied documents from Helen's files without stopping until late in the evening. For the next four days, I interviewed Helen and I copied documents.

I visited Helen again in 2003 and a last time in 2005. Each time she was open and honest and gave me full access to her records. I was often surprised at Helen's frank, personal revelations, particularly her admission that she did not believe in some of the basic tenets of the Mormon Church. Throughout her life, Helen had dreams that she believed were visions from God. She talked to me in great detail about them. She told me personal things about Aubrey, his business dealings, and their marriage that she had not told even her children. She asked me to include them in my account so that her family would know the truth.

Many times Helen asked to talk off the record. I respected her wishes. She was a very lonely woman; a recluse. Aubrey was gone and she didn't have any friends. She said that her children were too busy and she felt she could not confide in them for fear that they would think less of her. We spent a lot of time talking about things that had nothing to do with Fascinating Womanhood. At times, Helen was unkind. She often snapped at me, snatched things out of my hands, made demands, refused to cooperate unless she had her way, or simply walked into the other room and shut the door while I was talking to her. Once she called me at home in the middle of the night, livid, and threated to sue me for the "theft" of her materials. She was referring to the recordings of her voice. Later, she called to apologize.

Andelin never admitted to copying *The Secrets of Fascinating Woman-hood* booklets. In fact, I would discover this only after she died, when I saw the booklets for myself. Verna Johnson's daughter, Merrilly, who lives in California, had her mother's original booklets and kindly let me read them. This discovery made me sad. Andelin believed that because God had led her to the booklets they belonged to her, and so she had the right to do with them as she wished. Because Verna did not, in Helen's opinion, recognize the *religious value* of the booklets, she felt justified in taking possession of them, adding some of her own ideas, and then copyrighting the finished product in her name. Helen also believed that the teaching materials and ideas generated by FW teachers belonged to her. They were all part of God's work, she reasoned, and so she "protected" them by also copyrighting them in her name. Helen's belief in the rightness of her cause, and therefore the rightness of any behavior that furthered that cause, resulted in a string of ruined relationships. She broke with her oldest friend, Verna; with her cousin, Marlene Startup; with my mother, Alice Neuffer; with her closest confidant and political ally, Jaquie Davison; and with members of her church and leaders of the LDS Relief Society. Andelin eliminated any chance of finding common ground with her critics by attacking them personally, often cruelly. She avoided legitimate debate by promising God's punishment to those who disagreed with her.

For some reason, Helen trusted me with her story, and I am honored that she did. It was difficult, but I consider it a privilege to have worked with her. I don't subscribe to her philosophies but I respect her clarity and conviction. I also respect the voices of those women who followed Andelin. Their opinions are unpopular and many of their claims sound far-fetched and silly. But after reading hundreds of heartfelt letters I understand the truth of their experience and I think that their stories should be heard. Andelin and her followers are a historical treasure. I am convinced that in order to fully understand the feminist movement, one must also understand the fascinating womanhood movement that coincided with it.

A final note: After reading the description of my book in the University of Utah Press catalog, Helen's daughter Dixie wrote to me. She said that my claim that Helen was unhappy in her marriage was inaccurate. Her parents had a long, romantic relationship and were devoted to one another, she said. Aubrey, although often grouchy, she admitted, was a dedicated father and regularly told his children that he loved them. She said that her father was much more sensitive than her mother, and that my portrayal of him was one sided. This may be true. Aubrey died two years before I interviewed Helen and my depiction of him is based on her testimony alone. I met Aubrey once when I was fourteen or fifteen, when he and Helen visited our home. They were traveling to promote FW and my mother invited them to dinner. Helen was the star of the evening and Aubrey remained quietly in the background. I never got to know him.

Dixie, who owns a set of the original *Secrets of Fascinating Womanhood* booklets, disagrees with my claim that her mother copied them. She maintains that *Fascinating Womanhood* is Helen's original work and that her mother used only "a word, or a few sentences here and there," as inspiration.

INTRODUCTION

*I*n 1961 Helen Andelin, a disillusioned housewife and mother of eight children, languished in a lackluster, twenty-year marriage. A religious woman who also had high hopes for a romantic relationship with her husband, Andelin spent long periods fasting and praying, and seeking answers about the meaning of her life and ways to improve her marriage. That year a close friend introduced Andelin to a set of women's advice booklets, *The Secrets of Fascinating Womanhood*, written in the 1920s. While studying the manuals that she would later call "the hidden treasure," she had an epiphany that changed not only her life, but also the lives of millions of American women. Tailoring the information from the booklets to suit her situation at home, and closely following the instructions she found in them, Andelin experienced nothing short of a "miraculous" change in her marriage. Convinced that she could help others, she began leading small discussion groups for women at her church. Word of the classes spread, and Andelin, like a modern-day religious leader, eventually commissioned her most devoted followers to carry her vital "mission of charity" to thousands of eager listeners. At the urging of her fast-growing band of followers, she wrote and self-published *Fascinating Womanhood* in 1963. The book sold over three million copies and launched a nationwide organization of Fascinating Womanhood classes and seminars led by thousands of volunteer teachers.

At precisely the same time that Betty Friedan successfully initiated the rise of the second wave of American feminism with her landmark book *The Feminine Mystique*, Andelin's femininity movement also became the subject of intense popular debate. A charismatic and sought-after celebrity, Andelin appeared on radio and television, and in sold-out speaking engagements across the country, touting a brand of nostalgic political conservatism that large sections of the population found appealing. She also revived a genre of popular women's advice writing that not only supported the rising careers of such diverse women as Marabel Morgan, Phyllis Schlafly, and Roseanne Barr, but also uniquely contributed to the images of the family that have become firmly embedded in American culture.

So significant was the femininity women's movement that, in June of 1975, the *New York Times Magazine* featured a lengthy article on the nationwide FW phenomenon. Andelin's philosophy, no longer the tiny fringe movement that some observers had hoped it would remain, caught the attention of serious journalists across the country. Even the renowned sex researchers William Masters and Virginia Johnson wrote a feature article for *Redbook Magazine* in 1976 warning readers against *Fascinating Womanhood* and other advice books "that teach women to pretend." At a time when the renewed call for women's rights was at the forefront in the news, FW represented a significant aspect of a growing political and social backlash to the era's turbulence, which many feared was eroding traditional institutions and values. Andelin, having become a bestselling author and founder of the burgeoning FW organization, unquestionably agreed that marriage and the family were endangered as divorce rates spiraled and feminists questioned deeply rooted gender roles. To many of those feminists, Andelin's "Domestic Goddess" ideal symbolized some of the more retrograde, even ridiculous aspects of the backlash. Unable or unwilling to take her argument seriously, many feminists assumed, or at least hoped, that she and the numerous followers of her apparent fad would simply fade away.

But the views and goals of both Andelin and her FW movement were both more complex and more distinct than her critics conceded. Moreover, they endured. In fact, Andelin built a substantial and lasting following simply by addressing the immediate, felt needs of many women at a crucial moment in history when other reform movements did not. While Andelin regarded her work primarily as a religious calling, in time she and the women who followed her became a formidable political force with which feminist leaders eventually had to reckon. While Andelin's most enduring legacies have remained in the social realm, the strength of her movement derived from the fact that FW adopted the urgency and form of a charismatic religious revival. Only the efforts to routinize and eventually capitalize on Andelin's magnetic energy, ironically by those closest to her, would slow down the movement's growth. In 1977, exhausted by her public battles with both feminists and leaders of her religious community alike, Andelin left public life. Her movement, however, continued to flourish.

Andelin, only one voice in what by the 1980s had become a highly organized, well-funded, and motivated conservative movement, would continue to make a significant difference in the ways that Americans thought about the roles of men and women in marriage and politics, and in their understanding of family values as they negotiated the turbulent currents of social uncertainty. Andelin's story and the continued popular support for her philosophy illuminated in vital ways the modern culture wars that laid the groundwork for the dramatic upsurge in conservative political and religious responses to war, same-sex marriage, and anti-intellectualism issues that were dividing Americans by the turn of the twenty-first century.

This study of the femininity women's movement is part of a growing body of scholarship that seeks to expand the definition of women's historical involvement in politics by squarely facing the religious motivations and tactics underlying conservative politics. An understanding of Andelin's wide appeal as both a religious and political leader can augment the fast-expanding discussion about women's strategies to cope with—and shape—political and social change. The primary sources for this study are over thirty hours of recorded personal interviews conducted in 2001, 2003, and 2005 with Helen Andelin, several of her children, and former FW teachers. The project also draws on hundreds of private letters to Andelin from FW followers, as well as support materials such as teaching manuals, newsletters, and nearly one thousand completed Teacher Application Forms submitted to the Fascinating Womanhood organization. In 2002, after granting the author generous and unprecedented access to her personal files, letters, newspaper clippings, scrapbooks, photos, and family records, Andelin placed the bulk of her personal papers in the Special Collections archive of the Marriott Library at the University of Utah.

Chapter 1 traces Andelin's childhood, her formative young adult years, and her tumultuous twenty-year marriage, when her religious sensibilities and ideas about marriage were formed. Chapter 2 discusses Andelin's model of the Ideal Woman, Angela Human. Angela Human was a character that Andelin took from *The Secrets of Fascinating Womanhood* booklets and fashioned into the backbone of her message. This chapter also covers the daunting task of writing her book. Chapter 3, along with chapter 2, is an analysis of the main teachings of Fascinating Womanhood. Chapter 4 examines the fascinating womanhood movement at its height, when it became not only a national movement but an international one. It also provides in-depth demographic information, gleaned from Andelin's personal files, about the women who followed her. Chapter 5 reviews the challenges that Andelin faced in her efforts to convert both the leaders of the feminist movement and the Mormon Church to her message. The final chapter covers the direction the movement took after Andelin left public life. It broadly sketches the ways in which the fascinating womanhood movement has both evolved and remained relevant to large numbers of women, not just nationally, but on a global scale.

It is my hope that this study will provide a scholarly and evenhanded look at the philosophy and motivations of a crucial but often overlooked cross-section of individuals who have had a significant impact on the development of the modern-day woman. By locating Helen Andelin, and the movement she founded, within the larger historical context of women's reform efforts, I hope to expand the discussion of how women have participated historically in public reform and attempted to make sense of a disordered world.

One

BEGINNINGS

$\mathcal{J}$t was a mild day in February 1975. The Western Airlines jet taxied to a stop on the tarmac in Phoenix as the ground crew hurried to roll the stairs up to the passenger door. Helen Andelin, a middle-aged housewife from Santa Barbara, California, was fast on her way to becoming a national celebrity. A large group of loyal supporters waited anxiously for her to appear at the doorway. Except for a reporter from the *Phoenix Gazette,* the crowd was female. Mothers, wives, single women, young girls, and senior citizens brought friends, daughters, and neighbors to greet Andelin, and, they hoped, get autographs for their copies of her best-selling book, *Fascinating Woman-hood* (1963). A couple of other passengers exited before Andelin stepped out. When she did, everyone stood quietly for a moment, just looking. She was a handsome woman, stately, charismatic, and decidedly girlish. Standing at the top of the stairs, she looked like California's version of Jackie Kennedy. As she made her way forward, the breeze stirred her skirt. It was stylish, swingy, and pink, with large white polka dots. Like a movie star, she was tan and had pretty legs. Her dark, shoulder-length hair was teased on top and neatly curled into a flip.[1] Andelin smiled and waved brightly. As if a spell had broken, her admirers surged forward in anticipation, blocking the end of the stairway to get closer. It was both difficult to imagine and thrilling to believe that this glamorous woman was the mother of eight children. Declaring herself to be inspired by God and determined to show discouraged housewives how to save their marriages, this foe of liberated women everywhere looked more like the First Lady than a rising cult-heroine. Yet she had already sold a half-million copies of her best-selling book out of her kitchen. What the crowd at the airport that day probably did not realize was that the dynamic woman in the pink dress had initiated one of the most resilient and influential social movements in modern American history. From the typewriter at a table in her bedroom, Andelin, a regular wife and mother with an average education, an average income, and an average marriage, helped launch the Fascinating Womanhood movement.

Several factors rested at the core of how Andelin understood her life, her religion, her family, and her marriage—and how she eventually developed what would become the Fascinating Womanhood message. The first was a unique childhood shaped by both the financial devastation of the Great Depression and a spartan upbringing in the harsh, isolated conditions of the desert Southwest. Second, Andelin was raised in the heart of Mormon Latter-day Saint (LDS) culture. Reared by devoutly religious parents, she accepted a worldview that was both optimistic in its assumption of the basic goodness of all human beings, and heavily laden with endless striving toward personal salvation. Finally, because her family had moved often when she was a child, she yearned for stability. Andelin developed a heightened sense of nostalgia that eventually became part of her appeal to other women. She was smart, self-sacrificing, and dignified. She was also harshly judgmental. During her climb to the position of movement leader, Andelin developed strong survival skills. Outwardly, she was a confident woman; inwardly, she suffered painful insecurity. Driven by an acute sense of moral obligation and a crushing fear of failure, Andelin had a formidable will to succeed that often troubled not just herself, but those around her. Importantly, Andelin lived by the logic of immediacy. In this way, she identified with evangelicals, Christian fundamentalists, doomsayers, and other apocalyptic religious believers.

Andelin's memoirs often depicted loving parents, a close-knit family, and, at times, an idyllic childhood. Yet her life was also fraught with disappointment, uncertainty, and self-doubt. As a young girl, she relied heavily on classic Mormon understandings of family, individual purpose, and religious belief. As an adult she revealed an exceptional ability to reinterpret these beliefs by using both her own experiences and those of other women. She drew on several resources to help her make sense of her rapidly changing world and put them into a usable format that resonated with women worldwide. The majority of the content of Andelin's *Fascinating Womanhood* came from a set of advice booklets called *The Secrets of Fascinating Womanhood, or The Art of Attracting Men: A Practical Course of Lessons in the Underlying Principles by Which Women Attract Men—Leading to the Proposal and Culminating in Marriage,* published in 1922. Andelin copied the booklets at length and used the same title for her own work. In addition to the information from the booklets, she incorporated biblical writings, personal revelation, testimonials from other women, advice from her husband, and trial and error to formulate a philosophy that would make her famous.

On May 22, 1920, Helen Lucille Berry was born in the desert farming community of Mesa, Arizona. Her mother would have seven children, but Helen, the sixth in line, would be the only one born in a hospital. Helen's childhood was difficult. Her parents barely scraped by financially, and they moved many times; in later interviews, Helen said she often felt forgotten. In her memoirs, however, she described her childhood as "almost perfect."[2] Her parents, Anna May Whiting and Herbert Berry, like their parents before them, were pious Latter-day Saints who lived and breathed Mormonism. Anna May's ancestors were pioneers who, at the request of the Mormon leader Brigham Young, had helped settle the most uninhabitable regions of Arizona in the mid- to late-nineteenth century. Herbert's folks had come west from Kentucky and Tennessee to settle in the Utah Valley in the 1840s. Like everyone else in her small community, Helen went to church with a large, extended family. In addition to attending the regular services, she attended Sunday school, the children's group, christenings, baptisms, weddings, and funerals—all activities that recounted and reinforced the ethos of Joseph Smith, Brigham Young, and the men and women who followed them into Mormonism.

Helen's father served in leadership positions in a lay priesthood, and her mother managed equally demanding responsibilities in the women's auxiliary. On holidays, at special gatherings, and at the family dinner table, Helen took part in the ritual recounting of the stories of the persecutions and hardships of the first Mormon pioneers. She knew by heart the names of her dutiful ancestors who had become martyrs for the church either by giving their lives or by enduring incredible sacrifices to establish Mormon colonies in the western part of the country. It was these people who, when she was a child, Helen wanted to emulate—strong women who could go it alone if they had to, and independent men who could make something for their families out of the limited resources of the desert.

Helen's family lived in a gray stone house in downtown Mesa. Herbert Berry, who got his start as a sheep farmer, eventually fulfilled his lifelong dream by returning to college and becoming a dentist. In 1912 Herbert moved to Chicago to attend dental school. Anna May stayed with the children in Arizona. She studied for and passed the teacher's examination then took a job teaching grades 1 through 8 in the little town of Alpine, where she lived with her children in a small log house. Helen's mother milked a cow, brought in wood, and hauled water from a spring about a hundred yards from her house. Each morning she carried the youngest child to the home of a relative and took the three older children to school with her. Two years later Herbert graduated from dental school, returned to Arizona, and opened a dental practice. When a successful dentist several towns away offered him a partnership, Berry moved the young family to Prescott.

The country was in the throes of World War I, and the deadly flu epidemic. The flu hit Prescott particularly hard, and many people the family knew died. Schools and businesses closed, and Herbert eventually shut down his own business to stay home and help his wife care for their sick children. They recalled watching from the front window of their home for the hearse that often came by to pick up the bodies of the flu's victims. With growing panic they stood helplessly by as their daughter, Norma, already suffering from complications of the measles, became dangerously ill. The doctor recommended they take her to the warmer climate of southern Arizona, and the family moved again. In Mesa, a predominately Mormon town, Berry formed a partnership with another dentist in 1919; the following year, Helen was born.

Helen described how her parents followed the traditional pattern of male and female roles, recalling, "My father made the living while my mother stayed home, cooked delicious meals, managed the household, trained the children to be obedient, and taught us values." The family lived on a large lot in a nice part of town, where Anna May grew berries, tended fruit trees, kept chickens and a cow, and cultivated a large vegetable garden. "There was no doubt about my parents' respective roles in the family," recalled Helen. Although Helen's fondest memories of childhood included her mother's staying at home, the truth was that, for most of her married life, Anna May worked for wages, sold garden vegetables, assisted her husband in his dental practice, and brought in extra income. It was Anna May who "took charge of the family and was the one [they] looked to for a yes or no." This was indicative of Anna May's strength and unquestioned leadership within the domestic sphere—a traditional pioneer role that required great independence and physical skills. Later, Andelin up-ended this ideal of womanhood to include submission and femininity, traits that diminished the autonomy and physical capabilities of her mother, whose abilities she would later call masculine. She also included a romantic component she believed all marriages should possess—something that was not evident in her parents' marriage.

When Helen turned eight, she was old enough to be baptized in the newly built Mesa temple. Helen recalled, "The Spirit of the Lord was strong that day." She would never forget the "peaceful, holy feeling" she experienced just after her father baptized her.[3] "From then on during my youth," she said, "I could detect when an intense and powerful spirit" was present.

The Berrys purchased a home in Phoenix and, once again, Herbert set about building a new dental practice from the ground up. As the business prospered, Berry not only bought his family a new car but began buying old houses in the city and converting them into apartments. He even built an attractive, Spanish-style fourplex in the backyard of their large home. The family moved into one of the new apartments and converted the rambling old house into apartments as well. Before long, rents from the fourplex, the converted house, and other apartment buildings were adding considerably to the family's income. The Berrys enjoyed a period of financial stability and happiness. In 1935 Helen entered Phoenix Union High as a freshman. Life seemed perfect to Helen. Unfortunately for the Berrys and millions of other Americans, the stock market crashed in 1929—a calamity that ushered in the greatest financial crisis the country had ever experienced. While other parts of the nation felt the effects of the economic disaster immediately, it took several years for the Great Depression to catch up with Herbert and Anna May in Arizona. By the early 1930s, however, Berry realized he was in serious trouble. Overextended on real estate loans and unable to keep the rental units occupied, the family desperately tried to hang on until the storm passed. Although the steady success of his dental practice continued, Herbert eventually fell behind on his real estate payments. Not only were the apartments difficult to keep occupied, but the rents had dropped by more than 50 percent. Soon the family was without a car again and had to walk or take the streetcar. Forgoing all luxuries the family ate vegetables out of their garden, and Anna May bought damaged clothes at fire sales, which she washed, cut up, and sewed into swimsuits and quilts for her children. One day the company that owned the Berrys' piano came to the house to repossess it. Finally the bank foreclosed on their home.

Broke and homeless the Berrys moved to Holbrook, in northern Arizona, to live with relatives. Holbrook was a barren and dusty place. Herbert's newest office, which eventually became the family's living quarters, was in an old warehouse near the railroad station in a rundown section of town. Berry converted the front part of the warehouse into a dental office, and the family lived in the back. The situation was bleak; the family had hit rock bottom. Nevertheless, Helen's parents eventually worked their way out of financial ruin. In 1937 Herbert and Anna May built the first really nice motel in Holbrook. At the time, motels were just beginning to become part of the American landscape, and it was up to Helen to help get theirs open for business. At this time she became very serious about living the way that God wanted her to. Helen determined that in order to become a better person she would be willingly obedient and do everything her parents asked of her without her former habit of grumbling. Her first assignment was to make curtains for each of the motel rooms. Anna May bought several bolts of drapery material, sketched a design, and left Helen to figure it out. Helen accepted the job without complaint and finished the curtains. Anna May was pleased with her work, and soon the motel looked clean and cozy enough to open for business.

When guests began to arrive, it was Helen's job to work the front desk, renting out rooms to those who came in after the dinner hour. She wore a cowboy hat to fit with the Western atmosphere. Evenings at the motel were her favorite time. "The dust never blows past sundown," she wrote, and "the desert is calm and beautiful." Helen remembered this year of her life as difficult and demanding but important to her spiritual development. The income from the motel, although steady, was modest; there were few luxuries. The Berry family led an austere life—with plain food and simple pleasures. Helen worked without complaint. She put in long hours at the motel and described this point in her life as a time of spiritual searching. "I wanted to know what God expected of me and what I must expect of myself," she wrote. She believed that righteous living would aid her in her search. In addition to keeping her promise to herself to be obedient, she not only attended church as she always had, but read from a variety of religious works by LDS authors. She also read Mahatma Gandhi's biography, *Great Soul*, and books by American ministers such as Lloyd C. Douglas and Harry Emerson Fosdick. "Then, two things happened," she recalled. "The first was that the Spirit of the Lord came into my life as never before. I knew then what kind of a life I wanted to live."[4] The second was a visit from her great-uncle, Joel Roundy, from Hurricane, Utah.

In 1937, near the end of the summer, Roundy unexpectedly dropped in. Because he lived so far away, Helen had never seen him before. He took notice of Helen and announced that, with her mother's permission, he would like to give her a blessing.[5] Helen sat in a chair, and Roundy put his hands on her head and prayed aloud. She recalled that the blessing was unexceptional. However, at the end Roundy added, "You shall become a great counselor and advisor among your associates." Although living in the middle of the desert and working at the motel seemed unlikely to qualify her to counsel anyone, Helen took her great-uncle's words to heart. She believed it was her duty to find out what her mission was. In the fall the eighteen-year-old Helen was ready to leave Holbrook and attend college. She enrolled at Brigham Young University (BYU), where she shared an apartment with five other girls. Coming from the country, Helen was intimidated by the sophisticated city girls. College proved to be disappointing, and she became homesick. She described her year at BYU as lonely, boring, and bleak. It turned out that her social life was not the whirlwind of dances and dinner dates she had anticipated. Ill at ease with her roommates, she withdrew into more solitary activities, such as hiking in nearby Provo Canyon, studying in the library, and working on projects in the college sewing room. Helen's feelings of inferiority around her roommates increased, and she spent most of her time avoiding them. One day a young man she knew asked her to attend a Valentine's ball with him at one of the church meetinghouses in Provo. It was there that Helen met her future husband, Aubrey Andelin.

Aubrey was a handsome young man, and the couple were immediately attracted to each other. However, they didn't date until the following year, when Helen transferred to the University of Utah in Salt Lake City, where Aubrey was attending school. Their time together was brief, however. When spring came, the twenty-two-year-old Aubrey was called on a two-year LDS mission to the southern states. He reluctantly left school to return home to prepare, and Helen went back to Holbrook to work at the motel. They wrote letters but saw one another only twice more before Aubrey's mission. At their final meeting, he presented Helen with a ring but never proposed. Helen wore the ring proudly anyway, believing they would marry when he returned. Helen's accounts of her courtship with Aubrey portrayed him as both tentative and possessive. At one point he gave her his high school class ring, but after a short time he took it back because, she later said, he felt she was not committed to him. Helen said he never directly told her he loved her. Instead, he dropped hints or set up scenarios. Uncertain about her feelings for him, Aubrey even asked Helen's cousin to arrange a date with "a gorgeous blond" and then leak the information to make Helen jealous. Unseasoned and insecure, Aubrey proposed marriage only after he was safely in another part of the country; to Helen's great disappointment, he did this by mail. Sexually inexperienced, the couple prepared for marriage in much the same way their own parents had: they wrote to each other. Shortly after Aubrey left, the bishop from Helen's ward asked that she, too, serve on a proselytizing mission. In October 1940 Helen accepted an assignment to preach Mormonism for twenty months in Tennessee and North Carolina.

Although her mission was only moderately successful in converting non-members to the church, it proved to be an important stage in Helen's spiritual and social development. Disappointed by her inability to convince people to join the church, Helen immersed herself in the basic tenets of the Gospel. She adopted an ascetic lifestyle and also overcame her stubborn fear of public speaking—a skill later essential to her ability to lead other women. For Helen, inhibited and somewhat introverted, approaching complete strangers was excruciatingly difficult. On more than one occasion, she had the door slammed in her face. Helen had mixed feelings about her time spent as a missionary, recalling, "I gained a wonderful knowledge of the Gospel and a testimony based on logic and reasoning" but "lacking in spiritual conviction." At the time, however, she reasoned that a fervent testimony of the Gospel didn't matter that much. The important thing, she believed, was to keep the Commandments and live a good life.[6] One of the most significant things that happened to Helen during her mission was meeting Verna Johnson. Helen and Verna served as mission companions, living and preaching door-to-door together in a part of the country that was unfamiliar to them. They developed such a close friendship that, twenty years later, Helen would turn to Verna for support when she became distressed about her failing marriage. It was also Verna who would introduce her to *The Secrets of Fascinating Womanhood* booklets.

Anxious and lonely, Aubrey wrote to Helen every day. The couple planned to marry as soon as they both returned home. Then, in December 1941, a year into Helen's mission, the Japanese bombed Pearl Harbor. Terrified by what she and many other Americans believed to be a Japanese plan to take over the United States, Helen was equally worried that the twenty-three-year-old Aubrey would be called into military service and sent to war before they could marry. Aubrey was even more frightened by this possibility, and he got busy investigating how he could keep himself in the States. At the time, LDS missionaries were exempt from military service for the duration of their proselytizing assignment. Once home, however, Aubrey was eligible for the draft. To avoid it he tried to join the FBI and even sat for the exam while still on his mission. Unfortunately, he flunked the vision test. Hoping against reason that a speedy marriage would keep him from being called up, Aubrey decided to marry Helen immediately after his mission. In 1942, instead of going to his parents' home in Idaho to check in with the draft board, he took a train directly to Salt Lake City. Aubrey and Helen married two days later in the LDS temple; two days after that, the couple boarded a Greyhound bus and left for their future in Los Angeles.

Because his immediate goal was to avoid the draft and he had heard that defense factory work would delay his eligibility for military service, Aubrey looked for a job in one of the many busy defense factories operating in Southern California. He found assembly-line work within a week at a Western Gear factory, where he made parts for airplanes. Knowing that the job would not keep him out of the military forever, Aubrey searched for a longer-range plan. After learning that enrollment in medical school would keep him safely in civilian life, Aubrey decided to become a dentist. His acceptance into the program, however, was contingent on his first passing a number of science courses. Aubrey, a business major, had never taken science courses. Until he passed the classes and was officially accepted into the dental school, he remained eligible for military duty. He kept his day job, signed up for night classes, and hoped for the best. Eventually, the draft board in Idaho Falls caught up with Aubrey in California and ordered him to report immediately. The nearest draft board was in Wilmington. When he arrived as instructed, Aubrey was told he was in the wrong place and had to go to San Pedro the following Saturday. The delay, wrote Helen, turned out to be one of the advantages that turned events their way, as it gave them time to come up with a strategy. When Saturday morning arrived, Helen boarded a streetcar for San Pedro and bravely faced the draft board alone. After announcing that her husband had not come because he was working that day and could not get his schedule changed, she pleaded with the board to postpone his appointment until the following week. Remarkably, they granted Aubrey an extension. The following Saturday she went to the draft board again, obtaining yet another extension for her husband. Helen repeated this strategy three more times. If the draft board suspected a scheme, they did not say so. By the time Aubrey could not delay his appearance any longer, he had finished the necessary science classes and been accepted into dental school.

Safe from military service, Aubrey quit his job at Western Gear to study full time. He signed up for the Air Force Specialized Training Program (AFSTP) so that he could get his tuition paid: Aubrey was in the military but on deferred status. Helen got a job in the commissary at the Southern Pacific Railroad, earning enough money to make the rent and buy food. She continued to support Aubrey until he graduated. Aubrey finished school just a few months after the war ended in 1945. After passing the California dental board exam, he went to work for his father-in-law at Herbert Berry's newest and most successful dental clinic, in Lynwood, California. For the next several years, things went well for Aubrey and Helen—with one exception: They were childless. Even though they had been married for five years, Helen had still not conceived. She began taking a powerful new fertility drug that her doctor promised would help her get pregnant. Although she knew that because of the medicine she could become pregnant at any time, when the opportunity arose for them to adopt a child, Helen "felt prompted" to act on this good fortune. In January 1947 they adopted a son, Lane. Helen became pregnant within two months of beginning the fertility treatment. In 1948, only seven months after bringing Lane home, she gave birth to her second son, Brian. Helen stayed home to care for the boys while Aubrey's dental business continued to grow, but she became anxious about not doing enough for her spiritual life. She continued her search for wisdom, fasting, praying, and reading the scriptures. She asked God to tell her what her purpose was.

Eventually, Aubrey and Helen grew tired of city life. They left busy California for a quieter life in a smaller town in rural Idaho. On a trip to his hometown of Idaho Falls, Aubrey, somewhat impulsively, bought a dental practice in a nice building in the center of town. He bought a house as well, and the family moved in. The dental practice proved to be in an ideal location, and soon Aubrey was making a good living. Helen continued her spiritual search. Well versed in the story of the founding of Mormonism, she mirrored the pattern of the sect's teenage founder, Joseph Smith, by asking God directly for the answers to her questions. She recalled, "I remembered in the Book of James, the verse: 'If any of ye lack wisdom, let him ask of God, who giveth to all men liberally, but let him ask in faith, nothing wavering.' I began to pray earnestly for the answers."[7]

In 1949 she became impressed with a verse in Mormon scripture called the Word of Wisdom that read, "All saints . . . walking in obedience to the commandments, shall find wisdom and great treasures of knowledge, even hidden treasures."[8] The Word of Wisdom contains the LDS food code, which prohibits the use of coffee, tea, alcohol, and tobacco and gives instructions on eating meat sparingly. Helen, having long observed the Word of Wisdom, and believing that the scriptural promise applied to all Latter-day Saints, wondered why she had not received anything close to a treasure of knowledge. She reread the passage to see if there was something she had overlooked. When she reached the section that suggested eating meat only "in times of winter, cold, or famine," she believed she had found an answer. Perhaps, she reasoned, the family had not been strict enough in its observance of this portion of the commandment.[9] Maybe they needed to be even more "anxious to please the Lord." With Aubrey's permission, Helen began cooking vegetarian meals. Determined to live even more piously than she had before, she didn't even open a can of tuna fish. She and Aubrey followed their program so strictly that they didn't eat meat even when they were invited out to people's homes for dinner. Helen continued this practice in anticipation that one day the Lord would bless her with wisdom and "great treasures of knowledge."

In February 1950 Dixie, Helen's first daughter, was born. Helen described her as a pretty, dainty little girl with a dimple in one cheek. "How relieved and happy I felt, how blessed to have this beautiful little girl," Helen recalled. But her happiness in Idaho Falls was not to last long. Later that year Aubrey was called into active duty in the AFSTP and was assigned to Castle Air Force Base in Merced, California. Because the AFSTP had put him through dental school, Helen knew this day was coming. Still, it was difficult for her to accept the fact that the family would have to move. Despite her misgivings the Andelins returned to California and moved into military housing, and Helen resumed fertility treatments. Just as when she was on the drug before, an opportunity to adopt a child again presented itself. The Andelins jumped at the chance to take the baby. When Kristine was born in 1951, Helen was already several months pregnant with what would be the fifth child she would add to the family in four years. Six months after Kristine arrived, Helen gave birth to John. Although she seemed to manage this incredible workload well enough, Aubrey soon developed bleeding ulcers and had to be hospitalized. Shortly afterward, he was released from the air force on grounds of family hardship. In 1952 the Andelins returned to their attractive home in Idaho Falls, and Aubrey resumed his dental practice. Seven months later Helen gave birth to their daughter Ginny. Helen was happy to be home.

The war was over, and the couple now had six young children. Aubrey was doing well in his dental practice, and Helen was giving her best to her career in the home. Although there had been six children added to the family in five years, this period in Helen's life was peaceful. "I loved to clean, cook, bake bread and try to look pretty," she wrote. "I was enjoying myself and felt important."[10] Then, one night, Helen had a dream.

"I dreamed I was escorted by a male angel to the Celestial Kingdom," she wrote.[11] She was taken to a place where she recognized members of her own family, and she experienced a tremendous feeling of joy that was beyond any feeling she had ever had before. The happiness, however, was fleeting. Helen learned she must return to her earthly life to make improvements in herself. The angel took her to the site of a dilapidated old house where piles of bricks had fallen from the walls surrounding it. He instructed Helen to build a beautiful mansion out of what was left of the crumbling house. "The angel vanished," said Helen. Believing the dream was a message, Helen realized that it had to do with her lack of a testimony "born of the spirit." The bricks, she concluded, were her good works. Although crucial to the task at hand, they needed mortar to hold them together. That mortar was her testimony. Helen believed that without a spiritual conviction her good actions would not guide her toward eternal glory. In order to face the many tests and temptations and the responsibilities of life, she was certain she must have this conviction. She began to fast and pray regularly in search of the testimony she felt she must have.[12] She also continued to observe her food practices, care for her husband and children, and volunteer in her church.

Aubrey eventually tired of the sameness of small-town living and became restless; he wanted change. He told his wife he wanted new horizons, and made plans to take the family back to California. The thought of leaving her home was agonizing for Helen. Nevertheless, Aubrey rented office space in Fresno, fetched Helen from Idaho, and returned with her to California to find a house. Still hoping to make the best of a difficult situation, Helen agreed to the move but asked for two things: a house on a quiet street, and a school nearby. They looked at many suitable homes. To Helen's disbelief, Aubrey liked only one—a house on a busy interchange, far from the children's schools. The house did not have carpet on the floors, curtains on the windows, or landscaping in the dusty yard. Shocked at her husband's "inconceivable" disrespect for her requests, Helen remained speechless while her husband prevailed upon her to accept the house. "I was too polite," she said of the first real trial of the marriage. Later she wrote that she should have refused the house. "I had to pay a high price for being silent," she said. She came very close to having a nervous breakdown.[13] After purchasing the property in Fresno, the couple returned to Idaho to sell their house and pack up their possessions. Helen was overcome with panic about leaving her comfortable home and moving into the cold, noisy Fresno residence. However, for the sake of her husband, she found the courage to leave her contented life behind.

The family arrived in Fresno, and Aubrey enthusiastically set about building a brand new dental practice, supporting his six children, and helping his troubled wife get back to normal. But there were problems. The heavy traffic bothered him at night when he was home. And he had recently been called to serve as a member of the Mormon bishopric in the family's new ward. He had difficulty bearing up under the heavy responsibilities that the position entailed.[14] Helen remembered that the move was hard on him, and his restlessness increased. There were also problems in the marriage. "These were days of despair," she wrote. Having no other options, Helen tried to make the best of things. In 1956 Paul was born. That same year, having made a success of his business, Aubrey bought a lot on the outskirts of the noisy city, and the couple built a lovely, rustic farmhouse. The house was on a quiet street and was near both the elementary and high schools. Moreover, it was situated on a large lot with fruit trees. Helen, now the mother of seven, would finally experience the peace of mind she had sought. The family lived contentedly for four and a half years. But things had changed for Helen. Her relationship with Aubrey had suffered greatly over the years. He had become unhappy, and they were no longer as close as they had been.

In 1959 Helen decided that her husband was no longer in love with her. She began to realize that her marriage did not measure up to her expectations. "Instead of my marriage reaching the idealistic state I had planned, I had to admit it was quite mediocre. I was the taken-for-granted, neglected housewife who was often ignored."[15] Disappointed that her life was not the model of domestic happiness she had hoped for, she wrote, "I had my heart set on achieving the ideal marriage. I strived earnestly for this superior marriage, doing all I knew to measure up to my part by trying to become the ideal wife." She fretted, "My marriage had fallen . . . far below the dreams I once had." Ignored and undervalued by her increasingly difficult husband, she described herself as the "unappreciated little housewife, as taken for granted as the kitchen sink." Helen's disillusionment and sense of failure was so intense that, she said, "at times I would look in the mirror and ask myself, 'What's wrong with you?' Or, 'What must a woman do to be treated the way she would like to be treated?' I had to admit I didn't know." Just as she had in earlier situations with her husband, she blamed herself: "The teachings of my youth led me to believe that we make our own happiness, and if we are unhappy, we are to blame. So, I did a lot of soul searching to discover my deficiency." A key aspect of Andelin's spiritual search was her belief that prayer and strict physical discipline allowed one the necessary spiritual frame of mind to realize certain truths that would otherwise be missed. She began to pray earnestly for answers.[16] Believing that the ability to discern and interpret truth flowed from an inborn capacity given to all human beings, she assumed that "knowing" was her natural right.

While Helen looked desperately for a way to reverse the downward spiral of her marriage, Aubrey became even more discontented. For some time he had wanted to quit dentistry and follow the career path he had begun in college before the war, which was business. Having achieved some level of success in the dental business, and hoping to work his way out, Aubrey set his sights on real estate. Some time earlier he had joined in a partnership with several other investors in the land-development business. Beginning in 1960 he engaged in a series of land deals in the San Joaquin Valley, developing orange orchards into housing subdivisions. Having only limited experience in business and even less in real estate, Aubrey optimistically purchased six large tracts of undeveloped land. While working on still another land deal, Aubrey moved the family two more times. Helen was well into her sixth pregnancy and had seven children under the age of twelve to care for. The fact that her family changed residences so many times only exacerbated Helen's desire for stability. She began to suffer. Deeply disappointed, and fearing that she had failed as a wife, she became depressed. She continued to ask God for answers. One day she got a visit from her friend Verna Johnson. The year was 1961.

Johnson observed firsthand the problems in Helen's marriage. Verna encouraged her to stand up to her domineering husband and stop being a doormat. Surprised at Verna's frankness, Helen responded by confiding in her friend. She described her long-felt unhappiness, frustrations, and feelings of loneliness and failure. She said that her formerly adoring companion had become controlling, frequently busy, and unromantic. Aubrey, who she described as "spoiled rotten" by his mother, had become demanding and difficult to live with. Helen suffered a sharp hunger for the romantic love she had experienced while courting and as a newlywed. Verna wanted to help. She had been teaching marriage classes for over ten years in the San Francisco area and had counseled hundreds of married women. A set of advice booklets that her mother had given to her in her teens was the basis of her marriage classes, and she offered to let Helen read them. The booklets, she said, contained helpful information about what women could do to better understand men and make themselves more attractive to them. Verna promised Helen that if she would come to Oakland for a visit, she would share them with her. Given the fact that Andelin blamed herself for her marital problems, the idea that she could improve her situation on her own was an enormous relief. A week later she took the train to Oakland. Helen recalled that Verna had taken her into her bedroom, opened a wooden chest, and taken out a set of eight little booklets called *The Secrets of Fascinating Womanhood*.[17] The booklets, lessons in femininity and understanding men, proved to be just what Helen was looking for. Not only did they answer the immediate questions about how to make herself more attractive to her husband and improve her marriage, but they would become the foundation of the new code of behavior she would fashion and later share with women all over the world. Their discovery was a pivotal moment in both the pace and focus of Andelin's ongoing spiritual journey.

Said Helen, "I read the booklets without stopping, and as I read a ray of light came down . . . the precious light of truth." For Helen this truth was neither merely old platitude nor a quick fix to a present problem; it was a revelation from God. Verna, although she had been teaching from the set of booklets for over a decade, "didn't know what a treasure it was," said Helen. God, she believed, had answered her prayers. At that moment, she recalled, "I gained a glimpse into a whole new world, a celestial world, but one which can be experienced here on earth. Here was tremendous new insight into the man–woman relationship." Because Helen found the message in the booklets so stirring, she asked Verna if she could take them back to Fresno and type her own copies. Verna agreed, and Helen left with the booklets. Helen recalled, "As I returned home by train I guarded them with my life. . . . I could think of nothing else."[18] Although Andelin claimed that God had led her to "a hidden treasure," the fact was that the booklets she guarded with her life on the journey back to Fresno were not religious by any stretch of the imagination. They were the commercial endeavor of two modern-day self-help writers that instructed single women on how to get a man to propose marriage by mastering the strategies and tactics of winning men. Yet for her this new discovery was both religious and life-altering. While she never considered them to be the actual words of God, Andelin understood that the booklets contained fundamental realities that God had not only led her to, but had charged her with bringing to the world.

The discovery of the advice booklets profoundly affected Andelin, setting her on a course of self-improvement. The institution of marriage, she reasoned, was not to blame for the unhappiness of women. Nor were men to blame. A woman's unhappiness was her own fault. The failure of good women to have happy marriages was the result of error, the scarcity of proper information, and human weakness. A woman, believed Andelin, could find happiness and have the heavenly marriage she desired even without any deliberate action on the part of her husband. Helen copied the booklets word for word on her old Underwood typewriter. The answers seemed so simple, so practical, that she began to wonder if the new knowledge she had been led to was really as hidden from all women as it had been from her. She set out to find more information about the subject of marriage. First she went to the public library, but she was dismayed to find that the marriage manuals there had more to do with sex than with the love relationship between men and women. Having no luck at the local library, she searched the Bible; Andelin concluded that the wisdom contained in it applied mostly to men's problems. She acknowledged that a few choice verses from the writings of Paul concerning men's leadership over women, and the last chapter of Proverbs on the characteristics of a virtuous woman, were "essential." Still, she reasoned, when it came to scripture, the scope was limited. "The records of the Bible were kept by men. Ever notice that?" she asked.[19] While she continued to look for more information on the subject, Andelin took the booklets' lessons about becoming more feminine and attractive and applied them to the ailing relationship with her husband. His response, she said, was nothing short of miraculous. She observed, "My husband was like a different man. He began paying attention to me, to hurry home from his office and cut out-of-town trips short." Her once disinterested husband softened and became markedly "more loving and tender." While Helen credited the changes in her marriage to the information in the advice booklets, Aubrey's shift in attitude may have been the result of major changes in the family's life. While waiting for their eighth child, the couple moved to Clovis, a suburb of Fresno, and Aubrey left his dental practice.

Although he had experienced success in his field, Aubrey had never wanted to be a dentist. He had gone to dental school only to avoid the draft. Later he became resentful, feeling that that he didn't have a choice. Aubrey was prone to worry—and did so to the point of affecting the entire family. Over time he had become so unhappy with his profession that he avoided his children, and his relationship with Helen suffered. His misery reached a point where he became so irritable and melancholy that Helen served his meals to him in the bedroom. Fearing a reoccurrence of the bleeding ulcers that had hospitalized him while he was paying his debt to the AFSTP, Helen lived with the constant dread that her husband's despair might kill him.[20] Aubrey had been a successful dentist for fifteen years, but because of the unfortunate and isolating changes in his behavior, Helen urged him to quit. Relieved, Aubrey left the predictable and lucrative career of dentistry for the uncertainty of land speculation. After closing his dental practice for good and moving to the countryside to pursue his new career, he experienced a transformation. Even the children noticed the difference in his demeanor. Instead of retiring to his room early in the evening to eat his meals alone, Aubrey talked and laughed with the children, even holding and playing with the little ones. To his wife's great relief, he became more carefree and enthusiastic about his life and his future as a businessman. Grateful that she had encouraged him to set aside his profitable dental career once and for all, Aubrey credited his wife with saving his life.

As Aubrey grew more relaxed, the couple's marriage flourished. Helen believed it had more to do with her changed behavior than anything else. As she became more familiar with *The Secrets of Fascinating Womanhood* booklets, and as new insights occurred to her along the way, she continued to do everything possible to improve their relationship. Her efforts paid off. Aubrey, now adoring and attentive, began to voluntarily help her with things she could never have persuaded him to do before. So dramatic was the change in his behavior that "it was as though [she] had come into possession of some strange, magical power." Her formerly distant husband became so smitten with his new wife that he became poetical in expressing his love for her. This romantic side of her husband had all but disappeared after marriage. While engaged he had written her numerous love letters during their two-year separation. As beautiful as the letters were at the time, she noted, "They were nothing compared to the things he was saying to me now after twenty years of marriage." Finally, Helen realized she was actually achieving the ideal marriage she had always dreamed about and was doing it through her own efforts.[21] In 1962 Helen gave birth to their last child, a daughter they named Merilee.

In light of the extraordinary changes she was experiencing, Helen became increasingly anxious to share her insights with other women. With a growing sense of urgency, she organized a small class and began holding discussions with eight women in her church. Despite the demands of caring for a husband, seven children, and a new infant, she was determined to tell others how her marriage had dramatically changed as a result of what she had learned. Helen noticed that the women in the discussion group began to experience the same success she was having. The dull and uninteresting marriages of her students became romantic again. Troubled marriages and marriages previously thought unsalvageable were miraculously "rescued and renewed." Andelin's solution was both uncomplicated and optimistic. She believed that the right information, prayer, and a good dose of determination and hard work would allow any woman to make herself happier and improve a boring marriage—perhaps even save a doomed one. Word of the class spread, and women from many parts of the city wanted to sign up. Andelin taught more classes in what she now called Fascinating Womanhood, and soon the original group of eight women became a crowd of over 170. The surge of interest convinced Andelin that she had made an important discovery. "I knew I was on the right track," she said, "and was teaching principles women needed desperately." Andelin spread her message to anyone who would listen. Because God had led her to the booklets, she believed her efforts were a religious calling.

To accommodate the growing crowds, Andelin organized classes at the local YMCA and enlisted volunteer teachers. Soon women from a variety of backgrounds poured into the classes, and the project that the busy wife and mother had entered into with "a light heart" became one that she now viewed with soberness. Andelin, a sought-after speaker, did not yet anticipate that she would write a book and spearhead a significant women's movement. But she did understand the gravity of the challenges she faced. She believed that building a happy marriage was also a religious responsibility. With each class, she became more convinced that this philosophy was effective with all women who applied it. She started to appreciate the difficulties and unhappiness of the women she encountered. "I began to have a greater understanding of common problems," she said. "I became aware of the tremendous unhappiness that exists in marriages today and, surprisingly, with fine women who try very hard to be good wives." Many women, she realized, were in the same situation she had been: unhappy and disillusioned with marriage. She observed, "Most of them were worthy women who were putting forth great effort to make their marriages happy but not reaping the rewards. No one seemed to know what was wrong or have any real solutions."[22]

Andelin wasn't the only one taking notice of this general malady among married women. In her groundbreaking book, *The Feminine Mystique* (1963), the suburban housewife and political activist Betty Friedan branded the pervasive marital disillusionment that Andelin had described as "the problem that has no name." Friedan wrote, "[It] burst like a boil through the image of the happy American housewife. . . . The problem lay buried, unspoken for many years in the minds of American women. . . . It was a strange stirring, a sense of dissatisfaction, a yearning that women suffered" from one end of the country to another. "Each housewife," wrote Friedan, "struggled with it alone. As she made the beds, shopped for groceries, matched slipcover material, ate peanut butter sandwiches with her children, and lay beside her husband at night." According to Friedan, scores of women who had devoted their lives to housewifery remained, despite their dedication and hard work, "afraid to ask the silent question: Is this all?"[23] While the problems that Andelin and Friedan described were the same, the two proposed fundamentally different strategies to alleviate them. Unlike Andelin, who called for a return to traditional values, Friedan indicted the patriarchal structure resting at the very foundation of American social culture. She and other contemporary feminists advocated two popular strategies. The first was to incorporate women into the existing male-dominated system, where they would function as equals with the men who were already there. The structures of power would remain, but the focus and function of authority would change in order to include women. The other approach was to dismantle the system altogether and come up with a new social arrangement. Andelin, unlike Friedan, had no interest in gaining greater access to a man's world or changing social constructs. Nor did she have a quarrel with patriarchy. She believed that the restoration of conventional gender roles as spelled out in the booklets and the Bible was the only way to remedy unhappy marriages.

In formulating her new ideas about marriage, Andelin looked back to times that seemed better, wistfully recalling her parents' marriage during the happiest parts of her childhood as a model for improving modern marriages. She also looked to classical literature—the writings of Thackeray, Dickens, and Victor Hugo, and to the highly idealized romantic love depicted in Hollywood movies. Andelin melded the images of popular romance with the urgency of religious purpose to create an expectation of divinely inspired romantic love between husband and wife. Of the many women she knew in the same boat she had been in, women trying to make their marriages happy and failing miserably, Andelin acknowledged, "Their diligent efforts were obviously not enough. What they needed was knowledge, wisdom, truth—a light from heaven to guide the way. They needed to know what they were doing wrong, and how to make it right." Andelin became increasingly conscious of the fact that *The Secrets of Fascinating Womanhood*, written for single girls, did not address many of the problems of the women in her classes. She recalled, "I was teaching married women, so my knowledge had to expand. Some ideas came to me out of the blue; others were recollections of the past. But in a miraculous way the philosophy of Fascinating Womanhood fell into place." Finally came "the day the total picture of The Ideal Woman appeared before [her] eyes."[24] The Ideal Woman, an image Andelin had taken from the booklets and described as a revelation from God, was equal parts angelic attributes and human qualities. Together, these traits comprised a complete woman, a personality the booklets called Angela Human. The character of Angela Human became the most powerful illustration of Andelin's broader understanding of womanhood. Angela Human, or the Ideal Woman (From a Man's Point of View), was, she believed, what women everywhere sought to become.

TWO

THE IDEAL WOMAN

(From a Man's Point of View)

$\mathcal{J}$n 1965 the United States sent combat troops into Vietnam. Ultimately, fifty-eight thousand Americans would perish in this hotly debated war that lasted until 1973. Economic problems, racial unrest, and violent demonstrations against the war ushered in an era of widespread social discontent. It was the era of the civil rights movement. In 1961, Freedom Rides supporting racial equality began in the Deep South. Two years later nearly three hundred thousand citizens participated in the March on Washington to promote civil rights and racial equality. In 1963 Betty Friedan's *Feminine Mystique* sparked the second-wave feminist movement. And in November of the same year, a former U.S. Marine-turned-sniper named Lee Harvey Oswald assassinated President John F. Kennedy. The nation suffered, and the American family suffered. Divorce rates skyrocketed, and so did juvenile delinquency. By 1970 half of all marriages entered into would end in divorce. Marriage rates dropped as fewer young people chose to marry, and birth rates hit a historic low. As throngs of unhappy women left domestic life to seek economic freedom and fulfillment outside of the home, just as many struggled to hold their troubled families together. For those women seeking to recapture peace, happiness, and security at home, the homemaker Helen Andelin had the solution.

Andelin didn't talk about rights. She talked about love. "If he doesn't love you, your life will be an empty shell," she said.[1] Andelin called for women not to seek equality, but to find happiness in inspiring a husband's adoration and devotion—a kind of love, she said, that all women dreamed about. She called this love "celestial love." With celestial love even the worst marriage was salvageable. Celestial love was not something a woman waited for. She acted in order to get it. It was available to all women everywhere, provided they follow the right steps. Andelin not only had the steps, she had the vehicle—the Ideal Woman. The Ideal Woman that Andelin championed was ideal from a man's point of view. She was not necessarily appealing to other women. In fact, warned Andelin, she was likely to be an object of scorn among her sisters. This was because, Helen believed, most American women didn't know how to be happy, much less how to make a man happy. Other women's ideas of what it took to have a good marriage caused only confusion. "How do we know what is good, or for the good of our marriage?" she asked.[2] A woman who wanted to improve her marriage must not rely on her own notions of how to do it. Instead, she must be open-minded, adaptable, and willing to trust that Andelin knew what she was talking about. The idea, after all, was not to please other women. It was to please men. Of her discovery of the Ideal Woman, Andelin said, "I prayed with all my heart and soul. It came to me one day, after many, many months of searching . . . searching the Scriptures . . . teaching classes and having a smattering of knowledge, the ideal woman came clear to my mind."[3]

The Ideal Woman (From a Man's Point of View), or Angela Human, for Andelin embodied complete womanhood. The angelic side of Angela Human was composed of virtues that aroused adoration and worship and brought a man peace and happiness. Those characteristics were obedience, an unblemished character, the ability to understand men, the possession of a deep inner happiness, and the ability to become a Domestic Goddess. Alone, these traits produced a kind of holy love. "A man wants a woman he can put on a pedestal and worship from below, someone whose character is superior to his," said Andelin.[4] However, she taught, a man wanted more

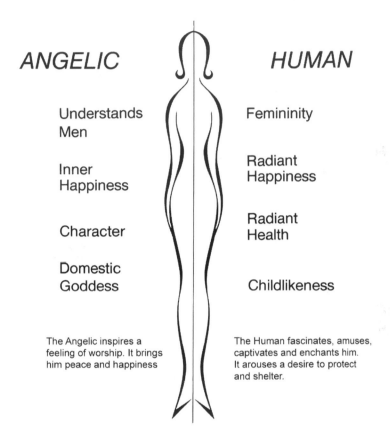

THE IDEAL WOMAN

ANGELIC   **HUMAN**

Understands
Men

Femininity

Inner
Happiness

Radiant
Happiness

Character

Radiant
Health

Domestic
Goddess

Childlikeness

The Angelic inspires a
feeling of worship. It brings
him peace and happiness

The Human fascinates, amuses,
captivates and enchants him.
It arouses a desire to protect
and shelter.

The angelic and the human qualities combine
to make a woman he can adore and cherish.

Together He Cherishes

FIGURE 2.1 The Ideal Woman from a Man's Point of View. Author's Collection

than an angel. To be an Ideal Woman, one must also possess the human qualities that fascinated, charmed, and amused a man. The virtues that made up the human side of Angela Human were femininity, radiant happiness, a fresh appearance and manner, and childlikeness. To illustrate her model for womanhood, Andelin turned to the Charles Dickens novel *David Copperfield*, in which David, a young and impressionable man, fell in love with two women but could marry only one. According to Andelin, each woman represented only one side of the Angela Human character. While possessing admirable traits, each lacked those qualities that allowed David to love completely and thus, said Andelin, were inadequate. Combining the traits of both women represented a complete model of womanhood.

Agnes Wickfield represented the angelic side of Angela Human. She was the woman who inspired David's worship. "Although her face was quite bright and happy, there was a tranquility about it, and about her—a quiet, good, calm spirit." Agnes was unselfish. She was a good housekeeper. She took care of her father, fixing his meals and running his house efficiently. Agnes and David became close friends, and she was the one he confided his hopes, dreams, and sorrows in. She gave him comfort, understanding, sympathy, and companionship. David realized, "As if in love, joy, sorrow, hope or disappointment, in all emotions, my heart turned naturally there and found its refuge and best friend." Agnes had a peaceful influence on David. She possessed a sweetness of character, and David loved her for it. Thinking about her soothed him, and David felt she was "one of the elements" of his "natural home." Not only did Agnes understand David, she possessed a deep inner happiness. She went about her work cheerfully. Agnes was an outstanding woman, yet David didn't marry her. Why? According to Andelin it was because she was so sober and self-denying that she lacked girlish traits. She didn't have the "fascinating little ways that stir a man's heart." She was too independent, too efficient, and too good. Although David loved Agnes, it was Dora Spenlow he married.

Dora had almost none of the traits Agnes had. She represented the human side of Angela Human. Instead of providing a peaceful, calm presence, she kept David stirred up. She made his heart beat fast, and he was wildly infatuated with her: "She was a fairy and a sylph . . . I don't know what she was, anything that no one ever saw and everything that everybody ever wanted. She had the most delightful little voice, the gayest little laugh . . . and the most fascinating little ways that ever led a lost youth into hopeless slavery." According to Andelin, "Her childlike ways, her dear little whims and caprices, her girlish trust in him, her absolute dependency upon others to provide for her, made an irresistible appeal to David's gentlemanly and chivalrous heart."[5] Dora enchanted David from the moment he met her. He was so attracted to her that he felt he couldn't live without her. Although he loved Agnes enormously, he loved Dora to the point of pain. While Dora bewitched David with her childlikeness and radiant happiness, she lacked character. She was not a good housekeeper, she did not understand men, and she was not obedient. David married her anyway, but she did not prove to be the kind of companion he wanted or needed. Not the kind Agnes had been. David loved both women, but, said Andelin, he never felt complete with either of them. Some critics say that Andelin misrepresented the Dickens story in order to support her own ideas. Andelin, however, believed that her interpretation of the novel was accurate. For her, Agnes and Dora were perfect examples of the angelic and human qualities that she believed a woman must possess in order to captivate and keep her man. For Andelin, these roles were not just the subject of literature. They were the embodiment of God's plan for womankind. The angelic side was who a woman was. The human side was how a woman behaved. By developing both sides, any woman, taught Andelin, had the capacity to inspire celestial love.

In the early nineteenth century, the ideal woman possessed four virtues: piety, purity, submissiveness, and domesticity. By adopting these virtues, said experts, a woman could enjoy both happiness and power within the domestic realm. Without them she was aimless in a world of uncertainty.[6] In the past, women had based their identities on mothering, physical attractiveness, love, and lower expectations of achievement and independence than men. Andelin, a traditionalist, upheld these views. "Women's needs are the same the whole world over—to make men happy, to understand the masculine nature, and to be loved," she said. For Andelin, a woman found her identity not by being like a man, but by understanding the differences between men and women. While a woman's greatest desire was love, she taught, the greatest desire for a man was admiration. A man wanted to know that his wife needed him and thought of him as her hero. He wanted someone to make him feel like a man. Rather than being his equal, Andelin said that a man wanted a woman he could protect, provide for, and guide. Andelin taught that women were not creatures able to thrive independently of their husbands. Rather, it was only within marriage that a woman found purpose, self-worth, and, most importantly, celestial love. Within marriage a woman had an identity. Outside of it she was adrift. A happy marriage, then, should be the highest goal of every woman. And to have a successful marriage, all a woman had to do was follow Andelin's simple prescription: Don't try to change your husband. Instead, change yourself. For many women, discouraged that their marriages weren't working out, Andelin's Ideal Woman sounded too good to be true. You didn't have to be special to become an Ideal Woman; in fact, you could be anybody. According to Andelin, a woman didn't have to be pretty or smart, have youth or money, or even come from a good family in order to find the happiness she was looking for. All she had to do was adjust her behavior. "Any marriage can be saved as long as the woman wants it to be saved," said Andelin. The simplicity and inclusiveness of her philosophy provided hope to regular women—many of whom, at some point in their lives, had considered themselves losers, failures, and even lost causes. Andelin spoke to women who already believed in marriage but were failing at it.

While the Ideal Woman must exhibit all the virtues of the Angela Human model, the two most important qualities were obedience and femininity. The obedient wife was a woman who knew her Bible and was willing to live by it. Scripture was unambiguous. God told Eve, "Thy desire shall be to thy husband and he shall rule over thee."[7] Andelin believed that a woman accepting this divine instruction could realize her true calling and thus willingly surrender to her destiny. It was a matter of character. She wrote, "The first law of Heaven is obedience, and it should be the first law of every home."[8] As a practical reminder of women's obedience to men, Andelin presented each of her students with a gold-painted dowel to represent her husband's authority. Then she assigned students to give the gold stick to their husbands in order to provide the couple with the opportunity to discuss their respective roles in a humorous manner. "The husbands like it, and often hang their sticks on the wall as a reminder and threaten to use it if the wife doesn't obey," she said.[9]

Obedience was good, but it was not enough. "Obedience alone is not our highest objective. There must be an accompanying spirit of sweet submission if we are to be charming women," said Andelin.[10] Love, she said, "will never blossom forth until we surrender to a man."[11] Andelin returned to scripture: "Wives, submit yourselves unto your own husbands, as it is fit in the Lord."[12] For those women who balked at her teachings, she said, "Some women feel that they are giving too much when they yield to a man's rule. I say they never give enough."[13] The fact was that many married women with children had no choice but to submit to their husbands, who were their only source of financial support and shelter.[14] Many of them literally had no place else to go. For these women, Andelin provided reassurance that their economic dilemma had social and religious meaning. All women, she taught, would be rewarded for willingly allowing their husbands to be the leader. "Give in to get what you want because this submissiveness will bring a strange but righteous power over your man," she wrote.[15] One student agreed: "I now forget about wanting my own way and apply the principles I learned in FW, and wouldn't you know, I get what I want without even asking for it." A smart wife, taught Andelin, yielded to her husband's decisions whether she liked it or not: "Not everything we want is right for us to have, and we can be grateful that men say 'no' to some of our requests."[16] Andelin taught not only that a wife must obey, but that she must teach her children to obey as well: "It is God's will that women put men above them and set a pattern for the children of total obedience to husbands."[17] When husband and wife couldn't agree, the Ideal Woman surrendered—even if her husband was wrong. Wrote Andelin, "The wife should never follow her own preference to that of her husband . . . for if the husband feels that he is right, but errs in judgment, the wife will be blessed for her obedience. Greater the sin of rebellion than the errors that arise from want of judgment."[18]

For many religious women who followed the Bible, obedience was nothing new. For some who were not religious, obedience was worth the discomfort it caused in order to save the marriage. Men and women, taught Andelin, had equal importance but different roles. "Leadership is just an office. It is just a job. It takes the faith of the woman," she said.[19] Submission, taught Andelin, was not oppressive; it was freeing: "Woman wins by surrender. She is victorious by yielding."[20] By doing as her husband wished, a wife relieved herself from the pressures of making difficult decisions. She was free to concentrate on raising her children, running her home, and improving other aspects of her personality. Obedience, taught Andelin, was not restricting; it was emancipating. And women believed her. "Her power is growing mightily by preaching utter female submissiveness," said one observer.[21]

Andelin's ideas on womanhood were not without precedent. As a Christian, she believed all of creation was based on God's laws of order, as spelled out in the Bible. Knowing these laws was enlightenment; practicing them was the fulfillment of a woman's purpose. According to scripture, God presided at the top of the chain of authority, followed by Jesus Christ. The husband was below Jesus Christ, and the wife was below him. Scripture says, "Wives, submit yourselves unto your husbands, as unto the Lord. For the husband is the head of the wife, even as Christ is the head of the Church."[22] All relationships, believed Andelin, were governed by these laws. "There is no such thing as chance," she said. "One woman succeeds in marriage because of obedience to law. Another fails because of disobedience to it."[23] Biblical law, she believed, governed not only the universe but also marriage. "Marriage is a theocracy," she declared, "not a democracy."[24] Her disciples agreed. "The Bible tells me what I am supposed to do as a wife and Fascinating Womanhood shows me how to do it," said one follower.[25]

While the angelic side of Angela Human was obedient, the human side was feminine. Femininity, a "gentle, tender quality found in a woman's appearance, manner, and actions, and in her general attitude," was a trait that any woman could integrate into her own personality by accentuating the differences between herself and men, not the similarities, wrote Andelin.[26] Femininity, she taught, was a way for women to empower themselves. "Femininity is very powerful," she said. "Ask any man if they don't feel the power of femininity when they come under its spell. They would do anything for a woman . . . [it's] just a natural response."[27] Femininity, she said, was "a campaign that should bring him to your feet." The feminine woman looked to a man for care, protection, and financial support; she displayed a lack of masculine ability, aggressiveness, competency, efficiency, fearlessness, and strength. And in a saying Andelin borrowed from *The Secrets of Fascinating Womanhood* booklets, such a woman never tried to "kill [her] own snakes." Feminine women, she taught, needed manly protection from danger. Dangers included strenuous work, going places alone at night, taking long-distance trips alone, spiders, mice, animals, snakes, storms, blizzards, and dangerous equipment. The woman who could take care of herself in dealing with any of these situations not only lacked femininity but was "repulsive" to a man. Andelin believed that the reason men stopped offering their chivalry was that women had become capable. She said, "If chivalry is dead, women have killed it," adding, "A man cannot derive any joy or satisfaction from protecting a woman who can obviously do very well without him. . . . He only delights in protecting or sheltering a woman who needs his manly care . . . or at least appears to need it."[28]

A feminine woman always radiated happiness—even if she was sad. A husband didn't want to see a depressed wife, taught Andelin, so a wife who was depressed should not be surprised if her husband left her.[29] A man, she said, was too involved in the masculine world of work to fuss over a woman who was out of sorts. After all, she asserted, life was much easier for a woman, who only has to "tend children, keep the house clean and smile." A feminine woman acted genteel in all situations. "Never slap men on the back, or drink by throwing your head back," she cautioned. And "shake hands with men gracefully," making sure not to grip too hard.[30] A woman who was feminine never took large bites of food, ate loudly, or talked with her mouth full. And she didn't wear pants—even around the house. Instead, she wore a feminine dress and apron. The feminine woman washed her face, put on makeup, wore attractive clothes, and did her hair properly. Andelin encouraged women who wore their hair short to grow it long and put ribbons and bows in it. Besides wearing feminine hairstyles, an important part of being feminine was maintaining a girlish figure. Andelin cautioned her students that a man might leave a woman because of just ten pounds of extra weight. An overweight woman could look masculine to her husband, even causing him to seek the companionship of a woman who took better care of herself.

Besides being obedient, maintaining a fresh, ladylike appearance, and staying trim, the Ideal Woman learned to keep her problems to herself. "The wise woman MINIMIZES her problems," said Andelin. "She works at them quietly and persistently. . . . She places her trust in God."[31] A woman who was feminine was careful about what she discussed with her husband. It was best if she didn't have strong opinions. Andelin urged women to avoid heavy subjects such as problems and feelings. She warned, "Airing feelings may bring a sense of relief to a wife, but this does not counteract the damage it does to the man. It robs him of his joy, his peace and comfort of his home and perhaps even his love."[32] Andelin taught women not to talk too much because this was a sign of weak character and self-centeredness. And she encouraged smart women to dumb themselves down. "A man doesn't want an intellectual woman," she said.[33] When a woman showed that she was more intelligent than her husband, she hurt his vulnerable male pride. For a less brilliant woman, Andelin taught that she didn't need to have a good head on her shoulders in order to follow a smart man's conversation. She need only listen and admire: "In his pleasure at having himself admired, the man seldom notices that his conversation is not understood."[34] The Ideal Woman had to accept that men were more temperamental than she was: they couldn't help it. When a man was cross, said Andelin, whose own husband was often cross with her, he was usually justified. Working in the pressure-filled world of the public sphere caused men strain and stress that homemakers didn't experience. If a wife was not careful, these pressures could lead to arguments.

Andelin taught that the Ideal Woman should never argue with her husband—even if she was in the right. In fact, when she was angry at her husband, she didn't confront or fight with him at all. Instead, she acted like a saucy child. Childlikeness, something more liberated women found disgusting, was one of the keys to Andelin's philosophy, and a crucial characteristic of the Ideal Woman. A womanly quality, Andelin promised, would "make slaves of men," childlikeness didn't come naturally to most women.[35] If a woman was having trouble being childlike, Andelin urged her to become a good actress. Andelin's "act as if" logic helped women overcome their reservations about behaving like an impudent little girl. While she encouraged genuineness, acting, if necessary, was one of the ways a woman could earn her husband's love. If practiced enough, explained Andelin, childlikeness could become second nature.

As she did in other aspects of her teaching, Andelin began her lesson on childlikeness with scripture: "Except ye be converted and become as little children, ye shall not enter into the kingdom of heaven."[36] While biblical scholars would cry foul at Andelin's misuse of the scripture, she found it an important tool to support her teachings and suffuse her philosophy with religious attributes. For Andelin, childlike anger allowed a woman to communicate her feelings without offending her husband. It was something a woman must learn if she was to heal a broken marriage. Rather than spewing hurtful comments during a fight, a woman needed to take the high road and treat arguments and disagreements lightheartedly—as a child would. She discouraged arguing, and advised, "Stomp your foot, lift your chin high and square your shoulders. . . . Or you can put both hands on your hips and open your eyes wide. Or, beat your fists on your husband's chest. Men love this!" After beating on her husband's chest, a wife could ask him, "How can a great big man like you pick on a poor little helpless girl like me?"[37] Or she could cry. But, Andelin advised, "Be sure it reflects the innocence of a child and not the emotional turmoil of a deeply disturbed woman. There is nothing which so frustrates a man as a hysterical woman."[38]

Rather than saying spiteful words that might insult a man's tender ego, a feminine wife must build him up—even when she was mad. It was better to call him an insufferable brute than a sniveling wimp. Andelin's favorite name was "big, hairy beast." Once a woman established that her man was strong and powerful, she could end the fight without damaging his pride. Andelin believed that because a man found a childlike woman so enchanting, he was more likely to give her the things she desired. "If you don't get things, you have not asked in the right way," said Andelin.[39] Some happy husbands of childlike wives gave them trips, jewelry, and cash. One delighted student reported, "In the past, he has always been very stingy with his money. Yesterday, he gave me money to buy groceries and told me to keep all the change for whatever I needed!"[40] A childlike woman, taught Andelin, got what she wanted. And it was fun. "I never realized how exciting it was to be a silly, frilly female," said one student.[41]

According to hundreds of letters from her followers, the rewards of obeying one's husband, being ladylike, keeping one's mouth shut, and sometimes becoming an actress were well worth it. Grateful students reported miraculous results: Their husbands stopped drinking, ended affairs, quit gambling, and even ceased cruel treatment and violent behavior. "After living FW the best I could my husband changed from a cruel, distant, selfish, unhappy person to a tender, loving and kind husband. We have never known such happiness together," said a disciple. There were plenty more like her. In one extreme example that Andelin published in her newsletter, an abused wife wrote, "At least once a week there was a horrible screaming argument and every day our conversation consisted of nothing but the most barbed sarcasm we could produce. The physical abuse continued. . . . Finally things got so bad I locked myself in our bathroom and tried to slash my wrists." After the woman had spent several months in the hospital and undergone electric-shock treatments, her sister told her about the FW classes. She attended and started living the principles—childlikeness, in particular. Her husband stopped hitting her. "We have not had an argument in months," she reported. "I've been showered with presents, compliments, and attention. And, I've been able to go off my medicine."[42] One thankful student said of the change in her husband, "I fell on my knees sobbing and thanking the Lord for answering my prayers."[43] Andelin continued to be flooded with similar emotional stories, but other women objected. "My dear, you've got to be kidding," wrote one woman. "I disagree. . . . I'm not a child, nor do I wish to be treated as a child, nor do women act that way when a so-called man is blackening her eyes."[44] Women complained that the FW teachings were degrading and that they manipulated men. Andelin was undeterred by these protests. She continued to maintain that all women, if they were willing, could enrich and even save their marriages. All they had to do was abide by simple behavior-modification techniques. "People think I'm going back in time," she said. "I'm not. The principles of truth are timeless."[45]

The appeal of Angela Human, and what made her so different from other female role models, was that she was attainable. Women who were in tiresome and unsatisfying marriages, women who were not trained for careers, and even women who were desperate could all, with effort, become Andelin's Ideal Woman. All women, Andelin believed, could change their unhappy situations into happy ones if only they followed the FW principles. Her conviction that all women experienced the same kinds of yearning for love, purpose, and marital happiness found a ready audience. Her deeply rooted religious beliefs and nostalgia for the past attracted large numbers of followers during a period of general insecurity and social unrest. The straightforwardness of the idea that all women were in the same unfortunate situation universalized Andelin's message and became central to its success.

From a religious standpoint, Andelin's philosophy answered ultimate questions. From a secular point of view, her system was both timely and easy for large audiences to comprehend. As her fan base grew and reporters began to write about her success, critics started to take notice. Psychologists, offended by her lack of credentials, called her dangerous. Feminist writers called her a religious fanatic and a fool. There was no such thing as a woman's essential nature, they said. And the belief that women were emotionally and biologically destined to be domestic and subordinate was demeaning. The Ideal Woman, they said, had nothing to do with the reality of women's lives. Undeterred, Andelin continued to teach women and pull in followers.

Andelin's students were encouraged and deeply grateful, and the numbers of women who considered themselves her loyal disciples exploded. "My life has become a fairy tale. I have finally awakened from a lifelong nightmare," wrote one thankful student. "Fascinating Womanhood has been the salvation of my soul, my marriage, and my family, and I will strive the rest of my days to live up to its teachings. Thank you, thank you, thank you!" said another. One woman reported, "He is proud of me now and is treating me more like a queen than [like] his cook, nursemaid, and baby-sitter." After fifteen years in an unhappy marriage, one follower declared, "I feel like a bride again. Thank you, Mrs. Andelin!" "Thank goodness our God is a truly merciful God, for I followed step-by-step the principles of Fascinating Womanhood and my husband responded miraculously," exclaimed another.[46] Students reported that formerly moody and resentful husbands began to treat them better and tell them they loved them after years of silence. Some said their husbands earned more money. Others became freer with their pocketbooks. Many husbands became more demonstrative and passionate. "He acts as romantic as a schoolboy," declared one supporter. And there were other rewards. One woman revealed that her husband gave her "a dozen red roses, a frilly nightie, and a new dishwasher." Other women reported that their happy husbands presented them with color TVs, trips to Mexico, jewelry, kitchen appliances, furniture, and draperies for the living room, sewing machines, and new cars.[47] Overwhelmed by her new success in a formerly unhappy marriage, one overjoyed student wrote, "God bless your work, Mrs. Andelin. I am the happiest woman alive."[48]

Buoyed by the many letters of thanks and testimonies of success, Andelin became determined to communicate to the legions of women she now believed needed to hear her message. At the urging of her growing band of followers, she decided to write a textbook to go with her classes. Spreading the Fascinating Womanhood message, she had come to believe, was her moral obligation. Andelin's desire for change was urgent, and she had little patience for those who might impede her work. Like teaching her classes, writing her book had become a religious calling. Her first thought was to get the little booklets back in print. She wrote to the copyright office in Washington, D.C., to see if she could republish *The Secrets of Fascinating Womanhood*. But the copyright, she learned, had long since expired. However, a new copyright could be obtained for the booklets, provided they were revised or improved. For Andelin, this was an opportunity. Her plans to write a book became a reality. She confided her plan to her disbelieving husband, who until this time had considered her "pretty dense." Although dumbfounded, to appease his wife, Aubrey agreed to support her.[49]

In 1961, without any sort of formal training, and "moved by [her] awareness of the desperate need for knowledge," Helen began to write. Using the title of the booklets that had given her a new purpose, she called her compilation *Fascinating Womanhood*. Writing the book took about two years. It was an excruciating process fueled by a gnawing urgency. "I knew it was a book that must be written, and it was more important than my own life," she recalled.[50] Because of the demands of her large family and the fact that her class materials were not organized in any particular way, Andelin's attempts to write at home were demoralizing and fruitless. She realized she would have to isolate herself for a period of time so that she could organize her thoughts and concentrate on her difficult undertaking. Fortunately, her husband, who throughout their marriage had grumbled at her every request, now had a lot more time on his hands. Grateful that he no longer had his dental practice, and delighted at his wife's improved demeanor, Aubrey was a changed man, willing "to do anything in the world" for her, said Helen.[51] Aubrey drove Helen to a San Francisco motel some 180 miles away, dropped her off, and returned home to the children. Helen holed up for a week, working sixteen hours a day to organize the basic structure of her book. It was not easy. Andelin, a college dropout with little work experience, had no background in writing. Feeling that she had taken on an insurmountable task, she endured headaches, nausea, and dizzy spells. Despite her suffering,

Andelin described the first of several revelations from God she would receive throughout her career. This one had to do with the Ideal Woman. She wrote, "The day the entire picture of Angela Human opened up to me was one of the most exciting days of my life."[52] She added, "I was given knowledge . . . almost as if the windows of heaven had opened up to me. A picture of the ideal woman fell before me."[53] She found herself "in touch with the infinite; in tune with the Lord . . . almost like being lifted up in the clouds."[54] At the end of the week, although physically and emotionally exhausted, Andelin had the basic outline of the book completed. "As I finished," she recalled, "I looked out the window and wept with relief for my most humble beginning." Although book sales would make her rich, for Andelin writing the book had little to do with money: she believed it was her mission.

Until this time, Andelin considered homemaking her career. Once she decided to write her book, however, she hired full-time help to take over her considerable housekeeping duties and care for her eight children so that she could write. On the weekends, Andelin and her daughters cleaned the house, did the laundry, and shopped for groceries. The writing was difficult, and Andelin turned to God for help. She recalled, "I began having a special fast day once a week . . . never did I sit down to the typewriter without first praying with heart and soul, and many times I had to stop in between for more prayers."[55] She began all writing sessions with prayer, sometimes sitting at her typewriter for long periods waiting for God to reveal to her the ideas she was looking for. She remembered that after a day's writing she "felt like a sponge that had been wrung out." She worked seven hours a day for nearly two months. She was close to finishing her first draft when summer vacation arrived and her children were all home from school. Andelin took a hiatus from writing for the summer and concentrated on her family. When the children returned to school in the fall, she once more hired domestic help and took up writing with renewed determination. She had to be drastic, she recalled. Cutting out all nonessentials, she resumed the work at hand, doing little else. She became so focused that, she said, "If I walked down the street and saw someone coming I crossed to the other side so I wouldn't have to talk to them." She noted that because she was so consumed in what she was doing, she lost friends. One of these was Verna Johnson. Helen recalled that Johnson had become increasingly "jealous" of her attraction to the booklets.

Andelin observed, "Verna wanted to keep the books secret. She didn't want to share. She was possessive of [them]."[56] Believing that the booklets were revealed to her by God, Andelin felt she could do with them what she wished. Offended at Helen's use of the material in the booklets for her own classes, Verna eventually withdrew from the friendship. But, as focused as Andelin had become on getting the information in print, Verna may have felt that Helen was the one who left the friendship first. Johnson had already established a large following of her own students in the Bay Area. When she invited Helen to Oakland, she had intentions of writing a marriage manual herself. In letters between the two, Verna confessed that she had been deeply hurt by Andelin's use of her treasured materials. Allowing Helen to return to Fresno with the booklets had been an extraordinary act of trust and friendship; Helen had violated that friendship by using her resources without her permission. Later, when Helen copyrighted the information in own her name, Verna gave up her idea to write a book and stopped teaching classes."[57]

Plunging into the final revision of her book, Andelin now worked at it sixteen hours a day, stopping only to eat and sleep. The writing, she recalled, finally began to get easier. Things started falling into place. God, she believed, was assisting her. And she had other help. Surprisingly, her once self-centered, distracted husband became a supportive partner. During all of this time, Andelin remembered, her husband was a tremendous help to her. Aubrey cooperated fully with his wife, rereading her book many times to help her with spelling, wording, and punctuation. Andelin credited her husband with giving her invaluable assistance on the subject of understanding men, which constituted 200 of the book's 380 pages: "My home was my workshop and he provided experience, inspiration, information and encouragement." At times, she reported, "I felt . . . the presence of my mother trying to help me from the Spirit World." Andelin's children also felt the importance of their mother's undertaking, even remembering it in their prayers.[58] Andelin rewrote the book seven times before it was finished.

The final draft of the book was completed in November 1963, but Andelin still felt it was too amateur. She sought the help of Phyllis Heald, a professional editor with Arizona Press Women, Inc., in Tucson, Arizona. Heald charged Helen fifty dollars and guided her through several revisions by providing valuable criticism and suggestions and helping with her literary skills. Andelin did not meet Heald until some time later; all of her editing assistance was via mail. In letters between Heald and Andelin, the editor expressed major concerns about the content of the book. Heald felt strongly about Helen's working title for her book, *Fascinating Womanhood*. She advised Helen not to use that title, that there were a set of little booklets written in the 1920s by that name that taught women to be timorous and coy and flutter their eyelids to be attractive to men. Heald, who felt that the proposed title sounded cheap, feared that Andelin's book would be negatively associated with the outdated booklets. She warned Helen that a publisher might argue against the book because "it is asking women, married women, to step aside and allow the new world of progress to move forward without their participation." And, she pointed out, Helen's manuscript encouraged women to "give up the gains they have made in the struggle for equality of opportunity in business, the arts and sciences." The "most vulnerable part of the book," Heald worried, was that it encouraged women to believe that "through application of her feminine intuition, instincts, charm, physical lure, patience, understanding and love, she can actually create a hero." Heald also expressed doubts about Andelin's Angela Human. If not carefully constructed, she warned, Angela Human could "give the impression of a Jekyll and Hyde combination." Heald ended her list of concerns with a note of support: "Of course, it is just as possible such a book could take the country by storm."[59] Except for noting that the title had been used before, Heald never made the connection between the booklets and Andelin's work. Perhaps she had never read them. Or if she did, she had forgotten. Andelin would take this lack of recognition as a good sign: "If only I could perceive the underlying truths in the little booklets, and others could not, they became even more of a 'hidden treasure of knowledge.'"[60]

Although Heald did not realize that she had plagiarized the booklets, Andelin was afraid somebody else might. She decided to seek legal advice. After looking at Helen's manuscript and the letter from the copyright office, a lawyer told her that citations were unnecessary. The information was public domain. Upon the advice of her attorney, and fearing that proper citations might confuse the reader, Andelin decided to leave them out. Twelve years later, when she asked her publisher about citing the booklets, she was again advised not to. It would only arouse "curiosity and become a nuisance," he told her. People would want to buy copies of the booklets instead of *Fascinating Womanhood*. Andelin posted a small notice in fine print on the publisher's page that said she had been inspired by materials written in the 1920s. Although she never gave credit to the authors of *The Secrets of Fascinating Womanhood*, Andelin was often reluctant to grant permission for other authors to use the material from her own book. She did so only if the other author agreed to use footnotes and include her book in the bibliography. In interviews forty years later, an uncomfortable Andelin said she wanted to give an "honest account" about what she had done with the booklets. Without admitting she plagiarized them, she did concede that the ideas were not her own: "I do not take credit for these ideas myself. God revealed them to me . . . [they were] pure knowledge from God."[61] Despite this explanation, Andelin nevertheless used the booklets liberally, copying much of them verbatim. Besides copying the title, she also used all of the main ideas, the sections on the Charles Dickens's characters, the Ideal Woman From a Man's Point of View, Angela Human, and the sections on childlikeness and understanding men. When questioned, she said, "It is rather complicated to explain which ideas came from the booklets and which were my own."[62] Later, in her autobiography and in her newsletters, she declared that her work was "written from scratch."[63] Andelin did use other materials in her book, too. One source she used liberally was scripture. She noted, "I take my ideas from religion. What greater source of truth is there than this?"[64] Another source was her observations of her husband, Aubrey. She said, "I only made a study of one man, but he was a very typical man." As well, she took suggestions from her students. Many of them brought related books and articles to class that she took advantage of. And she relied heavily on revelation that she described as "flashes from the eternal world."[65] Perhaps feeling guilty about copying the booklets, she later wrote, *Fascinating Womanhood* "was not a creation; it was a discovery."[66] Copied or not, the ideas resulted in huge book sales and changes in the lives of countless women. Once the editing was finished, Andelin obtained a copyright and made five mimeograph copies for students to read before publication.

Just before the manuscript was printed, Helen's cousin Marlene Startup invited Andelin to her home in San Marino, California, to speak about her soon-to-be-released book to an audience of about twenty women. They were "very nice ladies," Andelin recalled, and some of them were Startup's relatives. Andelin gave a two-and-a-half-day seminar in Startup's living room that covered the material she had been teaching in her classes for nearly three years. The women were so taken with the new information that seven of them approached her after the seminar and asked if they could become Fascinating Womanhood teachers themselves. From these seven women Andelin began her teaching program. The new teachers in San Marino began to experience the same kinds of success that Andelin had realized in her community. The classes were large; one of them registered over two hundred students. At the request of the teachers, Startup, a teacher herself, developed a set of teaching outlines, which she shared with Andelin. Helen mimeographed the outlines, compiled them in a bound packet, and distributed them to the San Marino teachers free of charge. Later she would copyright and publish the outlines and sell them for a fee to teachers in her nationwide teaching program. Helen never paid Startup for the use of the outlines, nor did she give her credit. The two women eventually had a falling out over teaching fees. "She caused a lot of trouble," said Helen. Startup broke from the Fascinating Womanhood organization and began teaching her own classes, under the name Joy of Womanhood.

In the spring of 1965, Aubrey hired the American Yearbook Company in nearby Visalia, California, to print the book. The first printing was just a thousand copies, many of which eager students had already purchased in advance. The books immediately sold out. The Andelins quickly placed a second order, and then a third. They continued to order more books to keep up with the demand. Soon local bookstores began ordering the book. In Salt Lake City, Deseret Book, the flagship book and supply store of the Mormon Church, began ordering books in batches of five hundred copies. Soon the demand was so great that the store began to order books in quantities of one thousand copies at a time. *Fascinating Womanhood* would eventually sell over three million copies. Its success, however, did not rest with the number of copies it sold but on its impact on marriages. This influence was evident in thousands of testimonials, many of which Andelin included in later versions of her book. From their home, the Andelins packaged books on the kitchen table and shipped them in large grocery boxes to eagerly awaiting customers.

Aubrey came up with a system of invoicing, and before long the couple had developed a rather amateur publishing company. This was the beginning of Aubrey Andelin's latest business venture, Pacific Press Publishers. Helen's mission to change women's lives, and Aubrey's newest financial endeavor, were off to a quick start. The newly recruited instructors began to teach the principles of *Fascinating Womanhood* in the suburbs of big cities as well as in smaller rural communities and outlying areas. "The classes spread far and wide," Andelin recalled, "one teacher leading to another, and soon we had a full-scale teaching program."[67] By 1966 the crusade to spread the *Fascinating Womanhood* message would see the participation of four hundred teachers in seventeen states. A movement was taking shape. In a few short years, Helen Andelin would become an iconic figure to whom thousands of American women would look for practical and spiritual advice. Andelin was not the architect of the Fascinating Womanhood philosophy. She was, however, its messenger. By imagining herself as the bearer of a crucial message, Andelin found a formidable amount of strength and determination. And her followers loved her. Of her discovery, she would later say, "I am a very ordinary person with average intelligence, no special gifts or talents. . . . But, I believe that because of my faith . . . the Lord blessed me with *a hidden treasure of knowledge.*"

As Andelin sold more books and became surer of herself, she began to speak to reporters about her newfound success. And she became increasingly critical of women who would not or could not save their marriages. Believing that a marriage succeeded or failed because of the wife, she placed the blame of a marriage gone wrong squarely on the woman's shoulders. To women who were not making progress in living the FW principles, she wrote, "Don't blame your husband. It is you who have failed."[68] She told one reporter, "We never have any failures unless the woman is too lazy to put all the teachings into effect."[69] To another she said, "If women have been unhappy with their role in the home it is because they have not given enough to it."[70] Following Andelin's lead, many women blamed themselves. Of the many mistakes she had made in her marriage, one woman confessed, "I hated myself with a passion I never knew existed. How could I have been so dumb . . . so blind . . . so stupid!"[71] Another said, "I can see where the many mistakes I've made have robbed my husband of his manhood."[72] "When I took the

F.W. course and read the book," said a reader, "I just couldn't believe how awful I had been. No wonder he behaved the way he did! I was doing everything wrong."[73] One fan said, "Looking back I can see that my husband's problem with alcohol was a very convenient scapegoat for my own shortcomings." And finally, a wife who had been married for seventeen unhappy years said, after discovering *Fascinating Womanhood*, "I read it cover to cover in two days, sobbing most of the time as I discovered what a selfish, ignorant fool I'd been."[74] When asked why she was so hard on women, Andelin answered, "I put a lot of responsibility on the woman because I write to women. If I were to write to men, I would tell them what they could do."[75] Besides, she explained, "Women are easier to correct and instruct than men. You might as well just face it."[76] Women seemed to respond to Andelin's tough-love approach. They attended classes, they bought books, and they wrote letters. Andelin had found a formula—and for thousands of women, the formula worked. Andelin's readers believed that by becoming the Ideal Woman, they could not only improve their situation, they could create their own heaven on earth.

Three

EVERYWOMAN'S
HEAVEN ON EARTH

*B*etty Friedan's critique on marriage, housewifery, and traditional sex roles left millions of homemakers dazed and confused. Prior to the publication of her book, male and female duties were well defined. Men worked outside the home as laborers, in factories, or at desk jobs, and women stayed home to raise the children and keep house. After *The Feminine Mystique* hit the bookstores, the home, long considered a refuge from the worries of the outside world, became a battleground in the war to define American womanhood. In 1963 Helen Andelin, responding to widespread reports of unhappy marriages, rising divorce rates, and increasing child delinquency, wrote her own book. In *Fascinating Womanhood*, Andelin, who had never heard of Betty Friedan, painted for her readers a picture of those happier times when the traditional objectives of men and women were unambiguous. In a country fraught with moral and social upheaval, for some, sticking to accustomed sex roles was comforting. Prior to Friedan there was little encouragement for women who chose not to follow convention. Three years before Andelin started teaching classes in California, Marie N. Robinson, a prominent psychologist and the author of *The Power of Sexual Surrender*, warned that women who turned away from what she believed to be their God-given roles were committing "sexual suicide." According to Robinson, the price that a woman paid for "deserting her true function" of wife and homemaker was "frigidity, restlessness, a soaring divorce rate, neurosis, homosexuality, and juvenile delinquency."[1] In the uncertain times of the early '60s, many women who didn't know which way to turn turned to Andelin.

Unhappily married women, noticed Andelin, remained as oblivious to the ways they could solve their marital problems as they were to the reasons for those problems in the first place. This, combined with popular images that were little more than simplistic caricatures of housewives, made for a great deal of bewilderment, disappointment, and anger. Tired, frustrated, and rebuked by other women, large numbers of American homemakers welcomed Andelin's unsophisticated solutions. She urged those women to shun more modern interpretations of womanhood and return to a time that seemed simpler and more innocent. And she provided plain instructions on how any woman, regardless of intellect, social class, appearance, or economic level, could do it. A satisfying marriage and happy home, she taught, was achievable for any woman. Women had no shortage of character, intelligence, or ability, she said. Nor, as Friedan charged, did they waste time, performing unimportant tasks. What they lacked was information and direction. For these women, Andelin had both. By following the principles of *Fascinating Womanhood* and living her part of God's plan, Andelin promised that any woman could turn her home into nothing short of a heaven on earth. All she had to do was learn to understand her husband, renounce a career outside the home, become an efficient and capable housekeeper, and satisfy her husband's sexual needs.

Success in marriage, taught Andelin, depended on husband and wife understanding their mission and living their respective roles. The trouble with modern society, she believed, was that the adoption of popular philosophies had resulted in a kind of social amnesia when it came to the original premise of and purpose for marriage. Modern women, she said, languished in unhappy, even tragic, marriages not because they were blindsided by an inherently unjust system, but rather because they had been deceived into thinking they were better off operating outside of their divine purpose.

Andelin argued that this deception resulted in women not receiving crucial training in how to be successful at marriage. Andelin's teachings eliminated equivocation by clearly defining the responsibilities of both men and women. To some it seemed to be a good alternative to the increasing struggles that came with being a contemporary woman. By simply doing one's prescribed duty, a woman not only pleased God, but created for her family a safe haven from the dangers and stresses of the outside world. By taking up her role as a homemaker, taught Andelin, a woman provided the calm, quiet, orderly place where children thrived, where women were happy, and where a man wanted to return after work. For scores of women, many without college degrees or significant career skills, Andelin's message was appropriate and relevant. At a time when Friedan and her followers charged that patriarchy was the root of female oppression, droves of ordinary women fervently supported it.

In order to live out the idyllic picture of the home as a heaven on earth, Andelin taught that a woman must understand the man's role as provider, protector, and guide. And she must accept her own part in the marriage. "A man is head of the household and woman is his subordinate helpmate," she said.[2] Man, she asserted, "was created in the image of God and was given dominion over the earth" and thus had dominion over his family.[3] Nevertheless, Andelin did not believe that men were more important than women. God had merely provided them with a different list of responsibilities. Men, she taught, were simple creatures who could and would misbehave if not properly cared for by a virtuous woman. If correctly understood and managed, any man had the potential of becoming a compatible, even outstanding husband. She contended, "A good woman can build or destroy a man. . . . By treating him the way he ought to be treated he will grow to be the man she dreams of."[4] Andelin believed that women were the moral guardians of the home, and that they were spiritually superior to their husbands. Still, a good wife, she said, must follow her partner. "The biggest problem in the American home today is the dominating woman—the woman who rebels and won't support the father as leader in the home," she said.[5] If a woman had trouble living her role, Andelin told her to pray: "The most important thing in living FW successfully is to pray about it day by day. . . . It is important to learn the principles, but in living it you will need God's guidance to succeed."[6] While her critics said that patriarchy was unjust, Andelin defended it as misunderstood and misused. Within the context of her greater mission, Andelin reworked patriarchy, identifying it not as a tool of repression but as a system for ordering families that actually freed women to live the kind of life that God had designed for them.

Andelin believed that the public was terribly confused about male and female roles; as a result, most men simply didn't know how to be men, and women didn't know how to treat them. Men were so different from women that it was "as though they came from another planet."[7] Thus, whatever mistakes men made were honest ones; it was up to the woman to overlook her husband's faults and allow him the freedom to correctly fulfill his role. Andelin instructed women to accept a man at face value and never try to change him. Rather than concentrating on her husband's errors, a wife must look to her own weaknesses instead. "Allow for his bad behavior and negligence," said Andelin. She promised that a woman who accepted her husband the way he was could transform him "from an apparently stupid, weak, lazy, cowardly, unrighteous man into a determined, energetic, true, and noble one."[8] Besides accepting him for who he was, a good woman admired her husband's manliness and made him the number one priority in her life. She was obedient, feminine, and entirely dependent when it came to things outside the realm of home and children. And she did everything in her power to please him. "Instead of trying to make him over," instructed Andelin, "try making him happy."[9] While a woman's deepest desire was for a man's love, taught Andelin, a man's deepest desire was for admiration. A man needed admiration for his manly qualities, his physical strength, his ability to provide for his family, and his sound decision-making ability. Andelin suggested that women find something to admire in their husbands every day. If a wife did not admire her husband, a marriage could be grim. One woman learned this lesson, reporting, "I was getting bitter criticism from by husband about the meals I fixed, that I was neglecting the children, etc. It was unjustified, for I had been trying especially hard to fix meals that pleased him and be a good mother. . . . He was so mean to me." Following Andelin's instructions to admire him at least once a day, even though he didn't deserve it, she reported that he stopped criticizing her and became tender. He even paid her compliments, and took her on long walks. She said, "It was just like turning off the cold shower and replacing it with a soft warm one."[10]

Andelin said that a man wanted to feel needed by those who depended on him. He was sensitive about his masculinity and could not stand to have it belittled, ridiculed, or treated with indifference. To protect a man's sensitive pride, Andelin taught women not to appear overly wise or to show a greater intelligence than her husband. When it came to bad behaviors such as drinking, gambling, chasing women, or being stingy, a man was not entirely at fault. "A husband would not be lazy, grumpy or unfaithful if the wife put to work FW principles," she told her followers.[11] One woman agreed, asserting, "Bit by bit, nag by nag . . . I changed him from a loving, tender, and very understanding man to a violent, uncommunicative, withdrawn tyrant. *Fascinating Womanhood* has saved my marriage and made my husband happy again."[12] When it came to adultery and alcoholism, Andelin often blamed the woman. "First check your own life. Are you the cause if it?" she asked readers. Had the woman "unwittingly contributed to a situation where [her husband] succumbed to a weakness? Most likely she had some part in it."[13] A man who strayed was not looking for sex, she explained; he was seeking appreciation and admiration. He wanted a woman who would make him feel like a king. A man's home was his castle, and a woman who did not treat him like a king could not expect his love or his fidelity. "If a man does not love his wife with his heart and soul, it is the wife's fault," she said.[14] Andelin taught that a woman who made mistakes with her husband needed to recognize and acknowledge her weaknesses, ask him for forgiveness, then commit to fundamental change. "When I called him a king and treated him as such, he had a desire to act like one," said one follower.[15]

Because a woman desired love more than equality, taught Andelin, she willingly deferred to her husband in all things. Being the leader was one of man's basic needs and was crucial to his happiness. According to the Bible, it was his destiny: "Let the woman learn in silence with all subjection. . . . But I suffer not a woman to . . . usurp authority over the man, but to be in silence."[16] Andelin further cited the passage, "Ye wives, be in subjection to your husbands."[17] A husband must have the freedom, Andelin said, to preside over his family as he saw fit. In his role as leader, a husband was at liberty to make plans and decisions unencumbered by the pressure of his wife or other family members. "Equality in running a family," said Andelin, "is the most impractical, unworkable arrangement ever conceived. Everyday decisions must be made and one person has to make them since two seldom agree."[18] In her article "How to Be a Perfect Follower," Andelin urged women to simply let go of the reins. Allow the husband to lead the family, she said, even if it looked like he would lead it into ruin. A woman must place her faith in God. For women who let their husbands lead, there were payoffs. A woman whose husband was in charge was relieved of tremendous responsibility, worry, and concern. A woman whose husband led, said Andelin, was free to function fully in her feminine role of keeping her home and caring for her children. Turning leadership over to one's husband brought peace into the household that would not otherwise be there if the woman were trying to make the decisions. A woman who stepped into the masculine role of decision making, said Andelin, could look forward to mental and physical strain, anxiety, tension, the loss of feminine charm, and perhaps even the loss of her husband's love. By following her husband's lead, however, a woman could be secure in his love, and free from worry. "Talk about women's liberation," declared one follower, "this is it!"[19]

A strong sense of self-esteem was one of a man's most prized possessions, taught Andelin. A good wife did all she could to encourage him to develop it. The most important way a man built his self-esteem was by providing for his family. It made him feel important. Moreover, it was God's commandment: "But if any not provide for his own, and especially for those of his own house, he hath denied the faith, and is worse than an infidel."[20] In addition to supporting his family, Andelin taught that a man had a need to gain status. It was not enough to be merely a paycheck. He hungered to excel in his work. A man wanted to be the hero at home, but he also wanted to distinguish himself in the world of men. A wife should understand this and support him in reaching his goals—even if it meant putting her dreams and desires on hold. To help a man succeed at work, a woman admired him and acknowledged and appreciated his efforts. She was careful not to overspend or yearn for luxuries. And she did her job dealing with the house and children to eliminate his stress when he came home after a long day. When a man walked in the door, a good wife had her housework done, dinner on the table, and the children under control. And she willingly took second place. "FW teaches that a wife should place her husband number one in her life," said Andelin, "but it is not possible, or even right, that a man place his wife first. A man must often neglect his wife and family in the responsibility he feels at work. . . . It is better to have ten percent of a one hundred percent man, than one hundred percent of a ten percent man."[21] When it came to a woman's role, Andelin relied on the Bible. Just as God had commanded Eve to serve and obey Adam, so were modern-day women commanded to serve and obey their husbands. For Andelin, being a good wife was a matter of character; it was a virtue that elevated the home to a place of importance and honor. "No success compares to the success in the home; no failure a worse failure," she said.[22] God, believed Andelin, measured a woman's worth not by her relationship with him but by her relationship with her husband. Being a successful wife and mother was not just a job; it was a religious duty. A happy home, taught Andelin, was not just a place where happy children resided; it was a place where honorable citizens were raised. Andelin, like Phyllis Schlafly and others who came later, connected motherhood to citizenship. Happy families, taught Andelin, meant a secure nation: "We who belong to the profession of housewife hold the fate of the world in our hands. It is our influence that will determine the culture of coming generations."[23]

In her quest to create a bit of heaven on earth, a good wife adopted Andelin's image of the Domestic Goddess. "Domestic Goddess," a term Andelin borrowed from the character Amelia in William Thackeray's 1917 novel *Vanity Fair*, demonstrated the practical and heavenly components necessary to achieve a happy marriage and successfully run a home. A Domestic Goddess was a cheerful, dignified, and capable homemaker. She spent her day keeping a clean, orderly home, cooking delicious meals, and wisely sticking to a budget. "She looketh well to the ways of her household, and eateth not the bread of idleness," said the Bible.[24] A Domestic Goddess beautified her surroundings, kept herself attractive and in good health, and took special care to see that her children were happy and well behaved. All of her energies went into being the best wife and mother possible. A Domestic Goddess learned the necessary skills and dutifully worked as long as required to achieve success and feel pride in her career in the home. However daunting her list of duties, a Domestic Goddess was never just a worker. She performed an invaluable service for her family while maintaining an attitude of appreciation toward the work she did. Her vocation was not meaningless toil, taught Andelin; it was "a sacred trust."[25] A woman's work lasted only about twenty years, Andelin reminded her audience. A man's work, however, lasted a lifetime. To critics who charged that *Fascinating Womanhood* advocated female slavery, Andelin shot back, "If it's slavery you are talking about, it is really the man who is the slave. He's the one who is tied to the inflexibility of a job since his role is to be the provider. She is the one who is free . . . nobody is making her punch a clock."[26] For some, the positive results of espousing the Domestic Goddess role were compelling. The revival of the domestic role resulted in the rejuvenation of traditional beliefs about the essential importance of the home. Elevating the significance of the home, and thus the housewife, gave hardworking homemakers the instant boost in status that many of them craved for performing thankless tasks year after year. They saw rewards for work that had previously gone unappreciated. Some *Fascinating Womanhood* devotees, who earned wages and continued to shoulder the bulk of domestic duties at home, quit their jobs and claimed the right to stay home. Those already at home eagerly took more pride in their domestic accomplishments. For them, the Domestic Goddess ideal outlined what many women felt was a more evenhanded designation of duties between husband and wife. Many women responded with relief and felt increased happiness. "I am grateful to FW for making me feel that my job as a homemaker is worthwhile," said one woman. "I've always known it, but Women's Lib made me feel guilty. Like I was a parasite for not going out and working."[27]

While, to her detractors, the Domestic Goddess was just another unpaid worker, she had great appeal to the women who embraced her. A Domestic Goddess did not bring home a paycheck, yet her contribution to her husband's financial success was of major value to her family and community. Not only was a woman who successfully ran her home freed from the burden of working for wages, she also enjoyed a greater amount of personal freedom than one might think. An efficient homemaker, said Andelin, had ample opportunity to pursue other interests, develop talents, and give service in order to enrich her life and make herself a better person. Andelin argued that this ideal woman stood for an important division of labor. A man had his work, and a woman had hers. For many women, caring for home and family made economic sense as well. Women who stayed home could engage in alternative forms of making money. Many Fascinating Womanhood followers gave music lessons, sold garden vegetables, babysat for their neighbors, cleaned other people's homes, took in sewing and ironing, and sometimes involved themselves in direct-sales organizations such as Amway or Mary Kay. Reluctant to give up these flexible but less conventional ways of supplementing the family income, women who stayed home opposed what they saw as the limitations of wage work. The feminist assessment that unpaid work was unimportant work rested on the philosophy that all work carried a monetary value. For most homemakers, this made little sense. Their experience of daily life required endless hours of work for which they never expected compensation. For many women, thinking in monetary terms about the domestic service that one willingly contributed without pay was insulting. Household tasks, they believed, had an intrinsic value involving integrity and responsibility, not money.

When it came to raising a family, Andelin taught that a woman's relationship with her husband always came first. Child-centered families jeopardized the marriage. A woman should make the strongest commitment to her husband, and place the children second. A good wife must say no to the kids, diligently carve out adult time, and focus on the marital relationship. In an article in *Family Circle Magazine*, the author Judith Sills supported Andelin's assertions. Like her predecessor, Sills said that the relationship between husband and wife should always come first. In families where the children were more important than the marriage, the heart of the household had shifted in the wrong direction. Marital love, she said, should always come before parental love. Like Andelin, Sills urged spouses to say no to the kids and find time to be alone. A strong marriage, not bending to the needs of the children, made for a successful family, she said.[28] As she honored and obeyed her husband, said Andelin, so must a wife also teach her children to honor and obey their father. She believed that the biggest problem resulting from a woman failing to honor the father as head of his household was juvenile delinquency. When a woman ceased to submit to the control of her husband, said Andelin, she lost control of her children. "The problems of rebellious youth can, in most cases, be traced to homes where the mother has been disobedient to the father or showed a lack of respect for his authority," she said.[29]

In addition to obeying her husband and relishing her role as wife and mother, a Domestic Goddess was a good housekeeper. The art of homemaking, in contrast to the images promoted by critics who saw keeping house as freeloading, was part of the long-standing models of domestic bliss in which women had been indoctrinated since Victorian times. In 1944 one rural Montana housekeeper put these beliefs into verse:

THE HOUSEWIFE'S SONG
I love to scrub the floors
And see their faces shine;
To dust the homey walls
And know that they are mine . . .
I love to wash the dishes
To see them sparkle bright,
And gently tuck the covers in
On every bed at night . . .
Of course these tasks are lowly,
But I love them—wouldn't you?
For it's life—and a good life is loving
The things that you must do.[30]

In 1963 Andelin communicated the same spirit of pride and joy in the domestic arts that the author of "The Housewife's Song" had written just nineteen years earlier. She understood that homemaking was serious business. She rejected Friedan's description of housewifery as mind-numbing, and the home as a "comfortable concentration camp." Andelin reminded women that there was a certain amount of pride—even enjoyment—inherent in any job performed with the right tools and proper attitude. In her book she provided a detailed outline and schedule of household duties that women should follow in order to be the most efficient housekeepers possible. Making beds, cooking, ironing, mending clothes, doing laundry, washing floors, and cleaning toilets all had their time and place in the schedule of a capable homemaker. Andelin recommended that cleaning be done rigorously and often, and that meals always be served on time. To be sure, running an efficient household, like any profession, took plenty of work. However, once a woman understood that homemaking was as important and personally satisfying as any other career, the focus shifted from the tedious nature of the work itself to the happiness one could realize from the successful completion of it. Any woman could become a successful homemaker, she believed, and there was no excuse for being a poor one. Andelin taught that women who failed at homemaking did so because they lacked character, were too busy with outside interests, had a poor self-image, made excuses, and even suffered demonic influences.[31] "A woman who is not a good homemaker," said Andelin, "is . . . a failure in life."

For the homemaker, running a tight ship paid off. A successfully run home was a place of peace and harmony. Good housekeeping eliminated chaos, saved money, and encouraged a cheerful spirit of teamwork. Importantly, said Andelin, an efficient household allowed a husband to be more successful at work and make a better living. Andelin believed that any woman could be an efficient housekeeper, provided she create a schedule, set definite goals and time limits, and vary her schedule only in emergencies. A good housekeeper never allowed herself to be crowded for time. Andelin suggested that to concentrate on her work a homemaker must eliminate all optional activities, such as attending baby showers and having coffee with friends or long conversations on the telephone. In order to be a good housekeeper, Andelin taught that a woman must face her work realistically. Not all women's work, she explained, was as pleasant as a man's. A woman must accept a certain amount of drudgery. A Domestic Goddess always maintained her femininity—even in the face of dirty jobs like cleaning floors and toilets. She put on a pretty face and accepted her work without complaint. While a Domestic Goddess willingly cared for her home and family, she never did men's work around the house. Men's work, said Andelin, consisted of mowing the lawn, washing the car, spading the garden, weeding, spraying for bugs, doing repairs, and painting. Such activities, which Andelin identified as physically destructive, detracted from a woman's feminine charm and could even be physically injurious. "Happy wives," she reminded women, "are helpless wives."[32]

When a woman thought of herself as the queen of her household, uncomplainingly accepted a significant amount of hard work, and displayed a genuine willingness to do whatever was needed, she brought "a sort of glory to her work as a homemaker." Rather than squandering her labor, Andelin taught that the Domestic Goddess was a purposeful, virtuous woman. By her consistent efforts she not only managed her own life the way God intended but added indispensable warmth of spirit to her household. Andelin reminded the legions of overworked and under-appreciated women that caring for their families was "a career of worldwide importance and infinite purpose," and that as Domestic Goddesses they could claim their position of honor in the home.[33] Andelin's esteem for the Domestic Goddess appealed to the rising numbers of women who, having made entire careers of family caretaking, began to realize that homemaking, once considered a noble undertaking, had become a dirty word. In 1965 Helen Gurley Brown, the founder of *Cosmopolitan* magazine, denounced the housewife as "a parasite, a dependent, a scrounger, a sponger [and] a bum." In a 1970 *Time Magazine* article, the feminist leader Gloria Steinem "castigated traditional women as 'inferiors' and 'dependent creatures who are still children.'" And some feminist extremists condemned women who made a career in the home as "traitors to their sex."[34] As the feminist critique against the besieged housewife grew more virulent, Andelin articulated a clear model of behavior and attitude that was both familiar and reassuring in the battle to define American womanhood.

A Domestic Goddess not only cared for her home, she stayed there. A woman's working outside the home, warned Andelin, usurped the male role, thereby damaging her husband's self-esteem. Because one of the basic needs of a man is to provide for his family, a woman's income threatened his masculinity and led to marital problems. A working wife deflated her husband's ego. In addition to the problems it caused in children when a woman worked, there was the danger that a man would lose his desire to support his family altogether. Women who worked outside the home, said Andelin, performed the sad disservice of letting husbands off the hook for their responsibly to take care of the family financially. Demoralized at having his wife perform his job, a man might respond by not working as hard, or not working at all. "When a woman lifts, a man tends to set his bucket down," she warned.[35] Andelin encouraged working women to simply quit their jobs and let the husband struggle to make a livable income. It would make him a better man. Sometimes quitting was the only way a woman could make a man accept his responsibilities. The feminist poet and novelist Erica Jong quipped, "Beware of the man who praises women's liberation. He is about to quit his job."[36]

For most American women, returning to the workforce, where they would have to compete with either men or seasoned career women, meant low wages and even lower status. Despite the efforts of the women's movement, there was little support for women who stepped outside the role of wife and mother to join the workforce. Although the women's liberation movement brought needed attention to the power imbalance between men and women, there were practical reasons that significant numbers of rational women preferred the Domestic Goddess role over the ideal of the empowered career woman. For millions of American women, the idea of the self-determining career woman proved to be merely that—an idea. The majority of women who worked outside the home did so in low-paying jobs with few benefits and fewer opportunities to improve their status. A woman who stayed home didn't have to pay for day care, a housekeeper, or meals. She didn't need her own car, and she didn't need a professional wardrobe. For many women, the cost of going to work offset the income they made. For Andelin's followers, staying home made sense. Even after feminists pointed out the inequities of housework, full-time career women still performed 90 percent of household chores. Andelin's viewpoint about the distribution of labor resonated with these overworked, career-minded "super-moms," women who, in addition to contributing to the family's finances, continued to shoulder the lion's share of the responsibilities at home. "Once I knew the roles and rules for marriage I was relieved of a lot of responsibility," said a former executive and FW teacher, Alwilda Braun. "Too many women try to be responsible for everything that happens in the family but they shouldn't. . . . I don't believe women should be garbage dumps for everything and everyone."[37] Andelin found wide support for her claim that providing an income in addition to performing the staggering amount of household and child-rearing duties expected of them robbed women of the ability to succeed at either task. Protecting a woman's right to her calling as a homemaker was only fair, she reasoned. She believed that *all* women were entitled to the right to choose housewifery over wage work. Her followers agreed.

Andelin, who supported her husband through dental school, taught that sometimes a woman was justified in working. Women could legitimately work outside the home, she said, in the case of compelling emergencies such as sickness, injury, or recovery from a drinking problem. She could also work to further a husband's education or training. As well, it was acceptable to work if her children were grown. In these cases, Andelin encouraged the women who wrote to her to be strong and keep working—but only until the crisis had passed. Then, she counseled, the husband must resume his rightful role as provider, and the working woman must return to her appropriate place as wife and mother. The money a wife made in her job outside the home, instructed Andelin, must be turned over to her husband for him to manage and distribute any way he chose. A woman should never work to ease her husband's workload, she added. As provider and leader of the family, it was his responsibility to take a second job if he needed to. If a woman had to work, Andelin encouraged her to take secretarial jobs or similar kinds of low-level work. Accepting a managerial or executive job posed the danger that a wife might outshine her husband and threaten his masculinity. When it came to equality in the workplace, Andelin said that neither she nor "any normal woman" believed women were "treated as an inferior" just because they were "kept out of certain positions in science, medicine, government, economic leadership, etc." She asserted that unequal pay does not cause a feeling of inferiority. She said, "We are paid less because of special consideration given to us as women, because we are not apt to be as consistent on the job as men." She held that if men were keeping women out of "masculine fields," it was because they had "respect for femininity, because they would like to keep women the gentle dependent creatures they were designed to be."[38] Andelin believed there were long-range implications of working: "If women continue to work, they will change our economy so that women will have to work. Our daughters will have no choice."[39]

While a husband ruled over his wife in all matters, Andelin drew the line at what she called a husband "putting his wife out to work." If a husband asked his wife to work, Andelin instructed her to say no. She advised one follower whose husband insisted that she work to simply resign. She asserted, "It's your right. He was commanded to earn the bread, not you."[40] Andelin, who supported women collecting Social Security for a lifetime of work, believed that all women had the right to financial support. A capable husband's refusal to support his family, along with adultery and physical abuse, she taught, was grounds for divorce. Andelin was hard on women who worked for luxuries or out of boredom. "I attack women who work when they don't have to," she said. "Our greatest problem today is juvenile delinquency and women should stay home and tend to their children."[41] She added, "Any woman who moves out into a man's world to conquer it and compete with him is a fool."[42]

Andelin didn't believe that women should train for careers. Suspicious of higher education, she felt that a woman's best training was what she could learn on her own. "Why study about the universe when we can't make our own marriages work?" she asked.[43] If a woman did go to college, Andelin believed, she should major in the liberal arts—not science, or math—or get a vocational degree. When asked about the case of widows or single mothers left without the ability to provide for themselves, she said, "If she trains for a career, there is too much chance she'll use it instead of staying home. It's not worth it just for the rare emergency that she might need the training someday."[44] Andelin wasn't the only one decrying the evils of the working woman. In a 1969 article in *Woman's Day* magazine, a writer warned that a woman's working, besides damaging a man's ego, made him defensive and overly sensitive. A working woman lost respect for her husband, and therefore nagged and criticized him for not being the sole supporter of the family, which further undermined his ego. In order to ease the difficulties it caused a man to have his wife work, the article, like Andelin, encouraged women to minimize their own successes. "Stop doing things better than he can," said Andelin. "It would be good if you could fail at something."[45]

But, in fact, Andelin was herself a serious businesswoman, and she made a lot of money. When the Fascinating Womanhood movement was at its height, she took to the road for months at a time to promote her book and give speeches. While she was traveling, and during the time she was writing her book, Andelin hired full-time help to care for her children and run her household. When asked about these contradictions, she justified herself by saying that her work was not a career. Rather, it was "a mission of charity" and "a benevolent service" that required sacrifice. Not all women believed her. One observed, "Mrs. Andelin, you are fooling yourself. You tell women to stay home and run their households and not have a career and that this is where they will find fulfillment. But you are the most professional of all women. In fact, you are a businesswoman par excellence. Many women follow your recipe and it does not work."[46] For women other than herself,

Andelin said of housekeeping and raising children, "To neglect these sacred tasks or turn them over to someone else is a serious dereliction of duty."[47] Not only did Andelin work, she was the star of the family. While her husband, Aubrey, traveled with her and was quoted in newspaper articles, he remained solidly in the background. Given these incongruities, Andelin explained, "In a way, I feel out of role because I never sought the spotlight. This was never my purpose. In the very beginning, it was only to help women, and I didn't plan to have classes. But the demand was so great—women kept coming to me."[48]

While a woman did not have decision-making power in her home, Andelin argued that she had an important power nonetheless. She taught that while a woman could never control her husband, she did have the power to influence him. A woman who practiced the principles of *Fascinating Womanhood*, she said, developed a magical power over her husband. If she took care of his needs and gave him his freedom, a wife could get most of what she wanted. For women who worried that their husbands would make mistakes with all of their newfound freedom, Andelin said, "Accept him and let him suffer the consequences."[49] Sometimes a man's bad decisions led to financial problems. In this case, a woman had to be adaptable. "Make all your dreams portable. Women should learn to be happy anywhere, in any circumstance—on a mountain top, or on a burning desert, in poverty's vale or abounding in wealth."[50] She asserted that a woman succeeded in marriage only if she adjusted to the man's way of doing things, "to his tastes, to his likes and dislikes, to his hobbies, [and] his pleasures." The woman who adjusted herself to fit her husband's "whims and pleasures is adored and treasured by her husband."[51] For the woman who couldn't adapt, or who questioned her husband, Andelin predicted dire consequences. Such a woman could count on her husband finding interests outside the home, including alcohol and other women.

A good wife lived within her husband's means. If a husband did not make enough to live on, it didn't mean that a wife should go to work. Instead, she needed to take the burden off of him by living frugally and making a dollar stretch. "If anything is killing man it's the extravagance of women," she said.[52] Thrift, taught Andelin, was not only a necessity, it was a virtue. Andelin waged what she believed to be a righteous struggle against consumerism.

She made her own bread and encouraged her followers to do the same. She warned against feeding the family prepackaged foods of any kind. She cautioned, "The next time you are tempted to feed your family ice cream, think of it as a mixture of anti-freeze, oil paint, and nitrate solvent."[53] She sewed her own clothes and dispensed recipes for homemade shampoo and meatless meals in her monthly newsletter. Rather than working outside the home for what she considered luxuries, Andelin urged women to cut out all nonessentials in order to make her husband's paycheck go further. "What do we need?" she asked. "Food, basic clothing and shelter. Then we do need some soap for washing, a broom for sweeping, and some pots, pans, and dishes."[54] Some of Andelin's suggestions for economizing were drastic. Sell a large home, she instructed, and move to a smaller, more affordable one. Sell one car and take the bus. Cut out music lessons for the kids. Don't take vacations; take the kids to the park or to the mountains for a picnic instead. Simplify meals by cutting out meat. Wear clothes as long as possible, and hand the older kids' clothes down to the younger ones. Shop at used clothing stores, and don't use fabric softener. Learn to sew. Get a side income. Breastfeed your babies. By breastfeeding her baby, Andelin pointed out, a wife could save enough money to buy a major appliance. Bottle feeding, on the other hand, "makes it all too easy for a mother to leave her baby for long periods of time to pursue her own self-interests." She said, "Every woman in America could live on her husband's income if she tried."

Andelin taught that a successful wife made her husband happy by understanding his sex needs. This presented a difficulty for Andelin's readers because *Fascinating Womanhood* didn't say anything about sex. In fact, it was probably the only marriage manual on the market that didn't discuss the topic of sex at all. Many bewildered wives wrote to Andelin asking for help. Believing that counselors gave bad advice and didn't work, Aubrey Andelin took on the subject of sex himself. In 1973, with suggestions from his wife, he wrote a pamphlet about sex that he sold under separate cover. *Fascinating Womanhood Principles Applied to Sex,* like *Fascinating Womanhood,* talked a lot about God and said very little about sex. A virgin at the time he was married, and not trained in any form of counseling, Aubrey nonetheless dispensed advice about sex with confidence. His advice was naïve, confusing, and often silly. *Fascinating Womanhood Principles Applied to Sex* taught virginity before marriage, restraint in sexual frequency, and how to say no. Masturbation and pornography were strictly forbidden. Perhaps the reason that the pamphlet said so little about actual sex was that Helen firmly believed that if a woman practiced *Fascinating Womanhood* diligently, a couple's sexual problems would simply go away. "If a woman really loves a man, she'll be turned on about sex," she said.[55] One happy follower agreed. After living Fascinating Womanhood, a formerly "frigid" wife said, "Our sex problems just weren't there any longer. . . . I have become his bride-lover again."[56]

While it said nothing about the act itself, *Fascinating Womanhood Principles Applied to Sex* said a great deal about women satisfying the sex needs of their husbands. While it was within a woman's right to say no, Aubrey suggested that if she developed a wholesome attitude and a feeling of compassion toward her husband's sex needs, she would feel more like having sex herself. One way a woman could have a better attitude about sex was to remember that God gave men a strong sex drive to encourage the creation of children. This drive had to be strong enough to overcome a man's reluctance to take on the burdens of a family. In being a willing sex partner to her husband, a wife was not only making him happy, she was serving a religious function. God commanded Adam and Eve to be fruitful and multiply. Modern-day couples should do the same, said Andelin. He promised that if a woman gave sex to her husband freely, she would learn to enjoy it. He wrote, "If a woman will have sympathy for her husband's sex needs, and learn to give of herself, adapting her feelings and life circumstances to his needs as much as she can, her sexual feelings will be increased."[57] Although *Fascinating Womanhood Principles Applied to Sex* advised sex in moderation, in interviews, Helen said, "There's no reason that a wife shouldn't be ready for sex every night." She contended, "Women spend too much time in the kitchen rather than in the bedroom."[58] She further said, "If a woman will give her all in sex to her husband, forgetting about her own lack of desire in her eagerness to please . . . she will awaken herself to a more pleasurable experience."[59] The Andelins encouraged women to accept a husband's erotic nature and to give wholeheartedly. A woman should make her husband number one, and make sex a priority. If these suggestions didn't work and a woman still didn't want to have sex, she should eliminate any resentment she may have toward her husband, use herbs to enhance sexual desire, or try to get herself in the mood by "awakening the senses." Andelin encouraged women to nourish themselves with good food, fresh air, and exercise, and look at the beauties of nature. "Sometimes a woman can 'turn-on' by watching a water-fall or the dramatic churning of the ocean," advised Aubrey. Additionally, she could eat the right kinds of food. Aubrey claimed, "Food with a sharp taste such as pickles, cheese, sharp salad dressings or foods with a 'zing' can help in its own way."

In the case of a woman who wanted the attentions of an uninterested hus-band, he warned that she should never pursue him. A husband, in his manly role, was always the initiator. Wearing makeup, perfume, and sexy nightwear and hurrying a husband into bed was the wrong approach for any wife. Instead, a woman should practice the virtues of femininity, dependence, and obedience. An "oversexed" tendency in a woman, taught Aubrey, was "unnatural." When a woman acquired the masculine traits of aggressiveness, boldness, and drive in her desire for sex, she could turn her husband off, or even drive him away. What could a woman do if she wanted more sex? Aubrey suggested that she fix her husband a delicious meal, dress in feminine nightwear, and make sure the children were in bed early. If a husband did not respond to these clues, a wife should practice reverse psychology. Ignore him. Read a book. Be too busy. In fact, it was Helen who contributed such ideas as: "[Wear] a high-necked flannel nightgown, no makeup or perfume and go to bed with the attitude of getting some sleep. . . . If he touches you move away as if you did not notice it. If anything will awaken his affections this approach will."[60] Thus, a woman who was smart and pliable could keep her husband happy and maybe even find some happiness herself when it came to the bedroom. "To me," said Helen, "there isn't any real true love in marriage without a very, very high type of sex life."[61]

For thousands of Andelin's followers, understanding men, letting their husband be the leader, embracing their career in the home, not going to work, and understanding a man's sex needs had their rewards. Besides get-ting more of the things they wanted, some newly feminine women expe-rienced dramatic physical changes as well. Several of Andelin's readers reported a cessation of menstrual cramps and irregular periods.[62] Others saw a rounding and softening of their appearance. One woman claimed to have developed larger breasts as a result of making her own bread. Some women insisted they had fuller hair and fewer facial lines. Some even lost weight and quit smoking.[63] Wives also reported getting material rewards such as perfume, flowers, clothes, vacuum cleaners, appliances, and trips to Hawaii. One woman even remarked that living FW principles cured her of suicidal depression. "I'd gotten so depressed I'd even considered suicide," she wrote. Recently separated from her husband of twenty-two years, she found *Fascinating Womanhood* in a bookstore. She eagerly read it front to back and immediately put its principles to work. After several months of following Andelin's advice, she succeeded in getting her husband to move back home. Not only did her desire to kill herself disappear, she was able to rekindle their love. "Now I want fifty more years with my wonderful husband," she declared.[64]

Andelin's simple message enraged her critics; but it electrified her followers. Women who attended Fascinating Womanhood classes spread the word to friends and neighbors, who also signed up for classes. Churches and YMCAs all over the country began to sponsor classes, and the Andelins couldn't ship books fast enough. Helen Andelin became well known on the lecture and seminar circuit. She gave interviews to radio stations. Newspapers ran stories about her. Before she knew it, she had created a large and loyal fan base. So grateful were her enthusiasts that one exclaimed, "After reading *Fascinating Womanhood* the light came on and I felt like shouting it to the world."[65] "Next to my Bible," said another, "*Fascinating Womanhood* is the most valuable book I have ever read."[66]

Four

HEYDAY

*A*fter its first publication in 1965, *Fascinating Womanhood* sold swiftly to an eager local market. In California, classes filled to capacity, and hundreds of women wrote to Andelin requesting lesson materials and volunteering to teach classes in their communities. In Utah, sales benefited from the fact that the Deseret Book in downtown Salt Lake City and the BYU campus bookstore in nearby Provo had posters and large displays of the book. *Fascinating Womanhood* became such a big seller in those two stores that eventually the BYU-sponsored Continuing Education System (CES) began hosting classes in Salt Lake City. For a while the classes packed in audiences of nine hundred students a week. Soon, bookstores all over the state began carrying *Fascinating Womanhood* as the message spread outside of the Mormon community. In time, women of all ages, races, religions, and economic and educational backgrounds were enthusiastically buying the book and attending FW classes. Andelin began channeling her energy into preparing teaching resources. The couple boxed and shipped books as fast as they could print them.

Although her book was a big success, Andelin ran into trouble with the Continuing Education System. The Los Angeles branch of the CES, formerly under the direction of Wayne Schute, had changed personnel. Schute had asked her to write a teaching manual that the CES could print for women who taught the church-sponsored classes. Unfortunately for Andelin, by the time the manual was finished, a new director had replaced Schute. Unlike his predecessor, Schute's replacement was not an enthusiastic supporter of Andelin or her book. He told her that without a PhD, she had no business writing such a book, and he informed her that the CES would no longer sponsor classes. Undaunted, Andelin wrote to her teachers, "The work of FW continues to grow. If we can't make it widespread quickly we certainly can slowly."[1] The Andelins bought a mimeograph machine and began printing *The Teacher's Lesson Guide: Fascinating Womanhood* from home. In response to the many women who wrote asking for authorization to teach classes, Andelin developed a simple set of rules, issued official permission, and made the *Teacher's Lesson Guide* available for sale.

By 1966 the Andelins had sold over forty thousand copies of *Fascinating Womanhood*. With book sales and the sale of *The Teacher's Lesson Guide*, the couple was making good money. Riding on a wave of success, they sought out a professional publishing company in New York City. Helen sent the book to Prentice Hall and waited for a response. The publishing house expressed interest but asked for heavy editorial work before they would agree to publish it. Unwilling to take advice and reluctant to make changes, the Andelins ignored the offer. Regretting their decision, two years later they traveled to New York to visit Prentice-Hall in person. One of the company's top executives agreed to meet with them. When they asked if the original offer still stood, the editor said he was no longer interested in the book. Besides, he added, they had probably already saturated the market. Flabbergasted, a disbelieving Aubrey explained that they had sold the books in a limited area, and that the market outside of California and Utah was almost untouched. The executive was unmoved and ended the meeting.

Next, the Andelins tried to contact Doubleday Publishers, to which they had previously sent a copy of *Fascinating Womanhood*. Doubtful the book would sell, the sales department had already rejected it, and the couple's efforts to see a company representative went nowhere. Hawthorne Books took an interest, offering the Andelins 15 percent in royalties. They declined because they didn't like the part of town where the publisher was located or the look of their office building. Making rash decisions would become a continuing theme in the Andelins' story. They often decided things based on feelings and intuition rather than information and hard facts. At the end of their disappointing trip to New York, Aubrey and Helen returned to Clovis to continue publishing and distributing the books themselves. That year, Andelin held a teachers' convention in Los Angeles, and four hundred women attended. She was a gifted motivational speaker, and the crowd loved her. She continued to teach classes and hold seminars throughout California.

One of the appeals of the Fascinating Womanhood system was that it required no special skills—and it didn't cost anything. The price of the book in 1965 was $6.50, but the classes were free. Teachers were unpaid volunteers, and courses were taught in church space or private homes at no charge. Teachers bought *Fascinating Womanhood* at wholesale and sold it to students at the retail price, making about two dollars per book. To offset the cost of their free time, many teachers set up elaborate display tables and sold related books and supplies to their students before and after class. Some of these items were daily-planning journals, candles, jewelry, lingerie, and motivational tapes. Teachers also sold makeup, vitamins, Bibles, and books on homemaking, nutrition, and childrearing. Sometimes students set up their own displays to advertise upcoming events, sell various items, and network. In 1969 Andelin allowed teachers to charge a fee. The cost of an eight-week course was fifteen dollars. Teachers used part of the fee to pay Andelin five dollars per student and supply students a workbook that they purchased from her for four dollars. One Fascinating Womanhood teacher and area director, Alice Neuffer, wrote a workbook for her own students and distributed it for free. She shared it with Andelin, hoping to get her feedback. Instead of providing a critique, Andelin hired a professional artist to illustrate the workbook, published it herself, and then sold it to teachers. Neuffer was neither compensated for her work nor given credit.[2]

Because they were having so much success selling *Fascinating Woman-hood* in California and Utah, the Andelins set up a ten-city promotional tour to publicize the book elsewhere and solicit teachers. Spreading the FW message became a religious crusade that, according to Andelin, was more important than her life.[3] While the Andelins' visits to the South and East were widely covered in newspapers, on radio, and on TV, the tour was not effective in terms of selling books. Not knowing what they were doing, the couple had no master plan to tie in aspects of book promotion and sales. They didn't do any advance work to booksellers before they went to a particular location, such as providing stores with book reviews, extra copies of *Fascinating Womanhood*, posters, or window displays. Nor did they set up in-store interviews or autograph signings. In fact, Aubrey's Pacific Press Publishers had not even seen to the task of making sure that books were available in the cities the couple planned to visit. Consequently, local bookstores knew nothing about the book, and potential customers could not find it. An interview and subsequent article in the *Atlanta Journal* resulted in over twelve hundred letters of interest in FW and FW classes.[4] But, recalled Helen, the reporter informed her by telephone that area bookstores did not know what the book was or where to find it. Women who were interested in teaching classes didn't know how to reach Andelin. While on their tour, Helen and Aubrey stopped in New York to meet with a literary agent. The agent thought he could get a publisher interested in *Fascinating Womanhood* and offered to take the Andelins on as a client. They said they would think about it and returned to California. The agent was busy and took more than a week to mail his formal proposal. Because they had to wait longer than they expected to, Helen decided the agent was unreliable. She wanted someone who appeared more eager, and rejected his services.

About that time, Deseret Book in Salt Lake City contacted the Andelins and offered to publish, promote, and distribute *Fascinating Womanhood*. With over five hundred dealers and national distribution, the offer was a good one. Impulsively, Aubrey turned it down. He wrote to Deseret Book, thanking them and saying that due to "unusual circumstances" he had to decline. The fact was, the Andelins were making a good living publishing the book on their own. Although untrained, they decided to handle the sale, promotion, and distribution of *FW* themselves. Having difficulty staying in touch with her growing band of followers, Andelin also began to publish a monthly newsletter. The newsletter cost twelve dollars for a one-year subscription and provided readers with instructions, encouragement, and information about upcoming events. Later, Andelin added an advice column.

As the number of subscriptions grew, the newsletter began to advertise books and teaching materials, and became a vehicle for Andelin's political views. The newsletter also discussed health food, hygiene, natural remedies, home schooling, and breastfeeding. It offered recipes for inexpensive meals, toothpaste, pancake syrup, and homemade cosmetics.

In 1967, during a time of rapid growth in the FW movement, the Andelins abruptly packed up, left Clovis, and moved to San Luis Obispo to rescue Aubrey's ailing student-housing project. Mustang Village, a thousand-unit apartment complex, was under construction just across the street from California State Polytechnic College (Cal Poly). Aubrey and his real estate partners hoped that their latest venture would produce a sizable rental income from the upper-middle-class students attending the university. The project, however, was in dire financial straits. Mustang Village was perilously over budget and behind schedule. Aubrey, who was still making payments on several other undeveloped tracts of land in Fresno, had made quite a lot of money from a series of timely business investments. Taking the cash from previous successes, he poured it into the Mustang Village partnership. Helen recalled that when her husband began doing well financially he also became a bit arrogant. He bought expensive cars and spent his money freely. Helen never chided him for his extravagance. "He works hard for his money. I think he should be getting some freedom from it," she said.[5] Much to Helen's dismay, however, as Aubrey became more successful, he began to ignore his children.[6] Rather than slowing down to concentrate on his family and the publishing business, as Helen had hoped he would, Aubrey continued his financial wheeling and dealing. He reasoned that every man needed to be tested by great wealth in order to prove that he could remain humble, regardless of his prosperity. "I felt he should also have the test of poverty," wrote Helen.[7] Soon he would.

Even as things took a dramatic turn for the worse, Aubrey continued to follow his dreams of affluence. He put even more money into Mustang Village. Soon Aubrey's business problems dominated their lives, according to Helen. The couple moved their publishing business to San Luis Obispo, and Helen started work on a second book. Word of *Fascinating Womanhood* continued to spread, and book sales continued to climb. Helen was inundated with letters from hundreds of women thanking her for her book, telling her of their successes, and inquiring about classes. In time, she was getting two hundred letters a week. Aubrey's real estate project sank deeper into trouble. Construction on the apartment building fell so far behind that Aubrey and his partners completely missed the crucial fall semester rental season. They knew that for a student-housing project not to open by fall was as serious as a department store's missing Christmas. Months later, when Mustang Village finally passed its certification for occupancy, the Cal Poly students, whom the entrepreneurs had counted on to rent the pricey new apartments, had already found other places to live. Instead of being 80 percent occupied, as they had planned, Mustang Village remained 80 percent empty. Aubrey, whose other land deals were not panning out, suffered one devastating financial setback after another. Helen, a survivor of her own family's ruin during the Great Depression, worried incessantly. She was increasingly burdened by the daily demands of her children and the steadily growing interest in *Fascinating Womanhood*. In order to keep up, she hired the elderly wife of one of Aubrey's employees at the struggling Mustang Village to take two-year-old Merilee during the day so she could work on her book, direct teachers, and answer fan mail.

Although her older children were in school, and her precocious toddler in day care, Helen suffered under the enormous pressure of the family's financial predicament and the logistical challenges of leading her expanding movement. Andelin was drowning in her work. She suffered migraine headaches and panic attacks. She feared the effects her mounting anxiety was having on her family. Having endured similar kinds of stress when she was writing *Fascinating Womanhood*, she knew that she needed to do something about her situation—and soon. Unfortunately, she would have to wait. The financial problems surrounding Aubrey's real estate venture were compounding fast. Making bank payments on an empty apartment building was nearly impossible. Nor could he keep up with the payments on his other properties. Book sales and teaching fees kept the family afloat while Aubrey desperately searched for a buyer. The couple began holding fast and prayer days every other day. Finally, after a year of debilitating worry and near financial collapse, Aubrey extricated himself from the massive weight of the failed Mustang Village project, taking a two hundred thousand dollar loss. When it came time to leave San Luis Obispo, the couple did not have the money to buy a home. Two buyers contacted them about the undeveloped lots Aubrey still owned in Fresno. Each buyer, within days of the other, offered cash for the building sites. Helen believed that the sale of the lots was an answer to their prayers. The proceeds were just enough for them to get out of town and buy a new home. Helen recalled a striking change in her husband as a result of the Mustang Village misfortune. After he lost the project, Helen said that her formerly self-important husband, who, while basking in his earlier successes, had had little time for his children, now began to pay more attention to them. His discouragement, she noticed, resulted in his increased devotion. "He loved them more than ever before," she observed.[8] Despite the Andelins' financial distractions, interest in *Fascinating Womanhood* books and classes continued to grow. In Maricopa County, Arizona, the county's conciliation court recommended the book to women seeking divorces, and a prominent psychiatrist, having learned about the classes from a FW graduate, recommended it to his patients. Adult-education programs continued to sponsor the classes, and churches continued to request them for their female parishioners.

After divesting themselves of the failed real estate enterprise and using the money they believed that God had given them, they moved to Santa Barbara and settled in a comfortable five-bedroom home in a small housing complex. It was an attractive place with a community clubhouse, tennis courts, and a swimming pool. Aubrey set up his publishing business in the garage, and Helen organized an office in a corner of the large master bedroom. She hired Mary Johnston as a full-time secretary. Johnston, a seasoned professional, proved indispensable, processing book orders and teacher applications, and helping Helen manage her crushing influx of mail. Aubrey tended to his remaining real estate ventures and, along with the older children, packaged books. The arrangement worked fine for a while, but the thriving business quickly outgrew the garage and makeshift home offices. Aubrey rented an office near downtown and took Mary with him. Johnston continued to help Helen with her correspondence, but her main job now was to provide secretarial support for Aubrey's publishing and real estate endeavors. Helen, by now, was no longer enjoying her work. She prayed to God to give her answers to her dilemma in dreams—dreams that would guide her actions. While up to this time Aubrey had been willing to support Helen's

FW business, she knew that packing and selling books was not his primary interest. He was still pursuing real estate projects and was not ready to give all of his time over to his wife's expanding organization. He grew restless. "It was easy to see it was not his dream," said Helen. Needing the money, Aubrey tried to get back into dentistry. However, he was too busy running his publishing business to devote the time he needed to build a new practice. He gave up his plans and tried to concentrate on Fascinating Womanhood. Of her husband, Helen later said, "I wonder if women can understand how much he sacrificed. He sacrificed all through the years."[9] Helen remained stationed in her bedroom office, writing, generating her newsletter, and answering fan mail. She was overwhelmed by her work. "As my book became widely known and I became more involved, not knowing how to reverse the situation, I became anxious. I was definitely *over my head* in this work," she said.[10] Late in the year, Helen was forced to take a break from her FW duties to undergo serious back surgery. At this time she also had a surgical facelift. She was forty-seven years old.

Andelin believed that spreading the word of Fascinating Womanhood was a calling from God. However, the logistics of shipping books, answering mail, training teachers, and running an office were strictly business. She struggled to integrate her religious mission with the business know-how it required. The resulting conflict intensified as Fascinating Womanhood grew out of its discussion-group stage and into an industry. In the beginning, spreading her message was a mission of charity. Now, however, the family needed her income. Helen did not foresee that turning FW into a business enterprise would dampen the effervescence of what had previously been a charismatic movement. Because she did not identify herself as a leader as much as she did a founder, her mission was not to garner public recognition. She recalled, "Instead of feeling lifted up in pride, I felt a tremendous weight of responsibility. So did my husband."[11] In order to relieve herself from her expanding duties, she needed to get her message into the hands of the right person, someone who could endorse it on a larger scale. Andelin became convinced that FW needed a successful, captivating leader to take it further in its development. She saw her public role as necessary but temporary. She believed that as soon as she found someone to lead the movement, her job as a public figure would end. The fact that Andelin viewed her leadership as transitory made it an increasingly difficult weight to carry while she searched for her miracle man. Her belief in male authority and her husband's business ideals precluded her from envisioning anyone but a successful businessman at the helm of her growing organization. She spent the next several years searching for this man, whom she nicknamed "Mr. X."

In 1969, having not yet found Mr. X, the Andelins established the Fascinating Womanhood Foundation in order to direct classes and provide lesson materials to the growing base of teachers. Helen also created the *Domestic Goddess Planning Notebook*—a calendar with areas to list appointments, household chores, and grocery lists, which she sold for six dollars. Aubrey continued his involvement by printing his wife's books, tending to business matters, negotiating the contracts, and controlling the finances. Later in the year, he began advertising for help. The money was coming in faster than they could handle it, and the business was too demanding for just one person to run. In *The Fascinating Womanhood Newsletter*, Aubrey wrote, "We are looking for qualified, aggressive men to work for us full or part-time in promoting FW. Good future and compensation."[12] It was undoubtedly because he was advertising in a woman's publication for a man to lead a woman's organization, that he didn't find any takers. That same year, Helen became acquainted with Jaquie Davison, a self-described "Jayne Mansfield type" from Ramona, California.[13] Jaquie signed up for one of Andelin's Fascinating Womanhood classes and found the message inspiring. Attractive and petite, with a sizable blonde bouffant hairdo and incredible energy, Davison quickly became one of Fascinating Womanhood's most successful teachers in the California area. She also became one of Andelin's most trusted confidantes. In 1972 Davison wrote her own discourse on womanhood, *I Am a Housewife!*[14] Her book, originally published by Aubrey's Pacific Press Publishers, became a success in its own right, selling thousands of copies in FW classes alongside *Fascinating Womanhood*. Davison was important to the FW movement, not just because she was a popular teacher but because she was integral to the political turn FW would soon take.

In 1970 the Hollywood publicist Irwin Zucker contacted Aubrey and offered his services to promote *Fascinating Womanhood*. The Andelins hired him immediately and paid him a thousand dollars a month to spearhead a publicity campaign. Zucker came up with the idea of Womanhood

Day "to preserve femininity, family life and a woman's place in the home."[15] He set up a nine-city tour so that Helen could publicize the occasion, drum up teachers, and sell books. Womanhood Day, which started as a counteraction to the women's liberation movement, was a day when Andelin's followers were urged to make their husbands breakfast in bed to honor him as the leader of the family, put fresh flowers on the table, sing around the house, dress and act feminine, and do something fun with the children. They wore slogan buttons, put bumper stickers on their cars, marched with signs, and passed out fliers. Women also signed a "declaration of dependence," in which they reasserted that the husband was the leader of the home. Women returned the declarations to the FW offices, where they were compiled and later used in political endeavors. Zucker called newspapers and radio stations which were happy to cover the story. Womanhood Day received national attention. Once again the Andelins failed to notify booksellers in advance of their appearances, so the effort did not do much to sell books. It did, however, bring nationwide recognition to Andelin. She appeared on fifty radio programs, and newspapers interviewed her at length. "Don't hide your candle under a bushel," she told women, "You are greatly needed in this work."[16]

The following year, Womanhood Day became Womanhood Week. During Womanhood Week, teachers in numerous cities offered a series of public presentations and workshops. Women decorated their homes, baked bread, and invited the public in for tours. They wore frilly aprons and caps, and handed out flowers, cookies, and FW literature. Teachers held press conferences and telephone and radio interviews in order to "influence the community by example and offset the destructive forces that threaten the family."[17] In addition to Womanhood Day and Womanhood Week, Andelin and Zucker established the Womanhood Movement. The goal of her movement was to alert the public to *Fascinating Womanhood* and seek the support of churches, adult-education programs, and women's clubs to sustain Andelin's efforts to save marriages. To support Andelin's Womanhood Movement, they created the Fascinating Womanhood League. Besides sending in a subscription fee of seven dollars and buying a three-dollar membership card, a league member had to promise to keep the card in her pocketbook, adhere to FW principles, attend political rallies, and commit to becoming "an essential part" of the Womanhood Movement. It was the league's purpose to "speak out as a voice of many and to gain support and strength for all [their] causes."[18] By 1971 the Fascinating Womanhood League was claiming seventy thousand members.[19]

In addition to establishing Womanhood Day, in 1970 Andelin published her second book, *The Fascinating Girl*. The book, a primer for single women, taught them how to attract and marry a suitable husband. Like its predecessor, *The Fascinating Girl* espoused the merits of femininity, childlikeness, and dependence. "There must be no trace of masculine strength, aggressiveness, or competence," wrote Andelin. "The feminine nature . . . is delicate, tender, dependent, submissive, and fearful of danger."[20] In order to get a husband, *The Fascinating Girl* taught young women "the six stages of winning a man." Much like selling a car or a house, an unmarried woman who wanted a husband had to learn to sell herself. "A salesman cannot win men unless he first has a worthwhile product, attracts attention to the product, turns the attention to interest, sees interest grow into desire and overcomes his customer's obstacles to buying it," she wrote. Once a girl mastered these talents, she learned how to "bring action to buy it."[21] In other words, she learned to get a man to propose to her. As in her first book, Andelin copied prodigiously from *The Secrets of Fascinating Womanhood* booklets. The plagiarism in *The Fascinating Girl*, however, was much more extensive. Andelin simply lifted entire pages from the booklets and inserted them into her work. As in her earlier book, she did not give credit to the authors of the booklets. She did, however, make an effort to let readers know that the information was not entirely her own. At the beginning of the book, she acknowledged the booklets and said that her work had been "freely adapted" from them. Classes in Fascinating Girl (FG) were popular. Teachers held them at the local YMCA, YWCA, churches, high schools, and private homes. *The Fascinating Girl* had sold one hundred and twenty thousand copies by 1993.

In 1970 it cost twenty dollars to take a Fascinating Womanhood course. Out of this, teachers bought workbooks for each student for four dollars apiece and paid a six-dollar-and-fifty-cent fee to the Andelins. Teachers provided their own meeting hall, refreshments, and advertising. Despite the fact that they made less than ten dollars per student for an eight-week course, women continued to teach the classes. And they continued to pay the Andelins for the privilege. As more political issues came to her attention, Helen worried constantly about the outside forces that she believed were intent on destroying the American family. At the urging of her husband and Jaquie Davison, her most loyal and politically conservative teacher, she began using *The Fascinating Womanhood Newsletter* as a political venue to decry the evils of abortion, government-sponsored day care, homosexuality, and the Equal Rights Amendment (ERA). These were issues that Andelin feared would ruin marriages, damage children, and obliterate the family. While political issues were never a part of the earlier FW movement, by the mid-1970s Fascinating Womanhood became synonymous with conservative political activism. Up until that time, Andelin had never had any interest in politics. Throughout her married life she had always voted as her husband had instructed. At election time he simply made a list of candidates for her to take to the polls. Because she didn't care about politics, she had no quarrel with appeasing her husband. "Why worry my head?" she said.[22] Thus, the new focus of the movement was an especially dramatic change for her.

Things seemed to be going relatively well for the Andelin family. Helen was a local celebrity; income from book sales, applications, and teaching fees provided a comfortable living; and the FW movement was expanding. Aubrey, however, was becoming agitated and restless. Unexpectedly, he decided to move the family to Utah. They sold their home and moved to a rented house in Springdale, Utah. The couple left their Fascinating Womanhood business in Santa Barbara, where Mary Johnston oversaw the day-to-day affairs. The family relied solely on the sale of Helen's books, supplies, and teacher's fees. The move proved difficult for Paul and Merilee, who were still in school. Paul, especially, became homesick for his friends in Santa Barbara. Within a short time of their arrival in Utah, their son John, twenty-one and having recently returned from an LDS mission in Brazil, moved home. The family of five was cramped in their small house, and Helen didn't have day-care for Merilee. The family was so unhappy that just five months after their arrival, they left the cold and snow of Utah to move back to sunny Santa Barbara. For the next few months, they lived in a rented house on Turnpike Avenue, just across the street from the high school. In April they bought a house in Hope Ranch, a Santa Barbara suburb, but lived in it for only a couple of days. "It was too glitzy," said Helen. Leaving all of their furniture behind, the Andelins sold the house. After that they purchased a condominium in a tidy, middle-class housing project. The backyard was attractive, and the house was already decorated and furnished when they moved in. The couple went ahead and bought the furniture, including the lamps and pictures. Helen re-enrolled Paul and Merilee in school and resumed her work. That year, she appeared on *The Merv Griffin Show*, was a guest speaker at a Youth for Christ national meeting, and spoke at a convention of the La Leche League and at a business convention of psychiatrists and doctors.

Just about the time the family was getting comfortable in their newest home and things were back on track with the FW business, Helen once again had reason to worry about her husband's business dealings. Aubrey had bought a share in a silver mine. Taking the seller's word that the mine would make them rich, Aubrey and his partners never tested it for silver. They spent a considerable amount of time and money searching for the silver but found none. In addition to their original investment, the financial blunder was costing the family over ten thousand dollars a month in mining expenses. Although Helen knew little about the specifics of her husband's business, she knew he was in deep trouble, and she feared for his health. Still believing that the mine really did contain silver, she asked the Lord to help her husband find it. As she had during difficult times in the past, she gave up food and spent most of her days praying. After a week, Helen became convinced that God had not heard her pleas. She sank into deep despair. One night, after a day of fasting, she got an answer to her prayers.

"That night," Helen wrote, "an angel appeared to me in a dream." Wearing a white robe, and carrying a tall staff in his hand, the angel delivered a message. Curiously, it had nothing to do with the disastrous silver mine, or her husband's impending health problems. "Satan," the angel told her, "is trying to take hold of your children." Alarmed and confused, Helen recalled that it took several days to "discern this strange answer." Finally, it came to her: The silver mine was of no consequence, nor was the family's future wealth or poverty. Instead, the angel's visit was to alert Helen to the true values in her life. Her children were what mattered, not the existence of the silver.[23] From that point on, she never worried about the mine or Aubrey's other financial problems. "I don't know what we finally did with the silver mine," she recalled, "or how much money we lost. . . . I had learned not to care." With a great deal of personal fortitude, Helen successfully detached herself from the turmoil of her husband's business affairs so that she could concentrate on her children and her work of spreading the Fascinating Womanhood message. Despite three major moves in one year, Andelin continued to write.

After his land-speculating business, the silver mine, and attempts to revive his dental career didn't work out, Aubrey directed his attention to making an economic success of his wife's organization. In 1971, just after Helen published *Lesson Outlines: The Fascinating Girl, A Course of Study,* Aubrey took over the Fascinating Womanhood empire and became its visible leader. He changed the name of the organization from Fascinating Woman-hood to the more business-friendly Andelin Foundation for Education in Family Living. Helen notified followers in her newsletter. Confused by the new name, and worried about the direction of the organization, teachers and students questioned Andelin about the shift in leadership. "I turned FW over to my husband once it became a man-sized job," she said.[24] In 1972 Aubrey wrote his own book, *Man of Steel and Velvet: A Guide to Masculine Development.* It was a guidebook for men, with a large section on understanding women. In the book, Aubrey instructed men that they needed to willingly take up the male role of provider, protector, and guide. "Don't be spineless or lacking in moral, physical, or mental strength," Aubrey wrote. He also encouraged men to emphasize the differences between the sexes. He asserted, "If men are truly men and women women, this contrast will keep the sexes attracted to one another and reduce the tendency to the unwholesome and destructive perversion of homosexuality."[25] While *Man of Steel and Velvet* never came close in popularity to *Fascinating Womanhood,* by 1998 it had sold a respectable three hundred thousand copies. So great was the demand for Helen's books and classes that Gladys Lee, a successful FW teacher in the Miami area, recalled that the Fleming H. Revel Company, an independent publisher the Andelins had already turned down, approached one of her students to write her own version of *Fascinating Womanhood.* Marabel Morgan, in her mid-thirties, and already holding FW classes of her own, asked Lee what she should do. When Lee contacted Andelin for advice, Helen told her to encourage the student to write the book—provided that she gave her credit for her ideas. Having never been possessive of the message to save marriages, Andelin had little interest in controlling those who were of the same mind. As long as she got credit, she heartily promoted any and all means of getting her teachings on marriage out to America, even agreeing to grant interviews with such men's magazines as *Playboy.*

Morgan pursued the publisher's offer, and in 1973, the former home economics major and college beauty queen wrote *Total Woman,* a book based on *Fascinating Womanhood* but with some steamy sex mixed in. Married since 1964 to her college sweetheart, Morgan told a story similar to Andelin's. She recalled watching powerlessly as her own "Cinderella" marriage swiftly changed course and eventually hit the skids. Fearful that the union would end in divorce, Morgan set out to save it. After attending FW classes, she decided that she could not expect to change her husband. Morgan resolved to change herself instead. "It is only when a woman surrenders her life to her husband, reveres and worships him and is willing to serve him, that she becomes really beautiful to him," she said.[26] Morgan received a hefty signing bonus and sold nearly six hundred thousand books in two short years. In newspaper and magazine interviews, she was often compared to her predecessor, and unacknowledged mentor, Helen Andelin. Andelin bristled at the frequent comparison to her younger colleague. "She imitates my format," she complained, "but, has given it a carnal, sensual approach."[27] To Andelin's particular dismay, Morgan, who she described as "dumb," didn't give her credit for using her material. Later, when she was asked to appear in an interview alongside Morgan on the television broadcast *60 Minutes,* Andelin declined.

While Aubrey showed outward confidence in his new role as leader of the Andelin Foundation, privately he was conflicted about being the figurehead of what was his wife's movement. Although initially enthusiastic about controlling all aspects of the business, he became increasingly uncomfortable with what would later become his press image as the head of a thriving women's club. The dilemma for the Andelins was that Aubrey could not maintain credibility by sitting quietly by while his wife became famous and made more money than he did. Nor could Helen, an advocate of childlikeness and dependence, show herself to be the powerful leader that she was. Because of his assertions about patriarchal leadership in *Man of Steel and Velvet,* the fact that Aubrey appeared to be riding on his wife's coattails by conveniently coming up with his own book was especially distressing. Living out the traditional model of marriage that they advocated was proving difficult for the Andelins. In time, Aubrey became as impatient as Helen to find someone else to act as Fascinating Womanhood's leader. Employing another successful man to work for him as a CEO would preserve Aubrey's position as the chief of the organization, and in a very public sense, the chief of his own household. Overseeing a manager would also remove him from the more "feminine" duties of office work and overseeing teachers.

By the end of 1972, Aubrey had become associated with Jim Parker, a successful celebrity–chiropractor from Irving, Texas. In addition to manipulating spines in his state-of-the-art clinic, Parker made a remarkable income from holding colossal chiropractic conventions around the country. Thousands of people attended Parker's conventions every other month. Parker's innovation was that he fashioned chiropractic work, long the underdog of the medical profession, into a kind of cutting-edge, direct-sales operation. In addition to maintaining expensive high-tech offices, practitioners, Parker urged, should provide clients the most complete and modern care by selling vitamins, positive-thinking books, and motivational tapes. They should also offer expensive in-house services like massage, nutrition therapy, and deluxe machinery, such as tilt tables, whole-body vibrators, and heat beds. Parker's new wave of chiropractic care swept many parts of California, Arizona, and Florida in the early 1970s. Emerging from their cheap, strip-mall offices, many chiropractors became the newly rich. They built huge stucco offices, drove luxurious cars, and lived in gigantic houses. Aubrey and Parker settled on an arrangement for Helen to teach FW classes to thousands of chiropractors' wives who attended the conventions and often needed to find something to do during the long meetings.

The conventions, like exclusive vacations, with fancy food and black-tie balls, were held in large cities, exotic locations, and sometimes on expensive cruise ships. Sales of Jim Parker's books, tapes, business supplies, and health equipment soared at these events. Sparing no expense, the Parker organization hired motivational speakers, political dignitaries, experts of all kinds, famous musicians, and even movie stars to inspire the participants. Dr. Joyce Brothers, the former president Ronald Reagan, the TV evangelist Dr. Robert Schuller, and the actors Zsa Zsa Gabor and Bob Hope were just some of the celebrity guest speakers at Parker's seminars. The arrangement was a good one for Aubrey and Helen. Given that most of what women learned at the Parker conventions was how to support their husband's chiropractic careers, the venue was a natural fit for promoting both Aubrey's book and what he understood as the basic premise of his wife's message—to show women how to help their husbands achieve financial success. Helen's seminars were a huge hit with the women, and the men came out in large numbers to attend Aubrey's new MSV classes. He was, by all accounts, a confident and talented public speaker with the ability to motivate others. Those attending the seminars benefited as well. By the end of the extravagant weekends, husbands had not only learned strategic ways of enhancing their doctoring business but could also take home newly minted Fascinating wives. Disconcerted with the public displays of wealth, excess, and waste at the conventions, Helen used the venue pragmatically. The Parker seminars were an effective way to spread her message; she was not interested in glamorizing her work.

Riding on the growing surge of public interest in his wife's work and the near guarantee they could sell ample books to the captive audiences at the Parker Chiropractic Conventions, Aubrey relished his new role as a celebrity author. In 1973 he edited some of the thousands of letters Helen's followers sent to her and published *Fascinating Womanhood Success Stories*. He also wrote and published *MSV: A Course of Study, Lesson Outlines* to accompany his book. And because his lone but ongoing complaint about his wife's book was that it did not adequately cover sexual matters, he wrote a sex manual. *Fascinating Womanhood Principles Applied to Sex* sold separately for three dollars. When asked why she didn't write the manual herself, Andelin said that her husband was "more qualified." In 1980 she added her name to the pamphlet as coauthor, and she included it in the 1990 edition of her book. The same year that Aubrey published *Fascinating Womanhood Principles Applied to Sex,* the Andelin Foundation instituted couples classes to support both Helen's and Aubrey's books. The classes were not well received. Women who took the Fascinating Womanhood course wanted to talk to other women about their problems and didn't like having men in the classes. They wanted a woman role model, not a man to listen to. With the couples classes striking out, Aubrey decided to concentrate on his own classes. Outside of the Parker seminars, he had difficulty finding men to attend them, and it was almost impossible to find men to teach them. In time MSV classes were abandoned.

Helen Andelin, 1940.

Aubrey Andelin, 1940.

Aubrey and Helen Andelin, Salt Lake City, Utah, 1942.

Helen Andelin and daughter Dixie. Merced, California, 1952.

Helen Andelin and family, Santa Barbara, California, 1970.

Helen Andelin, 1971.

Helen Andelin, 1975. *Washington Post*, n.d.

Helen Gurley Brown, Jacqueline Suzanne, Helen Andelin, and Adela
Rogers St. John on "The Big Question," *Santa Barbara News-Press*,
February 13, 1971.

Helen and Aubrey Andelin, 1976.

In 1974 taking an FW class cost twenty-five dollars. Seven dollars of the fee went to the Andelins, and teachers purchased workbooks for their students for four dollars each. Teachers made fourteen dollars per student for an eight-week course. They purchased *Fascinating Womanhood* at wholesale and sold it at retail, making another two dollars and fifty cents per student. Given the fact that the Andelins said that over three hundred and fifty thousand women had taken the course, fees from teacher applications, classes, and the sales of the books and workbooks were making them rich. Pacific Press published new lesson outlines, a new workbook, and a revised edition of *Fascinating Womanhood*. Women continued to request teaching materials, and students continued to take classes. It was a busy year for the movement. Unfortunately, the Andelin Foundation did not mobilize in time to celebrate Womanhood Day and Womanhood Week with news conferences, public demonstrations, and radio interviews; so they quietly urged women to recognize it at home. Despite this and other publicity errors, by 1974 *Fascinating Womanhood* had sold half a million copies in hardback, with no support from a major publisher.

For some time, Helen had wanted *Fascinating Womanhood* to be printed in paperback so that it could reach more people. As publishers realized that Andelin had a message that could sell, they began contacting her. Simon and Schuster offered to buy the rights to print the book in paperback. Aubrey, without consulting his wife, rejected the proposal. It is not clear whether he was holding out for a better deal or trying to figure out how to put the book in paperback with his own publishing company. Regardless, his saying no to the publisher made for a deep conflict between the couple. "It was one of the only times I was upset with him," said Helen. Despite her husband's actions, she continued to look for someone to print the book in paperback. In 1974, an FW teacher named Jackie Geoghan gave Helen the name of a writer in Seattle who had connections at Bantam Books in New York City. Helen contacted the writer and told him about *Fascinating Womanhood* and the number of books she had sold. Impressed, he called Bantam and made introductions. The publisher requested a meeting, and the couple flew to New York. Having reconsidered his earlier position, Aubrey was willing to listen. Bantam Books not only offered to publish *Fascinating Womanhood* in paperback, they promised a generous advance. This time, the couple saw eye to eye, and Helen agreed to an advantageous contract. Fearing they might lose control, however, the Andelins would agree to only a three-year contract. "We were very excited about what was happening," she wrote. She and Aubrey were in "full harmony with each other" about their decision. Helen agreed to do extensive publicity to promote her book.

Andelin continued her search for Mr. X. She made contact with Al Lippert, the president of the Weight Watchers diet program. With his extensive network, and his success in making Weight Watchers a national concern, Lippert seemed to Helen like the ideal person to advise her on managing Fascinating Womanhood. Although she had never met Lippert, Helen telephoned him one morning and simply asked him the secret of his success. She remembered that he was cordial, and the two had a friendly talk. His secret, he told Helen, was simply trial and error. Helen remembered that, after her initial conversation, Aubrey talked with Lippert at length, and according to her husband, Lippert even considered the idea of managing FW himself. Unfortunately, the two men were unable to settle on a suitable arrangement, and they parted ways. Aubrey negotiated this and all other business situations for the organization while Helen remained pretty much in the dark. She never knew what they talked about—only that the men could not agree. Andelin's quest for Mr. X took her to the business department at Brigham Young University. She knew that Weldon Taylor, the dean of the business school, was already familiar with *Fascinating Womanhood*. Hoping he could recommend a qualified business graduate to lead her organization, Helen explained their great need for Mr. X. Taylor told her the job she described was too much for an inexperienced graduate and suggested that her best bet was to steal an executive from another successful business. He gave her the name of five men. The first name on the list was the one the Andelins eventually chose. Sam Battistone, whose father had founded the successful Sambo's restaurant chain in 1957, was a member of the LDS Church and was a member of the Andelins' ward. When Aubrey contacted him about spearheading the growing FW business, Battistone was interested.

In 1975, just as Helen was about to begin her publicity tour with Bantam Books, Sam Battistone became the official CEO of the Andelin Foundation for Education in Family Living. Battistone, in his thirties and already an accomplished entrepreneur, sought to turn the Andelin Foundation into a successful corporate concern. Along with his assistant, Paul Rummel, Battistone oversaw all aspects of the operation. With the help of three secretaries, an office manager, a bookkeeper, a printer, and a high school student tasked with shipping the books, they ran the office, oversaw sales, took charge of the teaching program, and authorized expenses. It was Battistone and Rummel who came up with the idea to open a Fascinating Womanhood center. In March 1975 the foundation purchased a retreat center on several acres of land with panoramic views overlooking the city of Santa Barbara. The huge counseling complex had deluxe overnight accommodations for eighty people, fine-dining facilities, and large meeting and conference rooms. Battistone moved the foundation's offices into the Fascinating Womanhood Center and advertised it for rent to teachers in *The Fascinating Womanhood Newsletter*. For a while the center made money. Helen was holding seminars attended by twelve hundred or more women at a time, but only briefly. The FW Center could attract only women in the area. Teachers and students from other parts of the country were not willing to pay to travel to California. Interest in the FW Center declined, and Battistone's efforts to centralize the grassroots movement failed. He had trouble keeping the buildings occupied, and an attempt to hold a summer series of classes and lectures at the center never got off the ground. Eventually, Helen stopped teaching seminars there, and the foundation moved its offices to another location. Battistone sold the FW Center at a loss. Despite the failure of the center, the foundation continued to solicit new teachers by printing informational brochures and distributing them to businesses, libraries, and grocery stores. Large numbers of teachers continued to sign up. In 1975 *Fascinating Womanhood* was translated into Spanish, Portuguese, and Japanese.

In their efforts to make the Andelin Foundation a legitimate business, Battistone and Rummel began to require personal interviews for prospective teachers who lived within two hundred miles of Santa Barbara. Because the majority of potential teachers lived outside of California, this idea simply didn't work. Even the women who lived within two hundred miles would not agree to travel for an interview. Not wanting to pay the thirty-dollar application fee, travel for an interview, and pay the teaching fee, many women simply bought the teaching materials and taught the classes without authorization. The number of teacher applications dropped. Battistone and

Rummel lowered the application fee to fifteen dollars and began interviewing by phone. In 1975 the foundation reported eleven thousand teachers.[28] Still looking for ways to capitalize on the large numbers of FW teachers and students, Battistone and Rummel launched a line of Fascinating Womanhood jewelry. They also looked into introducing an attractive housedress and a Fascinating Womanhood recipe book. These ideas were short-lived. Other than the teachers who were required to buy supplies for their students, FW women weren't interested in buying anything. They just wanted to read the book and take the classes. Under Battistone's direction *The Fascinating Womanhood Newsletter* went from monthly publication to twice-monthly, and the price of a subscription went from twelve to twenty-five dollars. The newsletter, once a lifeline to Andelin, was now largely advertising space for books, teaching materials, and expensive conventions. While its overall message became more business-oriented, the newsletter continued to supply instruction to teachers, advice, and a steady dose of Andelin's political ideas.

At the time the Bantam publicity tour started in March 1975, *Fascinating Womanhood* had already hit the bestseller list. Andelin's nineteen-year-old son Paul was away serving a two-year LDS mission. The only child remaining at home was thirteen-year-old Merilee. Needing to travel, Helen sent Merilee to Utah to live with her older sister Dixie. With her children taken care of and her husband–manager by her side, Andelin embarked on a six-month national publicity tour to promote her book and find more teachers. Her personal beauty and frank opinions made her a popular guest on radio and television shows. *Fascinating Womanhood* seemed to explode into American popular culture, and Helen Andelin, who described herself as shy, became something of a cult figure. Newspapers and magazines photographed and interviewed her extensively during the tour. Helen was featured on the *Phil Donahue Show*, and *To Tell the Truth*. Leading TV personalities such as Barbara Walters, Larry King, Connie Chung, and Hugh Downs also interviewed her. While Helen made appearances on TV and radio programs, Aubrey usually sat in the audience. In newspaper and magazine articles, however, he was often photographed and quoted. Reporters, who sometimes chided him for using the title "Dr. Andelin" to make himself sound important, were very interested in "Mr. Helen." In an effort to show that her husband was his own man, Helen said, "My husband, who helps run the business, handles all the money. . . . I give it to him."[29] Described as "stern and snappish," Aubrey soon tired of staying in the background.[30] For much of Helen's tour, he talked to news reporters about his political opinions and his own book. "If men were really men, good chivalrous, respected *Man of Steel and Velvet* men, we wouldn't have women's liberation," he told one reporter.[31] To another, he said, "If women's libbers would read my book, they would say I'm their best friend."[32] Within six months, Helen had not only become a national hot topic, she had sold another half million copies of *Fascinating Womanhood*. One Detroit bookstore received a thousand copies of FW and sold out the same day. Fascinating Womanhood had teachers in all fifty states, the United Kingdom, Canada, Germany, Australia, South Africa, Japan, Brazil, and the Philippines. In 1976 Andelin took another publicity tour, visiting twelve cities in eighteen days. Bantam, having recently signed a contract with Aubrey to print *Man of Steel and Velvet* in paperback, hatched the plan of having the pair travel together in order to promote both of their books at the same time. Aubrey was interviewed along with his wife, and the Andelins became the media's example of the perfect couple. "Man was born to lead and woman to follow," said Aubrey.[33]

While *Man of Steel* generated interest largely in the mostly female audience, who bought it for their husbands, *Fascinating Womanhood* continued to sell like hotcakes. News of Helen's appearances was widespread, and huge crowds came out to see her. She held book signings and press conferences, and Aubrey was by her side. Helen was uncomfortable with her fame, recalling, "I just didn't feel I deserved it. . . . They were not awe-struck with me, it was the truth they were getting."[34] Although Andelin's growing audiences received her more enthusiastically than ever, those who criticized her were becoming more hostile and vocal. The personal attacks hurt her deeply, and she found it more difficult to shrug off the insults. In time, the increasingly negative reaction from women whom she felt God had called her to help caused her enormous physical and emotional distress. She suffered more migraine headaches, had trouble sleeping, and lost a significant amount of weight. When their book tour ended, Andelin returned to Santa Barbara to spend much-needed time at home. Although emotionally exhausted and in desperate need of rest, Helen remained unable to relax. Complicating the situation was the fact that Aubrey, on a two-month tour to promote his own book, was out of town. For the first time in her marriage, Helen spent long periods of time separated from her husband. She became worried, anxious, and depressed.

She was most troubled by the fact that, while her philosophy was finally getting attention on a national level, women from her own religious community were the victims of increasing marital unhappiness. She was shocked to learn that Utah, with its mostly Mormon population, had the third-highest divorce rate in the nation. This was horrific news for Andelin, and she felt like an "absolute failure." She wrote an impassioned plea to the president of the Mormon Church telling him she had the solution to the "divorce epidemic" plaguing the Mormon community and asking for a private meeting to discuss the FW program. His office promptly said no. He had never heard of Helen Andelin or her book. Stunned and bewildered, Helen searched her soul. She realized that FW was moving off track. Her instincts had told her that when Aubrey took leadership of Fascinating Womanhood, changed the name, and then placed the day-to-day affairs of the organization in the hands of businessmen who understood it as an entrepreneurial effort, the FW movement began to lose its way. It wasn't so much of a mission anymore as it was a sales operation. After more than ten years of encouraging, teaching, and helping women in person, Helen suddenly found herself alone in her clean Santa Barbara kitchen as her husband, two men she barely knew, and a huge publishing company commandeered her precious organization. In fact, every facet of her undertaking had been co-opted by men whose visions and goals were very different from her own. This realization prompted Helen's long journey through what would become an increasingly dark period of her life. As her growing distress fueled her insecurity about her qualifications to lead others, she began to accept the reality that the movement had permanently changed in ways she had never anticipated.

While her husband was out of town, Andelin decided to take a closer look at how Battistone and Rummel were running the company. After investigating the large amounts of cash the two had spent on things she considered unimportant, she became convinced that they were mismanaging the considerable flow of money that was pouring into the FW organization. Battistone "just didn't seem to think the money would ever run out," she said. "He was using our money and overspending." Alarmed, she telephoned

Aubrey, urging him to do something immediately. Her husband, who had never worked out a formal contract with Battistone, declined to speak with him over the phone. Instead, he told his wife to be patient and wait for him to return several weeks later. Helen's distress turned to panic. Some nights earlier, she had had a dream that convinced her that Battistone was running the foundation into the ground. Believing that her dream was a message from God, she decided to act. Without waiting for her husband to return, she confronted Battistone. Used to negotiating with Aubrey, he was reluctant to respond to her. The conflict escalated, and Helen took back control of the FW organization, ousting Battistone in a dramatic quarrel she would later regret.[35]

Because the classes were so popular, Andelin attempted to track, organize, and train the thousands of enthusiastic women who applied for permission to teach. In 1967 she introduced the teacher application, along with various other forms for teacher training, evaluation, and documentation that would evolve as the movement grew. The teacher applications provide ample evidence of the movement's appeal and revealed a social profile of its members. For example, Gilly Kuehn, a former high school English teacher from Orange County, California, began teaching FW to small groups in 1967. The mother of four sons and a daughter, she had been married to a successful Anaheim attorney for over twenty years. During her tenure as an authorized FW teacher, she taught over ten thousand women how to become more feminine, improve their marriages, and find a renewed sense of purpose in their lives. After finding *Fascinating Womanhood* on the shelf at a local bookstore, and later hearing about the classes, Kuehn decided to teach them herself in order to use her talents to benefit others.[36] She held the classes at the Alamitos Friends Church in nearby Garden Grove and donated all the proceeds of her teaching to charitable causes. At seventy-eight, she still teaches FW classes to women who request them.

Joan Kimble of Rock Hill, South Carolina, first heard about Fascinating Womanhood in the early 1970s at a Parker Chiropractic seminar she had attended with her husband in Fort Worth, Texas. Married for nearly two decades, she was active in her husband's successful business. Involved in the chiropractic industry since 1959, in 1975 she was named Chiropractic Woman of the Year by the Women's Auxiliary of the South Carolina Chiropractors

Association.[37] A highly sought-after FW teacher, Kimble, like Gilly Kuehn, also taught thousands of women throughout the 1970s. "I want to share the joy and happiness with others so they, too, can be loved and cherished," she said of her motivation to teach FW. "I believe it is right. . . . I believe it is God's way."[38] Experienced at juggling family and a job, Kimble advised, "If you must work, don't [surpass] him as the provider. He won't feel needed."

Forty-three-year-old Saundria Garner, of Winfield, Alabama, heard about FW classes from a friend. Married for twenty-five years to the manager of a local car dealership, the mother of four teenagers, and acting chairwoman of the local branch of the Eagle Forum, Garner wanted to become a Fascinating Womanhood teacher because of the feminist movement. Fearful that ratification of the Equal Rights Amendment spelled disaster for the American family, she added, "I think that women are in for trouble if this [bill] ever passes."[39] When asked about her qualifications to teach, she cited "twelve years as a Sunday School teacher and having seen a complete change in my husband as a result of FW." She taught Fascinating Womanhood classes until 1980.

Grace Chavis, a stay-at-home wife and mother from Plantation, Florida, took her first FW course in 1969. A devout Southern Baptist and the mother of two adopted children, Chavis said that until she took the FW course, she was "in rebellion against God." Living for two decades in an unhappy marriage to a career Navy officer who was "stern, cruel and verbally abusive," she credited *Fascinating Womanhood* with helping her find God and turning her life around. Andelin "changed my life totally," she said. After experiencing miraculous results in her own marriage, Chavis wanted to help other women. She applied to be an authorized teacher and in 1970 began teaching FW classes in the Miami area. She taught groups of up to three hundred women every month for twenty-seven years. "Eighty percent of marriages can be helped by FW," she said. "All a woman has to do is try." When Andelin was in Florida for her 1975 book tour, Chavis drove her around to radio stations for interviews, and the two became close friends. Of Andelin, she said, "It was a privilege to know her. She could convert the world if she wanted to."[40] Kuehn, Kimble, Garner, and Chavis represented thousands of women who joined ranks to become the movement's most ardent supporters—authorized FW teachers.

The teacher applications, while a vast source of information, have proved challenging to evaluate. Over the years, Andelin, a great organizer, continued to look for ways to run her movement more efficiently. Consequently, the applications changed form many times. Change intensified when her husband took charge of the movement in 1971 and required application fees, photographs, evaluations, and renewal forms for the teachers, along with a large, efficient-looking rubber stamp that said "APPROVED." Most unfortunate is the fact that Helen's near-obsessive tidiness resulted in the alteration and/or throwing away of years of applications to reduce clutter and save space. Many of the two-page applications that appeared after 1974 were streamlined for storage by simply cutting the back page off. Pictures stapled to the back were removed and glued to the front, covering up valuable information. Large photographs were cropped in order to fit in a smaller space before the applications were returned to the file. If a teacher moved or sent in a renewal form, information on the existing application was crossed out with a marker and updated. For a period of time, white adhesive labels bearing the teacher's name and address were affixed over the original information. There seemed to be no standardization of record keeping or storage. Against advice, Andelin discarded hundreds more and altered the remaining teacher applications to make sure they were neat before she sent them to the University of Utah archive in 2002.

The applications asked a range of questions: Applicants were required to relate information about their experience with FW, and were asked if they were married, and for how long, and if they had ever been divorced. They were asked to identify any parts of the philosophy they had difficulty accepting. Women were also asked where they planned to hold the classes and if they had previous teaching experience. One mother of seven said of her motivation for teaching FW, "God has ministered to me and many others through your book. He's laid it on my heart that I am to play a part in this ministry." Besides seeking permission to teach, she told Andelin that she was going to hand out one book a week for a year.[41] Beginning in 1973, women were asked to list the kinds of work that their husbands did. As the critics of Fascinating Womanhood became more vocal, and the application process became more sophisticated, other kinds of questions appeared. Some of these were: "Is Fascinating Womanhood manipulative?" "When is it acceptable for a woman to work outside the home?" and "Should men share responsibility in home chores and daily care of the family . . . in diaper changing and feeding babies?" All applicants had to attach a photograph and submit a processing fee. Application fees started out at five dollars and had increased to thirty dollars by 1975; Andelin stopped charging application fees after 1999. She said that between 1965 and 2005, over fifteen thousand women had requested authorization to teach FW courses.[42] In order to avoid the application fee, hundreds, perhaps thousands, more women taught classes without authorization. Many others operated under a more general kind of permission that the Andelin Foundation began granting to sponsoring organizations, such as churches and adult-education programs sometime around 1972. In a letter to the General Authorities of the LDS Church, Andelin reported that in the six years since the publication of *Fascinating Womanhood*, more than ninety thousand women had taken the classes.[43] Four years later she told the president of the Mormon Church, Spencer W. Kimball, "During the past ten years . . . over 350,000 women have been taught the principles" of FW.[44]

The majority of women who taught Fascinating Womanhood were white, middle-class, and Christian. Most of them had children. A very small minority of Fascinating Womanhood teachers were Asian, African American, or Hispanic. FW teachers were in their mid-thirties to late forties, and most of them had married in their early twenties; a significant number had married at eighteen or nineteen. Most lived in the Sun Belt South, in the Intermountain States, or on the West Coast. After 1974 the Andelin Foundation authorized teachers in Belgium, Australia, Canada, Puerto Rico, Indonesia, the Virgin Islands, New Zealand, Japan, and Russia. While a few had experience teaching in elementary and secondary public schools, most authorized instructors had no formal training in teaching prior to their FW experience. A small number had been vocational instructors in their jobs as public health care nurses, in the airline industry, or at beauty schools. Several women had advanced degrees. The majority of them had married young, had never graduated from college, and were full-time wives and mothers.

Many applicants described themselves as self-taught teachers of subjects as diverse as personal organization, crafts, sewing, meal planning, charm school, nutrition (for Shaklee or Amway products), makeup application, and

Weight Watchers. Others had backgrounds in modeling, 4-H, Lamaze classes, home schooling, midwifery, La Leche League, Al-Anon, and Girl Scouts. Questions about religious background were not included in the applications. However, many women said that they had heard about FW at church. Some said that God or Jesus Christ had led them to the FW message. Most women, when asked to describe their teaching experience, said they had served as teachers at their local churches, where they were involved in Bible study, Vacation Bible School, Sunday school, Missionettes, Christian Living, Aglow, and a variety of Christian teen groups. Baptist, Church of Christ, Latter-day Saint, Seventh-day Adventist, Catholic, and the Church of the Nazarene are just some of the Christian denominations identified in the teacher applications. A few women identified themselves as Jewish or Muslim.

Most women, it appeared, had tried their hands at some kind of home business, and they seemed to have relatively comfortable lives. Blue-collar husbands' careers ranged from truck drivers and day laborers to tank welders, press operators, cable splicers, machinists, and appliance repairmen. Most husbands held white-collar and management-level jobs such as hospital administrator, superintendent of schools, engineer, accountant, stockbroker, attorney, military officer, commercial pilot, or college professor. One husband was a successful TV producer in California, and another the president of a thriving oil company in Texas. One man, Tom Lantos, a Holocaust survivor, and former economics professor, was even a United States congressman. A good number of FW teachers were married to physicians, chiropractors, dentists, farmers, school teachers, salesmen, and police officers. The teacher applications peaked between 1975 and 1976. This surge in interest coincided with Andelin's extensive travel, her TV appearances, and radio interviews to promote her book. In 1977 the number of applicants dropped again, as did teacher renewals. FW teachers had a high burnout rate. One teacher in Las Vegas who taught classes of over three hundred and fifty women told Andelin, "I feel like I need plasma after every class." She finally wore herself out and quit teaching. Some women left FW to teach classes with their own materials or write books of their own. Others just wanted to stay home and live FW principles. The year that the teacher applications slipped was the same year Andelin left public life and retreated to her farm in Missouri.

While fewer women were interested in teaching FW classes, sales of the book continued at a steady pace. Despite her heavy travel schedule and severe bouts of anxiety, depression, and frequent headaches, Andelin continued to write. In 1977 she published *Study Guide: For the Fascinating Womanhood Home Study Course* for women who lived where classes were not available. For most of the 1970s, Andelin's popularity continued to climb. One writer described the interest in *Fascinating Womanhood,* and devotion to Andelin, as "a quiet revolution."[45] Another said, "The real phenomenon of our time is not the growth of the women's liberation movement, but rather the growth of the Fascinating Womanhood Movement."[46]

Five

ENEMIES

$\mathcal{A}$s Andelin's fascinating womanhood movement grew, the big question was, Whose version of womanhood would prevail? Would it be Andelin's nostalgic revival of the dependent, feminine housewife, or the feminist model of the independent, modern-day career woman? Andelin believed it would be hers. In her mind, there were only two things she needed to do in order to realize her goal. First she had to overcome feminist thought, and then she needed to get the endorsement of the Mormon Church. Much to her dismay, she never accomplished either one. The feminist movement continued to grow and was instrumental in passing legislation for legal and economic equality for women. And the LDS Church began to steer clear of Andelin and her movement. Although they had very different philosophies and goals, the feminists and some leaders of the Mormon Church had something in common: Andelin identified them both as her enemies.

At first *Fascinating Womanhood* sold to a mostly Mormon audience. In time, however, some Mormons began taking a closer look at Andelin's philosophy. In 1966 Reed Bradford, a professor in the BYU Family Relations

Department, published a book review of *Fascinating Womanhood* in the student newspaper. In it he said that Andelin's book was insulting and hypocritical and advocated a dishonest approach to marriage. He charged that *FW* was manipulative and gave hints on how to trap and keep a man. Pointing out that Andelin didn't have any credentials, he urged the BYU bookstore to stop selling the book.[1] On the department's book list, *Fascinating Womanhood* was listed as "not recommended." At first Andelin didn't pay much attention. *Fascinating Womanhood* was selling rapidly in Utah and the BYU Department of Continuing Education (DCE) was teaching FW classes to sold-out crowds. As her fame grew, however, so did questions about her teachings and motivations. One day a female student, representing the BYU Student's Union, asked her to speak on campus. Flattered and appreciative of the opportunity, Andelin willingly accepted. The following day the student called her to apologize, saying that approval for Andelin's speaking engagement had been cancelled. Andelin's dismissal as a public speaker was repeated at the more liberal University of Utah in neighboring Salt Lake City. "This struck me as being very strange!" Andelin recalled. "Even communists have been invited to speak on these two campuses." But to some Mormons, Andelin was more dangerous than a communist. She was a loose cannon, a publicity seeker, and a hypocrite with a following. Moreover, she was making a lot of money off of Mormon women. In time the DCE stopped sponsoring her classes.

Back in California, Andelin's marriage classes fell out of favor with her local bishop, and she was no longer allowed to teach them in Relief Society meetings. Her celebrity and her message of womanly dependence, along with her claims of divine mission, made her controversial in Mormon circles. Members began to distance themselves from her, and individual wards would no longer sponsor her classes or allow her to use building space to teach them. Soon Mormon bookstores stopped selling her book. "When *Fascinating Womanhood* began to be well known," said Andelin, "opposition appeared." Not willing to accept that the resistance to FW might have been broad-based, she accused individuals. She contended, "It sprang from the Relief Society President and [the] BYU Family Relations Department. . . . From there, it spread out among Church members."[2] Believing that those who disagreed with her methods were against her personally, Andelin identified all dissenters as her enemies. More convinced than ever that her work was a calling from God, she pushed past local opposition and began a crusade to secure the one thing she believed would lend unqualified credibility to her message—the sanction of the Mormon Church.

Historically, Mormon leaders have been accessible to rank-and-file members for advice, religious council, and arbitration. Beginning in the mid-1960s, the church took steps to change this policy by instituting a complex system of checks and balances on local and regional levels that limited access to high-ranking leaders—especially the president, who Mormons believed to be a modern-day prophet. Nevertheless, the idea persisted in some parts of Mormon culture that the leaders of the church were available to regular members. Andelin believed she had the right to a face-to-face meeting with the church president. Part of her heartbreak and later disillusionment was the denial of what she believed to be her basic right. Because it was too distressing to imagine that the Prophet himself chose not see her, Andelin interpreted her rejection as a blunder by uninformed aides. For a time this belief fueled an even stronger conviction that her message was of dire importance. She was convinced that if she could just get past his staff and talk to the Prophet *in person*, he would understand and believe her. Ultimately, she was sure, he would approve *Fascinating Womanhood* for churchwide use.

In 1966 Betty Friedan cofounded the National Organization of Women (NOW), a political group that focused on achieving political, economic, and legal equality for women. NOW focused on reproductive rights, equal pay, no-fault divorce, and an end to sexual harassment and discrimination in the workforce. The organization represented mostly white, middle-class women, and the movement it sponsored was called women's liberation. In the beginning, "women's lib" was often a source of media mockery. Focusing on the dramatic antics of fringe groups like SCUM (Society for Cutting Up Men), and conspicuous public demonstrations, the newly formed feminist movement suffered more than its share of public potshots. The message of equality, however, was one that was too central to American sensibilities for the media to ignore. The numbers of women who called themselves feminists exploded, and NOW was able to win some early legal victories. Some of these were the equal division of property in divorce laws, a woman's ability to open a bank account or borrow money without her husband's signature, entrance into jobs formerly considered too dangerous for women, and changes in common language that denied a woman an identity apart from either her husband or her father. Meanwhile, Andelin had been teaching classes long enough to see for herself the dramatic changes in the lives of thousands of women as a result of the Fascinating Womanhood philosophy. Scores of grateful women wrote her letters to thank her for saving their marriages. Many more bought her books and signed up for FW classes. Hundreds came to hear her speak. Helen described herself as a mediocre speaker, believing that it was her message that energized women, not her. She said, "I have no special gifts; only the truth." Borrowing the words of Jesus, she said, "My sheep hear my voice."[3] In January of 1967 Aubrey and Helen wrote to LDS President David O. McKay, requesting an appointment to see him. Unwilling to meet with the Andelins himself, McKay appointed one of his counselors, Alvin R. Dyer, to visit with the couple. The Andelins were given a respectful reception. Helen recalled that during their meeting the apostle "listened attentively and was sympathetic." Later he wrote a letter to them encouraging them to ignore opposition and pursue their work. Encouraged by what she saw as support for her cause, the Andelins pressed ahead. In March, Helen called Ezra Taft Benson, asking for a private meeting. Benson, who had served as the U.S. Secretary of Agriculture in both terms of the Eisenhower admin- istration, was a member of the LDS Quorum of the Twelve Apostles. Helen hoped that someone with Benson's well-known conservative political sen- sibilities would understand the urgency of the FW message. The telephone conversation did not go well. Rather than agree to her request, the harried leader curtly informed her that he did not know anything about *Fascinating Womanhood* and was too busy to spare even ten minutes to talk.[4]

Used to dealing with the folksy, approachable church leaders at the local level, Andelin was unaccustomed to the protocols of the sophisticated orga- nization the LDS Church had become in the twenty-five years since she and Aubrey had married in Salt Lake City. Closely following a business model, the church had, in the years after World War II, systematically streamlined itself to deal with the brisk postwar surge in membership. Not only did church rosters practically explode with new devotees in the 1950s and '60s, the church also became a virtual publishing empire, printing pamphlets, instruction manuals, music, Bibles, and other books. Increased membership, the fruits of an aggressive missionary campaign, along with a flood of printed material, resulted in a number of peculiar and embarrassing developments in the doctrine. Anxious that the troublesome heresies not get out of hand, the leadership of the church instituted the Correlation Program in the early 1960s to coincide with its projections for continued growth. The program's purpose was to identify, clarify, and systematize authentic LDS doctrine, while also rooting out those unwanted notions that had made their way into the minds of the general Mormon population over the years. To this end the church standardized all meetings, programs, and printed materials with unprecedented efficiency and decisiveness. The standardization of Mormon orthodoxy coincided with the nation's growing Rights Revolution. Thus, while the church was whittling itself down to a kind of barebones theological entity and emphasizing a more visible chain of command, Women's Liberation was becoming big news. Although Andelin was the furthest thing from feminism imaginable, she was, nonetheless, a female power to be reckoned with. And she just happened to approach church leaders with her ideas at the same time they were working furiously to batten down the hatches. Believing that the church she knew and loved was changing for the worse, Andelin reacted more sensitively to Benson's businesslike manner than a better-seasoned advocate for a cause might have. As she became increasingly vocal and emphatic, leaders in Utah became more remote, retreating to their offices at church headquarters and delegating duties to others.

While she never challenged ecclesiastical authority, Andelin chose to disregard formal arrangements of power and authority in order to fulfill what she believed to be a higher calling. Worrisome to church leaders was the fact that, in a tradition that emphasized personal revelation, Andelin's assertions of spiritual manifestations were impossible to refute. From outside the structures of official church power, she could lay claim to the overarching Christian tradition that affirmed the authority of spiritual gifts to all believers.Because Mormonism rested on its belief in personal revelation, church leaders had to admit that Andelin's spiritual power came not from the church but from her relationship with God. While the religion held that personal revelation was an essential part of daily life, such revelations were considered relevant only to the individuals who experienced them or to their close family members. For larger social problems the church's declaration that it represented the original Christian Gospel, fully restored, gave it, in the eyes of the membership, the authority to address these problems as an institution. Andelin's profession of heavenly revelation and worldwide relevance was problematic because she was forwarding the idea that, somehow, the "true and restored" church had overlooked the problem of divorce. Unable to categorize or control Andelin by means of the very values they espoused to the world, the leaders of the church, while they often agreed to listen, chose to ignore what she said. Rather than taking her seriously, they treated her with a kindly indifference that offended and enraged her. The result was an ideological split that Andelin described as "wrenching to the bottom of [her] soul." In what later became a crucial element to the underlying strength of the FW movement, and her own tireless efforts, Andelin began to see herself as more than merely misunderstood. She imagined herself a religious martyr. "A prophet is always hated in his own land," she said.[5]

Unwilling to abandon the struggle for church acceptance, the Andelins met with Apostle Howard W. Hunter. They told him of their great success with the books and classes and expressed their dismay at the opposition they faced from some members of the church. "He seemed very busy and preoccupied with straightening the papers on his desk," she remembered. She had the impression that he regarded them as intruders. Growing impatient with his apathy, she cried out, "If you knew what we were doing and what is going on, you would support it!" Hunter stopped shuffling papers and suggested that she speak with Belle Spafford, the president of the Relief Society. Hunter called Spafford on the telephone while the Andelins sat in his office. To Helen's great distress, Spafford was in a meeting and declined to meet with them. Disappointed and deflated, the Andelins left. A week later Hunter wrote to say that Spafford called back and decided to meet with them after all. Hunter tried to get in touch with the Andelins, but in their haste to meet with as many church officials as possible, they had not informed anyone of how to reach them while they were in Salt Lake. In his letter Hunter conveyed his good wishes and assured Helen that he would look at her book.[6]

Because of her rising anxiety and her inclination to take things personally, Andelin mistook the denial of church approval for a personal affront. The couple's scheduling mishaps further contributed to her belief that there was a churchwide plan to censure her. She believed she had been blacklisted.[7]

Rather than recognize these events as missed opportunities or intellectual differences of opinions, Andelin interpreted them as a betrayal by the beloved organization that had shaped her life. Especially unfortunate was her defensiveness and increasing paranoia that high-ranking LDS women were against her. So poignant was her distress with leading Mormon women who disagreed with her about *FW* that Andelin began to classify them all, especially Spafford, as her enemies. In time she adopted a strident, self-righteous demeanor that, while it effectively communicated her point of view, also annoyed and insulted even the most diplomatic church politicians. Believing she was engaged in a moral war, Andelin did not consider diplomacy, protocol, or patience. Unable to secure an audience with the president of the church or get the notice of his counselors, Andelin wrote to Dyer to ask that he take measures to quiet the opposition. She named certain professors at BYU and the General Presidency of the Relief Society as her worst enemies. While the Relief Society never took a stand against her work, Helen charged that Spafford herself had given the impression that the church was against it.[8]

Mormon leaders had reason to shy away from a charismatic like Andelin. At the same time it was standardizing nearly every aspect of its operations, the church was working diligently to establish its image as a friendly, mainline denomination. Long dogged by stories of gold plates, polygamy, and pioneer ambushes, the church was anxious to downplay its tumultuous history and shed its "peculiar people" label. Part of the LDS campaign to join the mainstream was to remind America that not only was Mormonism a Christian denomination but it also supported the family. What Andelin could not have known in 1968 was that, even as she failed to get notice from church leaders, the Mormons were gearing up to join the antifeminism fight. After the U.S. Congress passed the Equal Rights Amendment in 1972, fears of a constitutional challenge to the sovereignty of an all-male priesthood prompted the church to align itself with the Christian Right in order to begin an effective campaign to block approval of the ERA.[9] Even though Andelin became a tireless opponent of the ERA, the church navigated itself away from her, settling instead on another well-known, but more predictable and media-ready, conservative spokeswoman. In the early 1970s the church joined forces with professional politician Phyllis Schlafly.

In April of 1968 the Andelins again traveled to Salt Lake City to promote *Fascinating Womanhood* and Helen's sacred mission to save marriages. They hoped there would be apostles willing to meet with them there. Remarkably, even without a prearranged schedule, the Andelins were successful in getting meetings with some of the church's most prominent and hard-working leaders. The first person they met with was Elder Paul H. Dunn, a member of the church's elite First Quorum of the Seventy. While encouraging of their efforts, Dunn did not think they could get the church's attention. Next the Andelins met with LeGrand Richards, a longtime member of the Quorum of the Twelve Apostles. When Helen explained the success she was having with *Fascinating Womanhood,* he was attentive. Although Helen believed that he failed to understand how important her work was, she noted that Richards treated them "with great kindness and humility." He even accepted a copy of her book before they left his office.[10]

At the same time, groups of feminist protesters began to publicly oppose Andelin and her followers. A band of demonstrators picketed a Fascinating Womanhood class in Seattle, calling the eight-week course "Fascinating Slavery." One challenger walked into the class and shouted, "I don't believe [the] servitude of women is any solution to the social problems facing America!" Another provoked the instructor, demanding a debate on a local radio station. When asked to leave, the protestors did so quietly enough, but they remained outside with their husbands, who handed out "Fascinating Slavery" leaflets to interested passersby.[11] The protest was sparked by an article the *Seattle Post-Intelligencer* had run a few days earlier that quoted the well-liked Seattle FW teacher Glenda Boyer telling the reporter that it was deflating to a man's ego for his wife to work, no matter what he said. The editorial section of the paper was inundated with letters from both angry critics of FW and its passionate defenders.

Just after their return from a trip to Salt Lake City, one of Helen's students brought to her attention a bill that was working its way through Congress. The proposed Equal Rights Amendment stated, "Equality of rights under the laws shall not be denied or abridged by the United States or any State on account of sex." It sounded simple enough, but Andelin was alarmed. Not finding information about the hearings in the local newspapers, Helen's son Brian, a local attorney and an opponent of Women's Liberation, drove his mother to the Santa Barbara Law Library, where they followed the discussions with growing concern. Sensing a new and dangerous conspiracy against the family, and even America itself, Andelin concluded that feminists were "working at rapid speed to tie up the issue fast and furiously and get it passed . . . before the citizens knew anything about it."[12] She believed that feminists, who she thought of as a single monolithic group, were part of an "outrageous plot" and a "sneak attack" aimed at destroying the family.[13] Fearing that the passage of the amendment would ruin the country by undermining sex roles, Andelin began to warn her followers. She launched a criticism of the rising feminist movement in public meetings and in her newsletter.

In January 1970, Betty Friedan led the five hundred thousand-person Strike for Equality in New York City on the fiftieth anniversary of women winning the right to vote. That month's edition of *The Fascinating Womanhood Newsletter* urged supporters to help in starting a full-scale resistance to the women's liberation movement. In the beginning Andelin was diplomatic. "Although these groups have some worthwhile goals," she wrote, "the overall effects of their efforts arc negative and undermining to the family and marriage." Softening her attack, she asserted that the liberationists "are our sisters and we do not enjoy being in conflict with them." By October she was saying, "Their leaders are sick, confused individuals who have failed to find happiness and success as women. They are therefore not qualified to lead other women. . . . Some of them are admitted lesbians. . . . Every citizen of this country should be alerted to this danger."[14] Later she would explain to followers,

> Feminism centers around claiming *rights*, whereas FW centers around filling *responsibilities*, especially those in the home. The feminists want to assure equality of the sexes, whereas FW women want to preserve the *differences* between the sexes. Feminism teaches women to focus on *their* needs. FW teaches women to focus on their *husband's* needs and their *family's* needs. Feminism promises women a life of *freedom* and *equality*. FW promises women a life of *love* and *happiness*. Feminism is a *self-centered* philosophy, whereas FW is an *unselfish, giving* philosophy. Feminism ignores *basic religious*

principles, such as those taught in the *Bible*. FW is based on religious principles, *supported* by the Bible.[15]

Prior to 1970, Andelin had no personal quarrel with feminists. In fact, early on, she knew very little about them and, because she understood them to be part of the vast numbers of women she sought to help, she took very little interest in provoking or debating them. Protective of her own right to free agency, she also supported their right to believe as they wished. Early in the movement she thought of them less as moral rivals and more as simply uninformed, persuadable women who also desired personal happiness. Andelin believed that, given the proper information, feminists, like the women who read her book, would simply give up their incorrect ideas. "Our Womanhood Movement must have with it a spirit of love and concern for all women . . . not a spirit of antagonism. We are concerned about our sisters in the Lib Movement, for we feel they will reap nothing but unhappiness as a result of their misdirected efforts. We discourage their goals for their sakes as well as others."[16] Her repeated failure to get the attention of the church, the recent discovery of the congressional hearings, and the urging of her husband prompted her to confront feminists with charges that were uncharacteristically vicious.

Helen recalled that Aubrey strongly urged her to denounce her opponents publicly. He believed that in the tradition of biblical prophets, it was her duty to "call the feminists to repentance," even warning them of God's wrath if they did not change. Feminists, he believed, were teaching false doctrines, making a mockery of something sacred. Like the Bible's money changers in the temple, they needed to be driven out. Helen said that, because of her husband, she felt a great deal of pressure to carry out the public chastisements.[17] These exchanges and the livid responses of her critics fueled Andelin's efforts. She began to view feminists as she did her Mormon detractors, as her enemies. It didn't take long before she became convinced that they were part of a larger effort to silence her. As a result, throughout the early 1970s she became increasingly unkind in her public efforts against them. As with her experience with the Mormons, the rejection of "truth" on the part of some feminist thinkers was something Andelin failed to understand as an intellectual disagreement. Rather, she believed it was part of a dangerous scheme to destroy America. Andelin wrote to President Richard Nixon. Claiming to represent two hundred thousand women, she said, "We are disappointed you are supporting the Women's Liberation Movement. . . . We feel that the liberationists are sick individuals. . . . Their views do not represent the majority of women. . . . To support such a cause is to support a subversive element."[18] Andelin believed that feminist groups, along with homosexuals and the media, were part of a conspiracy to change the family structure from well-defined male and female roles to unisex ones. She feared that if these groups had their way, children would not be raised by their mothers but by day care centers. And she believed that the mixing of roles would lead vulnerable children into delinquency and homosexuality. She asserted, "Eminent psychologists claim [that] many homosexuals come from backgrounds where the masculine and feminine were never clearly defined. . . . They were hampered in their development into a distinct sex." She believed that "the feminists, the abortionists, and the homosexuals" were bent on ruining the country.[19]

To fight the liberationists, Andelin urged her readers to contact radio, TV, and newspaper outlets to speak out against the ERA. She encouraged them to become active in their school districts, write their legislators, and seek the advice of their husbands. "I think that each of us should consult our husbands . . . since men are better at politics than we women are." After printing several articles in her newsletter alerting her followers about the evils of the new bill, Andelin received a call from her friend Jaquie Davison, asking if she "could take the torch and do something about it."[20] Davison was a sought-after FW teacher on the Parker Chiropractic Seminar circuit. In 1970 she founded the Happiness of Womanhood Organization (HOW) in order to help stop the ERA.[21] Davison held news conferences and gave interviews in local and national newspapers. "It's time for housewives . . . to pull on the combat boots and battle those dragging the word 'housewife' through the mud," she told reporters. Politically energized by the threat of the ERA, Davison worked nearly twenty-four hours a day to stop the bill, even as she continued to maintain her FW teaching schedule.[22] HOW mobilized a march on the nation's capital, and Andelin flew to Washington, D.C., to participate in it. She held a press conference with Davison before returning to Santa Barbara. HOW, which distributed pink buttons that said "I Know

HOW," in 1972 claimed it had ten thousand members.[23] In her travels across the country, Davison met Phyllis Schlafly at a political rally. She claimed that she was the one who alerted Schlafly as to just how close the ERA was to ratification.[24] According to Andelin, "Jaquie passed the torch to Phyllis Schlafly," who, after meeting with the HOW founder, started her own campaign against the ERA in 1972. Davison said, "I was in on it two years before Phyllis Schlafly and her 'STOP ERA.'"[25] Andelin met Schlafly when they both appeared, one following the other, on a television program. Although they held many of the same political views, and Andelin encouraged her followers to attend Schlafly's rallies, the two were never associated with each other.

Sometime after that, Helen and Jaquie Davison had a terrible falling out. For reasons Helen did not share, Aubrey believed that Jaquie had "fallen into sin." He insisted that his wife disassociate herself from her friend. In interviews forty years later, Andelin expressed great sadness over her broken relationship with Jaquie. She wished that her husband had not "forced" her to end all contact with her "dear friend," feeling the break was too harsh.

In 1970 Helen and Aubrey showed up unannounced at church headquarters to meet with Joseph Fielding Smith, who had recently been installed as the new president of the church. Four years earlier, in his position as an apostle, Smith himself had signed the request from the office of the church historian asking for a copy of Helen's book and, later, the *Teacher Lesson Outlines* to place in the church archives. Unaccustomed to the workings of a large organization, Andelin understood all communication to come directly from Smith himself. She did not allow for the possibility that he signed documents generated by his large staff and thus would not remember her or her book. Because the Andelins had received a note from Smith acknowledging receipt of the materials, they were encouraged that perhaps he would respond positively to them. Incredibly, Smith agreed to a meeting. The couple spent close to an hour in his office yet remained curiously silent about the purpose of their visit. "We did not bring up the subject of *Fascinating Womanhood*," Helen recalled. She believed that, as a man of God, Smith should have been able to "discern" her mission without her explaining it. The Andelins left the meeting, and Helen concluded that it was "hopeless to get the attention of the Church."[26] For the next several years, she continued to hope that LDS leaders would take notice of her and listen to what she was doing to rescue marriages.

That same year, in Goleta, California, Andelin's followers picketed a public lecture by feminism's founder and top strategist, Betty Friedan. Three Fascinating Womanhood teachers led a group of women wearing aprons and ruffled dresses, carrying signs and feather dusters and pushing baby carriages outside the hall where Friedan was scheduled to speak. One reporter commented on the irony that the protestors were women "leaving their homes to picket Friedan for trying to get women to leave their homes."[27] The NOW president, arms folded across her chest, "look[ed] on amusedly as her fellow sisters protest[ed] her feminist attitudes."[28] FW loyalists continued to picket Friedan and other feminist leaders when they held press conferences and addressed large crowds; Andelin urged them on. In time some of Andelin's readers began to chafe at her shrill rallying cries against feminists. When one reader complained that the newsletter was devoting too much space to her strident political views, Andelin answered by saying, "We feel that Women's Lib *is* our concern since it opposes the very things we teach and will be destructive to the feminine world. We . . . will [continue to] speak out against issues that tend to destroy our work."[29] Andelin's readers also questioned her promotion of vegetarianism and natural remedies and her condemnation of circumcision. Nevertheless, *The Fascinating Womanhood Newsletter* became an effective platform for Andelin's objections to the creation of the United Nations, the birth control pill, legalized abortion, and government-funded schools.

As her celebrity status grew and her political views became more extreme, the rift between Andelin and her religious community expanded. The Andelins continued to plead with church leaders, who continued to avoid them. Then, according to Andelin, in the spring of 1971 the newest LDS president, Harold B. Lee, requested that the BYU Family Relations Department conduct a thorough critique of the Fascinating Womanhood program. Dr. Blaine Porter, dean of the department, agreed to undertake this task. At the end of his investigation, Porter compiled a report for the First Presidency.[30] When Helen asked one of her authorized FW teachers in Utah to drop by and get the report from Porter, he declined to give her a copy. Not realizing he had not shared the requested information only because he didn't know the teacher who was asking for it, Helen took his actions as an effort to discredit her. Several months later she traveled to Utah to confront him. Porter showed her the critique, which she described as mostly minor and picky, and he told her he could not endorse *Fascinating Womanhood*. Marriage, he said, could not be improved by talking to women alone. Both spouses needed to work together to create a strong marriage. In a letter to Andelin, he said, "It seems to me that a difference of opinion is a privilege we must charitably grant each other."[31] Andelin was furious. Porter was not the only disapproving person in the BYU family relations department. "I also confronted Dr. Reed Bradford," she remembered. Bradford, a well-known and respected professor of sociology, thought little of Andelin and her growing movement and wrote two articles in the student newspaper criticizing *Fascinating Womanhood* and warning against Andelin's approach.[32] Incensed, Andelin wrote to the president of the university to defend herself and complain about Bradford's public denunciation. Andelin often misinterpreted established protocols of academic inquiry and scholarly debate as personal attacks on her character. Her portrayals of Porter, Bradford, and others she believed were trying to condemn her were consistently negative.

As she continued her battle with the Family Relations Department at BYU, which she described as "almost like an animal," Andelin stepped up her campaign against feminism and its leaders. Aubrey joined her in the cause. As president of the Andelin Foundation for Education in Family Living, he wrote letters, traveled with his wife, and granted newspaper interviews. Publicly engaged in denouncing the feminist agenda, Helen continued to complain to church leaders that she had been treated unfairly. Aubrey wrote to Finn Paulson, the regional representative for the church, to protest "unsupportive comments" the leader had made about the FW program while on a trip to Brazil. He also claimed that Paulson was the one who had discouraged the sale of *Fascinating Womanhood* in church bookstores.[33] As the effort to get the approval of the church continued, Andelin fought even more vehemently against her feminist rivals. Her main strategy was to taunt them. She said, "Betty Friedan is a personal failure. What's she doing talking about success?" She told reporters that Friedan was not pretty, that she "never dated in high school, she was rejected by men, and her husband beat her up."[34] She claimed that many feminists hated men and were homosexuals. She even had unkind words about the women's rights leader Susan B. Anthony, asserting, "She was an old maid who had a distrust and dislike for men."[35]

In an interview with the *Daily News* in New York, Andelin said of feminist leaders, "They are misfits caught between two worlds. They have rejected the feminine world and are forcing their way into a man's world where they will never be anything but a second-rate man."[36] Like a religious zealot, she called for repentance. While this street-preacher type of energy invigorated her message, it widened the split between her and her feminist sisters.

As Andelin became more politically active, her detractors grew in numbers. She was frequently invited to speak at college campuses, and at the University of California, Los Angeles, Helen spoke to an audience of 2,500 students. The appearance ended badly. During her presentation, she said that a woman didn't need the right to vote. She was booed. When she talked about a married man being the head of the house, the men applauded loudly and the women continued booing her until she had to quit speaking. The audience remained so hostile that Andelin had to leave the stage. Aubrey led her out of the building. At California State College, where Andelin faced a panel of nine feminist academics, "the feminists became very rude and ugly in speech," she remembered. Speaking to a largely female audience, she was unable to get a word in to answer her challengers. "The lady who invited me rose and defended me and sharply rebuked the audience," she remembered.[37] The audience didn't listen. Finally, she said, "Aubrey came on stage, put his arm around me and led me away." At other places where crowds got particularly antagonistic, Aubrey became accustomed to walking onto the stage and dramatically whisking his wife to safety.

On a nationally televised program in Toronto, Canada, Andelin debated her philosophy of marriage with the famous bandleader, Artie Shaw, who opposed her assertion that the man should be the head of the household. Shaw, she recalled, was pleasant, but the live audience was aggressive and belligerent. "I felt an evil influence in the room," she recalled. Frightened, she believed she saw "Satanic looks in some of their faces." Aubrey, who usually accompanied his wife to speaking engagements, was not able to come on this particular trip. "I defended my point of view by quoting the word of God," she said.[38] When she returned to Santa Barbara that evening, she spent the rest of the night in prayer. The chief editor of *Cosmopolitan Magazine*, Helen Gurley Brown; the feminist author Jacqueline Suzann, and the novelist Adela Rogers St. John faced off against Andelin on another TV program. Rather than debate them Andelin quoted Scripture and predicted God's wrath if the women didn't change. They quickly tired of her, and finally stopped talking—ending the interview.[39] After a particularly antagonistic crowd objected to Helen's presentation at a graduate student seminar, Aubrey told a newspaper reporter that the audience was "the most despicable bunch of libbers," he had ever seen. "I call them the Children of Darkness who can't see the light. They're not moral people. They have to *gang* together."[40] Andelin had other critics. The famous sex researchers William Masters and Virginia Johnson, in an article warning readers of the dangers of do-it-yourself advice, said that Andelin was taking advantage of women who were searching for answers anywhere they could find them. Andelin was not a qualified marriage expert, they pointed out, and they took particular offense to the Andelins' sex manual, "where women control when and how often to have sex and practice moderation so as not to 'spoil' a husband as little children can become spoiled if you give them too much candy."[41] Berean Bookstore, a large supplier of Christian books in the Midwest, California, and Arizona, stopped carrying *Fascinating Womanhood* when they found out Andelin was a Mormon. When one dubious reporter accused her of seeking fulfillment outside the home, Andelin had a ready answer, "I do this as a benevolent service; not for fulfillment. . . . I've always put my husband and children first. If other women did the same as I, it would be fine."[42] She pointed out that she had been a full-time wife and mother for twenty years before she wrote *Fascinating Womanhood*. To another reporter, who accused her of making money at the expense of unhappy women, she said, "The profits of my book have been used to further this work and to compensate those who devote time to it. . . . I personally have not received any financial benefits."[43] Asked one journalist, "Can you imagine what would happen to our schools, our hospitals, our factories, our stores if the married female employees quit tomorrow?" Andelin answered, "Is not the success of the home even more important than the success of our schools, our hospitals, and our industries? . . . If women quit work, all men would be able to find jobs. . . . Besides, any work outside the home can be done by men. This has been proven in many societies." As her list of enemies expanded, so did her following; thousands of women signed up for FW classes.

One of the most easily identified parts of Betty Friedan's *Feminine Mystique,* was her treatise on the evils of unpaid housework, which, she said was symptomatic of the much deeper condition of inequality between men and women. Friedan objected to the gender-based division of labor and the societal assignment of unpaid work to the improperly identified weaker sex. Home, she argued, was an exploitative prison, and housekeeping was restrictive and demeaning. Although housework was only part of Friedan's larger critique, it quickly became a weapon in the woman-to-woman combat that followed. Housework, Friedan charged, expanded to fill the time allotted to it. She quoted family experts as saying that "most housework . . . 'can be capably handled by an eight-year-old child.'" She added, "Women pay a high emotional and physical price for evading their own growth."[44] Immature women, women who did not contribute to society, and those avoiding growing up, all hid behind the safety of housework, she said.

By focusing on the kinds of work women customarily did, and assuming that most women disliked these tasks, Friedan and others failed to notice the more positive aspects of conventional homemaking that Andelin extolled: self-respect for a job well done, personal pride, creativity, self-sufficiency, and, in some cases, the ability to earn extra money. Despite the broader analysis of gender equality that Friedan had aimed for, the crux of her critique, as it took hold among the public, was that traditional women's work was degrading. Certain jobs were beneath one's dignity to do. "It is expected that women do for love what no man would do for money," she said.[45] While privileged people have always had others perform tedious and boring household chores for them, rural families, much of the lower middle class, and the urban poor did these jobs themselves. These duties were necessary, and were shameful only to those who had the financial means not to do them. For women accustomed to doing all kinds of work, excelling at humble tasks such as sewing, caring for children, and cooking meals provided important sources of personal pride. While arguing her case for equality between men and women, Friedan also promoted a darker parallel, that the heretofore honorable work of countless poor and middle-class American women was, in reality, humiliating. By shaming the housewife, Friedan offended much of Middle America, splitting the women's rights movement and creating a class argument. In was in this cultural war zone that the reassuring messages of *Fascinating Womanhood* flourished. This disparaging of housework not only contributed to the vicious public counterattack against feminism, but it created a considerable amount of space for Andelin's more comforting message that traditional women's work was noble.

In the late '60s and early '70s, the feminist movement marched forward. But as the 1970s progressed, the organization suffered a series of setbacks. Friedan, who left office as president of NOW in 1970, took issue with the ideological turn the movement began to take. She charged that the group "focused too many resources on lesbian issues" and said that "too many feminists hated men."[46] She opposed its increasingly narrow radicalism, and encouraged women to give up extremism and sexual politics and to place more emphasis on families. Friedan eventually fell out of favor. Critics like Phyllis Schlafly, who accused feminists of supporting a "chip-on-the-shoulder" dogma, claimed that Women's Liberation was never trying to help women in the first place, but only seeking to advance its radical agenda at the cost of women.[47] In 1972 Congress passed the Equal Rights Amendment and sent it to the states for ratification. The ERA was quickly ratified in twenty-eight states. Among its endorsers were the AFL–CIO, the American Bar Association, and President Richard Nixon. Nationwide adoption of the proposed amendment seemed sure. By the mid-1970s, however, an astonishing upsurge of opposition to the amendment emerged. Encouraged by the battle cries of the conservative Republican leader Phyllis Schlafly, state legislatures fought the ERA with ferocious determination. Schlafly argued that passage of the new bill would result in the loss of the privileges and protections that American women already enjoyed. One of these was lifelong financial support for housewives. She feared that passage of the ERA would eliminate child support and alimony for stay-at-home wives. "Even though love may go out the window, the obligation should remain. The ERA would eliminate that obligation," she said.[48] Schlafly's other example of female privilege was women's freedom from the draft. During the years of the escalating Vietnam War, the idea of mothers and daughters being conscripted into the military was terrifying—as were TV and magazine images of women soldiers in communist China and the Middle East. Schlafly and others also argued that passage of the ERA would lead to mothers' losing custody of their children in divorce, compulsory government-controlled day care centers, and unisex bathrooms in schools and other public buildings. In response to the opposition, five states rescinded their votes. In 1979 the bill was just three states short of the number it needed for ratification. Congress extended the deadline, but by 1982 the proposed ERA still did not have enough votes to pass, and the amendment died.

In 1973 fifty million people watched openly gay Billie Jean King overwhelm Bobby Riggs in the televised "Battle of the Sexes" tennis match at the Houston Astrodome. In the same year, the Supreme Court upheld *Roe v. Wade,* giving women the right to a safe and legal abortion. Those alarmed by these events fought back. The Andelins joined the pro-life movement and became active in anti-homosexual efforts. Andelin continued to use her newsletter to project her political beliefs. Abortion, she feared, would encourage sex before marriage.[49] When it came to the menace of homosexuality, she wrote, "Do you know that there is a bill in Congress which, if passed, will remove existing discrimination of homosexuals in employment, housing, and federal programs? Think how dangerous it could be to have homosexual school teachers who may influence students. . . . They could even become social workers and public officials." The harm in giving homosexuals equal rights, according to her? "It gives a certain *acceptance* to the practice. This is just what the homosexuals want. . . . Please write to your Congressmen and appeal to others to do so."[50] The Andelins, immersed in conservative politics, toyed with the idea of joining the John Birch Society. Aubrey, who had been an avid supporter of Barry Goldwater in 1964, was attracted to the organization. They read some of the literature and were interested in joining.[51] They attended a number of Birch Society open houses and a political rally. Helen even wrote a pamphlet for the Society about one of her FW teachers who was a member. The Andelins invited representatives of the organization to meet with them in their home. Ultimately, they decided not to join. Aubrey felt that the organization was "all talk and . . . didn't actually do anything." He later told reporters who asked about his affiliation with the John Birch Society that Fascinating Womanhood was "independent and non-aligned."[52] By the mid-seventies a new brand of political activism was fast gaining ground. As Andelin promoted her personal politics, a more militant brand of right-wing, pro-family, female activism began to stoke the increasing national fears of the ERA, homosexuality, abortion, and same-sex bathrooms. One John Birch Society pamphlet warned, "Look Out! THEY'RE PLANNING TO DRAFT YOUR DAUGHTER!!" While many of Andelin's followers eventually identified themselves with Christian conservative politics for a variety of reasons, it was some feminists' belittling of the housewife's work that, in large part, associated their movement with organized labor, communism, and anti-Americanism. This association prompted a strong reaction by more-radical conservatives. Women's involvement in the new right-wing groups was "another version" of women's liberation, said one writer. While the goals were very different, the fact that women were rushing into the political arena, even for reasons that seemed to limit their freedom, was, in fact, liberating.[53] Andelin's fans kept sending in letters about how their marriages had been transformed by living the Fascinating Womanhood philosophy. One enthusiast from Seminole, Florida wrote, "Every day is just like a miracle before my eyes. I never thought that ever again I would be honored with gifts, flowers, love notes, the door held open for me, a sweet smile or tender touch. . . . I could go on listing."[54] Said another, "It seems like all I am doing is setting back and letting him spoil me. It really makes you feel like you are in the clouds." One woman wrote, "I've been showered with presents, compliments, and attention."[55] A happy housewife reported, "He has decided to give me a grocery allowance."[56]

One reason for Andelin's remarkable appeal despite vigorous opposition was that she refused to play by the rules of intellectual argument. Armed with an effective self-proclaimed credibility that did not rely on the approval of anyone, Andelin became a powerful opponent in public debate. Because of the importance they placed on their own qualifications as trained scholars and religious authorities, Andelin's critics underestimated her strength. Believing that she had been called by God, Andelin discounted the conventional categories of knowledge and relied instead on "spiritual gifts." She said, "When you're speaking the truth you speak as one having authority. You don't need to back it up."[57] Thus, her run-ins with critics of all persuasions often resulted in a fireworks display that seemed to make her only stronger. It also reconfirmed her status as a champion for regular women. Because she used the combined criteria of experience and testimonial rather than evidence and logic, Andelin was a formidable foe. She was living proof that a leader of a movement didn't need logic—only conviction. "Techniques do not make a great writer," she told her critics. "Great thoughts do."[58] While she was often booed by live audiences, it was nearly impossible for her detractors to wage a war of words against her on radio or TV. Some of Andelin's unwillingness to conform was due to her inexperience. Mostly she just refused to bend to convention. She simply said what she wanted to. Public discussions with Andelin had the disconcerting consequence of making her sophisticated, formally educated challengers look exactly like the kind of women she was trying to help in the first place—frustrated, unhappy, and unfeminine. In contrast, Andelin's personal magnetism, over-the-top femininity and prim self-righteousness often got the best of even seasoned journalists. Most didn't agree with her message, but they loved her anyway. Reporters often commented on her looks and the way she dressed. In Chicago one journalist described Andelin as a "soft-spoken, gracious power." Another said, "There was a heady smell of Chanel No. 5 in the Pick Congress hotel room where Mrs. Andelin combed her long wavy brown hair before meeting the press." Starstruck reporters said that Andelin was beautiful, smelled good, had a nice voice, and looked younger than her fifty years. They pointed out that she had nice legs, knew how to do her makeup, and walked and talked like a lady. One reporter described her pretty "daffodil yellow dotted Swiss dress with tiers of tiny ruffles across its skirt." Andelin, she noted, had even sewn the dress herself.[59]

One of the consequences of her growing fame was that it drew public attention to the troublesome issue of credibility. Andelin did not have a college degree, nor was she qualified as a marriage counselor. In fact, she had no professional training at all. Admitting she had only a modest education, limited experience in worldly matters, and very little knowledge of history, Andelin claimed to be an expert just the same. Firm in her conviction that knowledge was not the possession solely of formally educated people, she followed a more populist impulse by defining and maintaining her own criteria for what constituted truth. Andelin held that the events of everyday life were just as authoritative as any published study or report. When it came to marriage, she had little patience with intellectual arguments. Because she had been married for two decades, was the mother of eight children, and belonged to a large extended family, Andelin steadfastly believed that she was as much an expert on families as any book-trained authority. Plus she had the Bible. When asked about their qualifications for counseling married couples, Aubrey told a reporter, "We are students of the Scriptures. I cannot think of any better credentials."[60]

Eventually Andelin began to listen to her readers about the fact that her political involvements were taking away precious momentum from the Fascinating Womanhood message. After all, it was the marriage relationship that Andelin saw as essential, not politics. She began to backpedal. In a 1974 interview after a speaking engagement at Loma Linda University, she reversed her organization's earlier involvement in the anti-ERA movement by saying, "I personally oppose the ERA, but Fascinating Womanhood doesn't get into it. I feel there would be more lost for women than gained." But, she added, "Women's liberation [has] nothing to do with the program."[61] By 1975 her challenge to Women's Liberation was much more diplomatic. Instead of referring to her feminist critics as failures and misfits, she began to once again call them her sisters. She told her followers that she was tired of arguing with them and wanted to get on with her own program. In one interview she said it was "unchristian" to disparage the feminists. She insisted that she was not antifeminist and that the ERA was unnecessary, but asserted that none of her family had worked against it.

An official for the Girl Scouts said they had received a form letter with signatures calling for Betty Friedan and "others of a like persuasion" to resign from their board of directors. The petition had been circulated from state to state and signed by seventy-six women who described themselves as "dedicated teachers of Fascinating Womanhood." Claiming to have no knowledge of the petition, Andelin said, "We just have other things to do. We're interested in the happy home. This is my ministry."[62] While she enthusiastically agreed to support one of Phyllis Schlafly's trips to California and Arizona by alerting her followers, Andelin did so on a provisional basis. It was something she was willing to do because she had the means and the organizational network to help, but she didn't want to involve herself publicly in the cause anymore. She continued to speak out in her newsletter against Women's Liberation, homosexuality, and women working outside the home. She also supported a variety of conservative causes.

Despite the fact that *Fascinating Womanhood* had been in print for over ten years, Andelin worried that Mormon women were not getting her vital message. She was scheduled to give an FW seminar in Salt Lake City in August and hoped that maybe she would have some luck with the newest church president, Spencer W. Kimball.[63] She wrote to him of her success in "saving and restoring" thousands of marriages over the years, and asked if it would be possible to see him. He never answered her letter. Later she called his office only to receive a "rather cool" answer from his secretary who explained that it was not possible for her to meet with the church president. "This affected me profoundly," Andelin remembered. It was not Kimball's busy schedule that bothered her but rather the way his secretary had of making her "feel rejected." Demoralized by the slight, Andelin fell into a deep depression. "I was sick in bed for a week," she remembered. So intense were her feelings of rejection that, several times in the middle of the night, as she recalled, "I broke into a cold sweat and had to change my clothes. . . . I seemed to have a condition that was out to destroy me."[64] She was anguished by her failure to see Kimball in person and was stung by her belief that the church had "treated [her] like an outcast." She was distressed that the church office building was designed so that visitors couldn't get direct access to the elevators. "It's enough to make your blood run cold," she said. In May of 1976, after she had sold over a million books, Andelin wrote to Kimball again. Troubled about the still-climbing divorce rates in Utah, she explained to the president that there were alternatives to divorce. She pleaded with him to meet with her personally. But Kimball remained silent. A few months later, she saw the church president's picture on the front page of the local newspaper. Kimball was smiling widely as he shook hands with the actor, Telly Savalas, the star of the popular television show, *Kojak*. In 1976 *Kojak* was the TV program that leading observers rated the most violent in America. Andelin couldn't believe that the president of the Mormon Church would rather shake hands with a movie star than talk to her about saving marriages. In August, when the Andelins were in Salt Lake City, they tried to see Kimball again. They were met with another one of his personal secretaries. This time the secretary said that Kimball had received Helen's letter, which had impressed him. The Andelins stayed in the city for several days to see if there was a chance that the Prophet would make time to see them. Because he was preparing for an LDS conference in Europe, a meeting never worked out, but Kimball did send a message through his secretary asking Helen to be patient. Months went by, and in November, after no word from the LDS president, Aubrey called his office again, but to no avail. He continued to call. Finally, in early February 1977, two years after their original request, the Andelins were summoned to church headquarters in Salt Lake City.

Kimball did not meet with the Andelins himself but instead assigned the task to General President of the Relief Society Barbara Smith and the prominent church elders Gordon B. Hinckley and Marvin J. Ashton, both members of the Quorum of the Twelve Apostles. The day before the meeting, the Andelins held a special fast and prayer day in hopes that they could deliver the FW message appropriately and also that Smith, Helen's perceived foe, and the brethren would receive it in good faith. They arrived at the church office building fifteen minutes early for their appointment and waited in the reception room. Shortly after they arrived Helen saw Barbara Smith walk into Hinckley's office. They waited another thirty minutes to be invited in. Before they sat down before the three leaders, Aubrey asked if he could open the meeting with a prayer. At first the elders said no. "We sat in silence, dumbfounded by their attitude," Helen said. Since proper protocol indicated that one of the brethren should suggest prayer if there was to be one, not Aubrey, his asking to pray was likely an affront to basic etiquette, and a serious social error. In a more informal setting, rejecting an offer to pray with a member of the church would be unheard of in the normally genteel LDS society. The fact that the Andelins did not differentiate between local custom and the reality that they had, quite unbelievably, secured a meeting with three of the highest-ranking church officials was an unfortunate one. Hinckley reconsidered and asked Ashton to pray, which, Helen recalled, "he did very briefly." After the perfunctory prayer, the Andelins learned that they had only thirty minutes of their allotted hour left. Barbara Smith had taken the other thirty minutes. Later, Helen would say that Smith had used the time to "poison their minds" against her.[65]

"I talked first," Helen remembered. She gave a brief description of what she believed to be her vital work of saving marriages. She told of her successes and the profound changes she had witnessed in thousands of couples. With great emotion, she urged them to read *Fascinating Womanhood* and endorse it for churchwide use. When they hesitated, she exclaimed to the puzzled leaders her intense frustrations with those she believed to be the opponents of FW. Helen later recalled, "I said my worst enemies were the feminists, the abortionists, the liberals, the BYU Family Relations

Department, and the General Presidency of the Relief Society." To the leaders, Andelin's impassioned indictment was a regrettable display of rash and unprofessional behavior. Lumping Smith together with abortionists and other enemies was uncalled for and embarrassing. To make matters worse, Aubrey tried to pin Smith down. Without regard for her position, he turned and asked her directly if she thought *Fascinating Womanhood* was manipulative. Helen remembered that Smith, now on the spot in front of her male colleagues, squirmed. After a moment she straightened up in her chair and forthrightly answered, "I certainly do, and I do not think it fitting for the LDS woman."[66] Hinckley, steering around what might have become a quarrel, asked Helen what she expected of the church. Andelin asked for a "formal and extensive investigation" of *FW*. She offered to come to Salt Lake herself to conduct a test case involving twenty unhappily married women. The elders, she proposed, could interview each woman before the class "to have accurate knowledge of the condition of her marriage." Then, after they completed the FW program, the leaders could interview the women again to see how their relationships with their husbands had changed. Andelin was certain that they would agree to her plan. Instead, Hinckley ended the discussion by saying he would turn the entire matter over to Barbara Smith for further investigation.

Helen was stunned. Hinckley had just turned the analysis of the entire Fascinating Womanhood program over to one of her "worst enemies." This came as an incredible blow to Andelin. She could hardly fathom the fact that a "member of the opposition" was now in charge of critiquing the philosophy she had hoped the church would officially adopt. She walked out of Hinckley's office, sat down in the first chair she could find, and burst into tears. She said later, "I had always trusted the leadership of the Church. Now I suffered painful disillusionment. . . . What were they afraid of? I am just an ordinary Saint and a housewife. Why were they [afraid]?"[67] Powerless to accept what was happening, she cried bitterly. As Sister Smith walked out, she patted Helen on the shoulder. Smith never did conduct Andelin's proposed investigation of *Fascinating Womanhood*. "I have never seen her or heard from her since," she said.[68]

Because church leaders had not recognized her divine message, Andelin could interpret the meeting only as a monumental failure. While, in reality, the people in Salt Lake City were making an effort to better understand her, she took their reluctance to embrace her program wholeheartedly as a catastrophe of epic proportions. The outcome of the meeting shocked her and Aubrey to such an extent that they were "sick in bed for two days." After their return to Santa Barbara, she continued to suffer with persistent and painful doubts about the church. "I knew the Gospel was true," she said, "but I did not know about this present administration." She described the LDS leaders, who she once understood as men of God, as "uninspired men in business suits." After all, they *should have* recognized what she was talking about. She believed that their inability to do so signaled a lack of spirituality and moral strength.[69] Aubrey sent a final letter to Hinckley and Ashton, appealing one last time for their attention. Leveling aim directly at Barbara Smith, he wrote, "what hurts the most" was that Smith's statements during the meeting were "almost a direct transcript of the phrases made by the women's libbers, free-love advocates, pro-abortionists, homosexuals and liberals of all kinds." Making no distinction between Smith and others "who want no restraints and who deny the God-given role of women," Aubrey wanted to know for what reason they could be so offended. He said, "Knowledgeable people cannot be relied on."[70]

After what she believed to be the unsympathetic treatment from those she hoped would understand her vision, Andelin thought about leaving the church. She decided to ask God what she should do. Aubrey agreed to support her no matter what she decided. Abstaining from food and water, Helen spent an entire day in prayer. "I prayed to the Father and the Father answered . . . word for word," she recounted: "God said that *the Lord Jesus Christ is watching over His Church. Stay with the Saints.*" It did not matter whether the brethren were out of line, or not. Helen understood that the behavior of individual men was of no consequence to an all-knowing God who, she believed, guided the unfolding of history itself. Most important for her was that she knew the most valuable thing she could do was remain a participating, active voice in her church. To leave would be to abandon those thousands of LDS women statistics told her would eventually end up divorced. Andelin's realization that the Mormon Church would not officially adopt her message only spurred her on. She discarded the idea that she needed the endorsement of any organization. Being rebuffed by church leaders only added an element of urgency to her burning sense of mission. It also added a component of outrage that, for Andelin, ultimately proved empowering. She declared, "I didn't write *Fascinating Womanhood* for the Mormon Church, I wrote it for the world."[71] Maintaining that her insights were authoritative in their own right and did not require the permission of any religious organization, she continued her work. Andelin kept her differences with the church to herself and out of her public discussions. She may have feared alienating Mormon women, who the church was not formally acknowledging were suffering from escalating divorce rates, or this may have been a sign of her loyalty to the church despite the shortcomings of its leaders.

What Andelin failed to realize was that there were genuine reasons that large numbers of LDS women objected to her philosophy. Rather than being part of a churchwide plot to discredit her, many LDS women who agreed with Andelin's emphasis on the family nevertheless found her methods for achieving marital happiness offensive. Offspring of resilient pioneers, Mormon women could scarcely imagine themselves as frivolous, saucy, and helpless. Moreover, childlikeness and defenselessness were simply not Mormon virtues. While LDS women willingly agreed to the decisions of church authorities, many of them chafed at the idea of subordinating themselves to individual men. LDS women took issue with feminism's indictment of patriarchy and the denigration of housework, but they objected to the fact that Andelin's teachings encouraged women to pick and choose the jobs they would perform, based on their sex. For Mormon women, refusing to engage in the "masculine" jobs of paying bills, mowing the lawn, or washing the car simply because these were "men's" work did not make sense. Andelin's own mother and sisters, used to heavy farm duties, were good examples of this broader understanding of family work. While her Relief Society sisters Spafford and Smith would never disagree with Andelin's objective to save marriages, Andelin's instructions to perform only ladylike tasks were, at least to Smith, materialistic. Many LDS women also objected heartily to Andelin's instructions not to wear pants, even while engaging in housework. Mormon women dressed for comfort and function and were not about to let Andelin tell them how to dress. For many Mormon women, Andelin's teachings were as off-putting as they were to her feminist opponents.

Tired of fighting women's liberationists, and having failed in her attempts to get the blessing of the Mormon Church, Andelin was exhausted. Nevertheless, she continued to write supplementary teaching materials, give speeches, and hold conventions. Her books continued to sell, and classes in *Fascinating Womanhood* and *The Fascinating Girl* were being taught in adult-education programs, community colleges, and high schools across the nation. Teacher applications kept coming in, and so did teachers' fees. Despite the income the Andelins were having financial problems. Their miracle man had left the business one hundred thousand dollars in debt, and they didn't know how to manage their money. Employees had to be let go. The Andelin Foundation for Education in Family Living went from a flourishing concern back to a two-person operation. Helen, with the help of a secretary, continued to answer letters, process teacher applications, and generate her newsletter from her home office. The workload was overwhelming. Aubrey began to search for other avenues of income. The couple agreed to a few limited tours to promote their books, but by 1977 Helen wanted to get away. When Aubrey suggested they take their remaining profits and leave Santa Barbara, she agreed. Believing that they were called by God to start their own religious community, the Andelins and their adult children moved to a farm on the outskirts of a small town in Missouri, and Helen left public life.

Six

FARMVILLE

$\mathcal{A}$fter her grueling publicity tours, the falling out with the FW CEO Sam Battistone, and her emotional devastation at the continued failure of LDS authorities to take her seriously, Andelin was ready to leave the public spotlight. She wanted to be free of the leadership of Fascinating Womanhood so that she could return to her first career—that of wife and homemaker. Andelin stopped teaching and she turned down opportunities to speak publicly and be interviewed. Aubrey, tired of the rigors of the FW empire, was ready to retire from his wife's venture and pursue other interests. In 1977, at the height of the fascinating womanhood movement, Aubrey and Helen, along with their son Brian, traveled east in search of a parcel of land big enough for the entire family. They ended up in rural Missouri. California was an expensive place to live, and the couple worried about their adult children. "We felt we were in for the troublesome last days,"[1] said Helen. Finding a site he liked, Aubrey made a quick decision to purchase 170 acres of farmland on the outskirts of the small town of Pierce City. He named it Farmville. A home place had long been a dream of the Andelins. The trouble was that

Helen didn't like Missouri. She would have rather moved to North Carolina or Arizona. But Aubrey and Brian loved the Farmville property; to them it felt like home. They saw Farmville as a final residence where the family could establish a safe haven. Outnumbered, Helen felt unable to protest. She recalled, "I didn't really agree with coming to Missouri. . . . But, I never put my foot down. I practice what I preach."

For Mormons, the "last days" refers to the time in history just before the Second Coming of Christ, when the saints prepare for his arrival. In the last days, Mormons believe that there will be anarchy, wars, destruction, widespread crime, plague, and famine. All of these "signs of the times" tell believers that the Second Coming is near. In order to prepare for this period of chaos and gear up for the appearance of the Savior, Mormons ready themselves to endure the pandemonium by storing food and becoming self-sufficient. The LDS Church's website currently recommends a short-term and a long-term food supply. According to Mormon doctrine, Jesus Christ will first appear in Independence, Missouri. Because of this belief, some Mormons who believe the end is approaching move to Missouri to bide their time. It was Aubrey's plan to create a self-sufficient religious community to wait for the Second Coming. Aubrey imagined Farmville as a utopian community where everyone would live in common. Each family would contribute their finances to a joint pool and disperse the funds to individual families as needed. They would eat meals together and have community projects like vegetable gardens and beef and dairy cows. Before they purchased Farmville, Aubrey made a tour of a Hutterite community. He believed that the family farm could operate the same way. He wanted to see his granddaughters wearing aprons or floor-length pinafores, with their hair tied back in braids like Amish children, and his daughters wearing bonnets and long dresses with aprons. Helen thought Aubrey's dream was childlike, but he was so passionate about it she didn't want to object. She said, though, that she never had any intention of wearing an ankle-length apron, nor did she think such clothing was feminine or practical. Shortly after Aubrey and Helen moved, five of their children, along with their spouses, also moved to the family refuge. In addition to his family, Aubrey also led two hundred other members of the church to Missouri in order to await the disasters of the last days. Helen's firm belief in the impending Second Coming of Christ made her agreeable to her husband's desire to abandon her huge fan base of supporters for a life of seclusion. Her frustrated fans wanted to know, Where was Helen Andelin? Not forgetting her followers entirely, she hoped to delegate her mission to someone else, a task that proved more difficult than before.

Brian bought a building in downtown Pierce City, and his parents moved Pacific Press into it. Aubrey kept the publishing business going. Fascinating Womanhood was still a big business. Aubrey hired a secretary to run the office and a high school student to pack and ship *Man of Steel and Velvet*, *The Fascinating Girl*, workbooks, and lesson outlines. Aubrey remodeled the floor above the office and built an apartment for he and Helen to live in. After just a few months in their new home, Helen began to suffer from the remoteness of the place. Bored and isolated, she became terribly home-sick for the West. She worried about the thousands of disciples she had left behind. While she no longer wanted to be accessible to her followers, she struggled with letting go entirely. Helen hated the apartment. Once she learned that Pierce City had been the site of many Ku Klux Klan lynchings, she became convinced that the building was home to evil spirits. In fact, she believed that the whole area was cursed. Her children thought she was overreacting. Because of Helen's fears, Aubrey built a storage building on the Farmville property to keep books and supplies in, and the couple moved into a two-bedroom cottage that was on the farm when they bought it. Helen was deeply troubled that she did not feel the same way about Farmville that her husband and children did. She feared it represented a personal failure on her part, a misunderstanding of mission—even a lack of favor with God. She prayed to make peace with her situation. In time, some of their LDS neighbors also had difficulties adjusting to life in Missouri and gradually left. Some of the children couldn't find work and had to move away. While the feelings among the adults about their new home were mixed, for Aubrey and their sons Brian and Paul, being at Farmville felt like living on hallowed ground. Helen continued her personal struggle to come to terms with her self-enforced exile. No longer having young children to raise, interviews to give, or classes to teach, she had a hard time dealing with the slower pace of her new life and the geographical distance she had put between herself and her followers. FW was at its most successful, and it was difficult to move. All of her contacts were in California.[2] She had little choice but to pray and wait for spiritual confirmation that she was in the right place after all. Twenty-five years later, Farmville still didn't feel like home. "I'm still having a hard time in Missouri," she said.[3]

Feeling a sense of obligation, and fearing that the movement was going backward, Andelin decided to throw herself into her work and try to lead from afar. She attempted to revive the idea of the Fascinating Womanhood Center, and Aubrey rented office space in downtown Monett, a nearby town of just under eight thousand people. The center was open weekdays to hold classes and sell FW materials. She advertised classes in *Fascinating Womanhood*, *Man of Steel and Velvet*, and *The Fascinating Girl*, as well as classes on motherhood, homemaking, and health. In her newsletter, she told readers that she planned to come out with FW lessons on tape, in addition to house wear and shoes that would help women look more feminine at home. If the Fascinating Womanhood Center succeeded in Monett, she believed it would be the first of many throughout the country. Andelin prayed for its success. Unfortunately, the center didn't get enough interest to justify keeping it open. There were other problems as well. Aubrey, still looking for lucrative business opportunities, was "swindled" by a con man to whom he lost a million dollars in assets. While not giving the specifics of the failed venture, Helen said that her husband, a trusting person, had been taken advantage of.[4] When it came time to renew their three-year contract with Bantam, the Andelins decided to let it run out and went back to publishing and distributing *Fascinating Womanhood* themselves. They hoped to make more money publishing *FW* in hardback than they had made in royalties for the paperback edition. Teachers complained; they wanted the cheaper paperback. Andelin told them, "FW is a way of life and that calls for investment in the hardback book. . . . FW is serious business which requires commitment and dedication."[5] Without a major publisher and a paperback edition, the Andelins couldn't keep up. Book sales dropped perilously, and fewer women wanted to teach classes. Realizing that they had made a mistake, the Andelins approached Bantam and asked for a new contract. Bantam took them back.

From Missouri, Andelin made several attempts to find a suitable leader for the FW organization. She contacted Sam Battistone and asked him to return; he declined. She advertised in her newsletter for "a dynamic man to lead FW" but got no response. Nothing else seemed to pan out. While her frustration over the dramatic slowing of her movement continued, Andelin dutifully published *The Fascinating Womanhood Newsletter* and kept up correspondence with her fans. Still passionate about her message, she had lost her ability to deliver it. She was just too far away. She looked for, but was unsuccessful in finding, a way to honorably quit without sabotaging her movement. In 1981, she turned the leadership of FW over to Bob Forsyth, the husband of her eldest daughter, Dixie.[6] Dixie, a full-time homemaker, and Bob, a psychologist and family counselor, eagerly accepted the challenge to take up their parents' enterprise. With FW safely in the hands of a new leader, Helen and Aubrey decided to leave Missouri, and moved to Arizona. They would live between Arizona and Missouri on and off for the next eighteen years. The Forsyths hired a secretary and renamed the organization Family Living International. Taking over the publishing company, they worked hard to make a success of the business. But Forsyth, not having run a business before, met with financial difficulties. Family Living International was not as profitable as he had hoped. Unwilling to let Forsyth actually take charge of the business, Helen became consumed with anxiety about his leadership. She was not satisfied with the direction the organization was going. And she worried about the money. Although she said she didn't want to lead FW anymore, she couldn't give it up. One night, she had a dream that foretold the death of the Fascinating Womanhood movement under Forsyth's direction. Fearful that she had once again made the wrong move, Andelin decided she wanted the business back. She and Aubrey quarreled with the Forsyths. Dixie and Bob sought legal advice. Ginny's husband, Robert, tried to mediate. Ultimately, the Forsyths gave up their dream of running Fascinating Womanhood and returned the organization to Helen and Aubrey. Ousted from the organization, Dixie and Bob distanced themselves from Aubrey and Helen and joined the Amway Corporation. Once again in charge of Fascinating Womanhood, Andelin, now sixty years old, had lost some of her vigor. She resumed her correspondence and her newsletter, but FW was a movement without a leader. Under the control of Bantam, *Fascinating Womanhood* continued to sell at a steady pace. The Andelins continued to print, sell, and ship the *FW Lesson Outlines, Man of Steel and Velvet, The Fascinating Girl,* and the *FW Workbook.* Eventually, Helen and Aubrey mended fences with the Forsyths and, surprisingly, decided to join Amway themselves.

The couple worked diligently at their Amway business and became direct distributors. They attended rallies all around the country and got many of their friends to join. In addition to selling soap and vitamins, they toiled away selling books and conducting marriage seminars on cruise boats and at other expensive sales conventions around the country. Helen even wrote an article for Amway's *Achieve Magazine.* In time, Aubrey became acquainted with one of Amway's most successful "evangelical capitalists," Dexter Yager.[7] Yager, considered the "grandfather of network marketing," had made his first million dollars by age thirty in the Amway business. By 1986 he was making ten million dollars a year and contributing hundreds of thousands of dollars to the Republican National Committee and other conservative causes. The Andelins taught classes for Yager and other established distributors, just as they had at the Parker Chiropractic Seminars in the early 1970s. Shortly after meeting Yager, Helen had a dream in which God confirmed that her involvement with him was vitally important to the growth of Fascinating Womanhood.[8] Certain that they could get some kind of a partnership going, the Andelins met with Yager and presented the idea. But Yager was doing well enough on his own and wasn't interested in promoting FW. Deflated, Helen and Aubrey continued along in their Amway business for several years and promoted Fascinating Womanhood any way they could. Eventually, they became restless and moved to Houston, Texas, to be near their sons Lane and Brian and to try to get them to join Amway. When that didn't work out, they returned to Arizona. While in Arizona, the Andelins ran their business from a distance. They had their mail forwarded and hired their grandson in Missouri to ship books.

In response to the Supreme Court ruling *Roe v. Wade,* which gave women the right to a legal abortion, the country experienced a dramatic conservative turn that set off a ferocious cultural backlash against feminism and other liberal reforms.[9] The new Christian Right, coupled with an upsurge in nostalgic conservatism, exploded into mainstream culture. The Christian Right, a kind of evangelical insurgency, was an ultraconservative political response to the perceived evils of modern society. The movement believed the moral character of the nation was in jeopardy, and it sought to restore decency and integrity by infusing public policy with religious philosophies. So popular was this evangelical trend that much of the same language and goals expressed by the Christian Right also worked their way into large, direct-sales organizations like Amway. Amway experienced huge boosts in membership and revenue during this period, and took on a decidedly Christian corporate personality attractive to the Andelins.[10] Legalized abortion, said the Christian Right, was government-sanctioned murder. Lesbian and gay rights, sexual and reproductive freedom, and the legal distribution of pornography, they believed, were ruining the country. They supported a return to traditional family values, the upholding of the death penalty, and the maintenance of superior military strength. As the Democratic Party became increasingly associated with the pro-choice movement, the ranks of the Christian Right began to associate themselves with the Republican Party. In 1980 Ronald Reagan, supported by the evangelical Christian conservatives, was elected president of the United States. He continued his support of evangelical causes until he left office in 1989. For Helen, it may have appeared that efforts to tear down the American family had either diminished or that religious conservatives were slowing the decline of American morality. Her interest in politics waned. However, in the early 1990s, when the democrat Bill Clinton became president, Andelin became convinced that the nation had taken a turn for the worse, and she resumed the fight for her political causes. For her, the level of interest in FW served as a kind of national barometer of morality. She attributed the dramatic decline in teacher applications not to the fact that she was no longer a conspicuous leader but to the belief that more women were rejecting their God-given roles by working.

Despite its gains for women's equality, the feminist movement began to fragment as it struggled to encompass a growing list of explosive and emotionally divisive issues such as race relations, gay rights, and legalized abortion. These conflicts, in addition to the conservative backlash, wounded the movement. Even some devoted feminists began to lose interest. The conservatives were gaining ground. Phyllis Schlafly, in her book *The Power of the Positive Woman*, quoted a 1974 Roper Survey commissioned by Virginia Slims that said that only 2 percent of the women surveyed would choose a career over family. She agreed with Andelin in saying that to encourage men and women to act outside of their God-given roles was "as wrong as efforts to make a left-handed child right-handed."[11] People began to listen.

Betty Friedan, who in 1970 argued that feminism should remain mainstream, began speaking out against feminist radicalism. In the March/April 1979 issue of *The Fascinating Womanhood Newsletter*, the headline read, "Women's Lib Leaders Admit: 'We Were Wrong about Marriage, Motherhood, Beauty, and Men.'" The newsletter quoted Friedan as saying, "This period of rejecting motherhood and housework is over." Underneath a picture of Friedan in which she was smartly dressed in a polka-dot blouse and wearing lipstick, the report continued: "In the beginning women in the movement were ready to throw out the baby with the bathwater, to act out of rage. . . . They now realize they're denying themselves something important when they deny their softness, prettiness, nurturing abilities, earthiness and domestic qualities."[12] The article not only proclaimed that morality had overcome error, but praised feminists for finally seeing the truth. The same newsletter reported that *Fascinating Womanhood* had been translated into Spanish, Portuguese, Japanese, and Indonesian and was being translated into French. Fascinating Womanhood classes were being taught in Germany, Ireland, Spain, Mexico, Puerto Rico, El Salvador, and Canada.[13] In the United States other conservative writers had already begun to use Andelin's work.

In 1972 Elizabeth Rice Hanford wrote *Me? Obey Him?: The Obedient Wife and God's Way of Happiness and Blessings in the Home*. Following Andelin's lead, Hanford, and subsequently other authors, called for wives to be submissive to their husbands. She drew heavily on the Bible and on Andelin's teachings. Hanford quoted scripture to back up her statements regarding obedience in the marriage relationship. Like Andelin, she said that submission, rather than being oppressive, gave a wife freedom. She asserted, "If you would know true freedom, you must submit to your husband's authority."[14] Like her predecessor, she taught that submission, in a magical way, gave a wife her deepest desire—love. Hanford urged women to be dependent and allow husbands to make the decisions. She taught women to say, "I will obey you implicitly . . . and trust you to make the right decisions for me."[15]

In 1981 Friedan penned *The Second Stage*. It was the same year that the first female Supreme Court justice, Sandra Day O'Connor was sworn into office. In *The Second Stage*, Friedan admitted that the feminist movement had neglected the family. She argued for a kind of "new thinking in feminism" that expanded the cause to include economic justice for both men and women in order to preserve the family. She decried feminism's "preoccupation with sexual identity politics" and the incessant disparaging of men. Declaring she was for human liberation versus simply women's liberation, she encouraged women to work with men instead of against them.[16] At the very moment the feminist movement was under the greatest attack from the Christian Right, Friedan outlined the more gender-integrated approach to women's rights that she had been formulating since the mid-1970s. Chiding the younger feminists who had since taken leadership of the movement, Friedan warned against the dangers of "pseudo-radical cop-out sexual politics."[17] Feminist leaders, who disagreed with her insistence that the women's movement shun its more radical manifestations and remain mainstream, accused her of "reversing the revolution."[18] At the height of the conservative backlash, the liberal women's movement became hopelessly mired in organizational infighting. Friedan was not the only one who was put off by the increasing militancy of Women's Liberation. Scores of other women, who also believed in equal rights but could not identify with the personalities and lifestyles of such leaders as Gloria Steinem, left the movement.[19] As feminism became more diverse, so did the stereotypes of feminists. Feminists were depicted not only as anti-family but also as man-haters and lesbians. With the heartbreaking defeat of the Equal Rights Amendment in 1982, and growing public support for competent and highly visible conservative women like Phyllis Schlafly, it seemed the feminist movement had been effectively chopped off at the knees. Hollywood movies and TV programs portrayed career women as worn out, unhappy, and infertile. Magazine articles found fault with the feminist ideal of the single-minded career woman and began to devote space to the more traditional subjects of marriage and motherhood.[20] In 1986 Helen Gurley Brown's own *Cosmopolitan Magazine* published an article entitled, "How Not to Get Dumped on His Way Up." The article encouraged women to lose weight, wear perfume, be sexually available, and put their mate first. "His ego must be fed forever and ever—Don't forget!" said the article's author, Marian Tremper. "He doesn't have to give an inch. You do."[21]

In the same year that Friedan published *The Second Stage*, Andelin, back in Missouri, wrote her final book. Rather than directing her efforts toward marriage relationships, as she had in the previous sixteen years, she concentrated instead on writing a practical childrearing guide for parents. From her bedroom office at Farmville, she wrote *All about Raising Children*. Not able to find a publisher, the Andelins published it themselves, and Helen advertised it in her newsletter. When the Equal Rights Amendment was finally defeated, Helen Andelin was living quietly on her farm in Missouri. With Andelin out of the limelight, interest in the Fascinating Womanhood movement died down. The book still sold briskly, but soon fewer people knew who Helen Andelin was. The movement she started, however, was not over.

In 1985 the Andelins left the Amway Corporation to serve a sixteen-month proselytizing mission for the Mormon Church in Australia. With their mission president's blessing, they spent much of their time teaching Fascinating Womanhood and Man of Steel and Velvet classes. Shortly after their homecoming, they returned to Amway and starting building a new business. Once again, they became direct distributors. But the couple, now in their mid-sixties, seemed to run out of the stamina or interest necessary to continue plugging their books at Amway conventions. They eventually abandoned their distributorship. Having forgone the idea of finding a new Mr. X to run her organization, Helen settled back into writing newsletters, answering mail, and teaching an occasional local class. The leader of the once-vital FW movement was now officially retired. Her message, however, did not retire with her. In fact, the ideas that she so ardently expressed from the 1960s through the 1980s again became fashionable in the public mind. FW was still going strong—even with an absentee leader. In the post-Reagan era, Andelin's philosophies about the revival of traditional gender roles reemerged in best-selling marriage manuals written by charismatic gurus who became overnight celebrities and sold hundreds of thousands of books. In 1986 Willard F. Harley, Jr., a psychologist and marriage counselor, wrote the national bestseller *His Needs, Her Needs: Building an Affair-Proof Marriage*. The book, a widely used marriage manual in Christian circles, spelled out how to respect the differences in male and female needs in order to have a lifelong love affair. According to Harley, the man's primary need was sexual fulfillment. His other needs were recreational companionship, an attractive spouse, domestic support, and admiration. "A man's need for physical attractiveness in a spouse is profound," said Harley.[22] He urged women to dress attractively and always look their best. As far as domestic support went, a man needed just what Andelin taught in *Fascinating Womanhood*—peace and calm when he walked in the door at the end of the day, a happy wife, quiet children, and a good meal. In order for a man not to be temped by women outside the relationship, he needed to be admired. Next to sexual fulfillment, said Harley, admiration was a man's greatest desire.

Like Harley's work, Andelin's writings were also brought back into popular culture by an up-and-coming new comedian. In 1988 Roseanne Barr burst onto the American scene with her TV show *Roseanne*. In it she played an overweight, slovenly housekeeper who sarcastically referred to herself as a "domestic goddess." Domestic Goddess, a term she got from Andelin, was the basis for her stand-up comedy routine and her television show. Barr grew up in Salt Lake City, where her mother attended Fascinating Womanhood classes when Roseanne was a teenager. Barr made Andelin's Domestic Goddess a household word. Barr's manager called Andelin on two occasions to thank her, in the comedian's stead, for her inspiration, and to make sure she wasn't too offended by the parody. Andelin, who had never heard of Roseanne Barr and wanted to get her message out any way she could, told him she was glad that Barr was using the term and gave her blessing to the comic.[23] The show ran until 1997.

Helen, having moved with Aubrey to her hometown of Mesa, Arizona, continued to stay in touch with her followers through her newsletter. She tried to think of ways to keep her movement alive and at the same time remain in the background. In her May 1989 newsletter, she announced another name change for the organization; it became Fascinating Womanhood Today. The new name, she said, was an effort to strengthen the FW message, clarify its teachings, and restructure the organization. She told readers of plans for an upcoming video series to be produced in Los Angeles. The videos, to be used in FW classes, would be dramatic reenactments of how one should, and should not, treat a husband. She said that there would also be videos of success stories, and called for her readers to send theirs in. These plans were wishful thinking. The Andelins were out of money, and they were running out of teachers. Helen never gave up her idea of a video series, but she was never able to execute it. While in Arizona, the Andelins entered into a contract dispute with Bantam. Helen claimed fraud, saying that Bantam had shorted them on royalties and wasn't doing enough to publicize the book. She wanted the rights to her book back. Bantam, which claimed no knowledge of wrongdoing, gave in. Once again, the Andelins went back to publishing *Fascinating Womanhood* themselves. While in the United States things had slowed down since the book's heyday, the movement continued to grow internationally. By 1989, FW classes were being taught in sixteen countries.

Meanwhile, the fight against feminism was still on. In his article *"The Myth of Feminism: Lies, Damned Lies, and Statistics,"* the author Nicholas Davidson argued that feminist leaders had distorted statistics into "myths" that needed to be exposed. Women didn't *want* to be at work, as the feminists had claimed, but would rather be at home taking care of their children. "Nine out of ten women do not desire full-time employment outside the home," he said.[24] Citing polls of working women between the ages of twenty and forty-five, Davidson said that most women worked only because they felt they had to because of pressure put on them by the feminist movement. The writers Linda Burton, Janet Dittmer, and Cheri Loveless said much the same thing. In *What's a Smart Woman Like You Doing at Home?* the authors claimed that women who were "rediscovering the merits of home and the pleasures of rearing children . . . are a majority."[25] They called the exodus from the workforce by successful career women a revolution. Condemning books and articles that sang the praises of the successful working mother, Burton, Dittmer, and Loveless sought to "expose the gap between what the media says about mothers and what mothers say about themselves." They challenged the notion of the "supermom," women with exciting careers *and* fulfilling family lives.[26] As Andelin said years earlier, women simply couldn't give their all to both. Something had to suffer, and it was usually the children. They talked about problems of day care and absentee childrearing. Nurturing a child, they said, was much more challenging than working outside the home. More women than you might think, said the authors, were giving up good salaries, promotions, and tenure to make the choice to stay home. Andelin took notice, saying, "In 1972 I predicted that if women didn't stop going to work they would change the economy so that they would have to work. Look at what's happened. Most women no longer have the choice. For those who still do, I say they should leave their filing cabinets, their typewriters, their fancy business suits, and their mahogany desks and just stay home."

Andelin, now seventy, worked quietly on a major revision of *Fascinating Womanhood*. She rearranged the chapters, added more about femininity, and inserted more success stories. The Andelins eventually patched up their differences with Bantam and renewed the partnership. In 1990 *Fascinating Womanhood* was reissued as a trade paperback. Aubrey, still suspicious of people in the publishing business, negotiated the contract himself. The Andelins continued to move between Arizona and Missouri. While Aubrey wanted to create a family legacy at Farmville, Helen, a self-described city girl, didn't want to be isolated there. Although Bantam took care of sales for *Fascinating Womanhood*, Helen still had an office to run. Not having a secretary, she did the work herself. Because she felt it looked bad for her to be running a one-man show, she answered her phone and processed teacher applications under the assumed name of Elsa Holman. She didn't want to be identified, she said.[27] Holman, a pseudonym that Andelin began using in the 1970s, sounded too much like a spy to her son Brian. He came up with the name Meredith Lawrence. Andelin used both names and continued to look for a respectable way to get out from under her heavy FW duties. Meanwhile, *Fascinating Womanhood* was being read by a new generation of post-feminist authors.

At the time *FW* was reissued, relationship experts began to pick up on the ideas that Andelin had been forwarding for twenty-five years. In the 1990s, popular marriage and relationship manuals that advocated a return to 1950s-era middle-class values, including traditional gender roles for men and women, surged into bookstores. P. B. Wilson's highly popular *Liberated through Submission: God's Design for Freedom in All Relationships* (1990) broke with what had become conventional relationship literature since the mid-1970s, and encouraged women to submit willingly to the authority of their husband's rule. Like Hanford, she mirrored Andelin's teachings by arguing that submission did not put women down; it set them free.[28] Vehemently criticized by feminists, Wilson's "marriage Bible" went on to sell over one hundred forty thousand copies. Its popularity coincided with the founding of the colossal nondenominational Christian men's organization, Promise Keepers. Established by the former University of Colorado head football coach Bill McCartney, Promise Keepers was a conservative organization that encouraged men to be more masculine and to dedicate themselves to Jesus Christ in order to change the world. Promise Keepers drew so many followers that in October 1997 the C-SPAN news station broadcast the assembly of the 1.4 million men who attended the Stand in the Gap demonstration on the National Mall in Washington. D.C.[29] The Promise Keepers' assertions of masculinity and their calls for male responsibility sounded a lot like Aubrey Andelin's *Man of Steel and Velvet,* written two decades earlier. Adding evidence to the fact that the tide in public thinking about marriage and family had turned, in 1992 John Gray's *Men Are from Mars, Women Are from Venus* became an instant bestseller and launched a nationwide, multimillion-dollar public career for an obscure and otherwise nerdy California marriage and family therapist. Gray, like P. B. Wilson and others, drew heavily on Andelin's philosophy.

Gray, like Andelin before him, concentrated on the "innate" differences between men and women. It was as if, as Andelin had said earlier, they were from different planets. Each complemented the other in a "magical and perfect way," Gray asserted, calling his observations "gender insight." He agreed with Andelin's claim that a woman's greatest need was to be loved and cared for. Men, on the other hand, craved admiration. A man, in his quest for admiration, felt the need to prove his power. Gray said that a woman was guided by her feelings, and a man was driven by his intellect. When a man had a hard day at the office, or when he felt controlled, corrected, or confronted by his wife, he retreated to his imaginary "man cave" and put up a wall of reserve. By accepting and admiring him, a wife could get her husband to come out of his cave and give her the love she wanted. Like Andelin, Gray instructed wives not to complain, offer unsolicited advice, or ask her husband too many questions. Rather a wife must accept her husband as he was. "Relax and surrender," said Gray.[30] When properly understood and treated, a man would become a "knight in shining armor." If, on the other hand, he was misunderstood, he might simply walk away from the relationship. It was only by understanding and accepting the differences between men and women, said Gray, that both sexes could live in harmony.

In 1992 Andelin disconnected her telephone. She no longer received her mail at home but told fans to send it to her publisher. She stopped sending out and accepting teacher applications. But the letters from women who wanted to talk to her kept coming in. They asked advice; they sent her their success stories, thanked her, and asked permission to teach classes. Some women asked for personal meetings—even offering to travel great distances to see her. Feeling that she owed them for their loyalty, Andelin continued to answer the letters of persistent fans. Trying to free herself from some of her commitments, she sent a query to Bantam Books and asked if they would publish and promote *The Fascinating Girl*, which, in an effort to sell more copies, she had recently renamed *The Secrets of Winning Men*. Her followers didn't like the new name, and neither did Bantam. They rejected the book. Bantam executives felt that the Christian skew of the book might be off-putting to non-Christians. Besides, "winning men" sounded manipulative. They didn't think the book could be mass marketed; the relationship book market had been saturated and it was very hard to launch new titles, they explained.[31] Realizing that changing the book's title had been a mistake, Andelin restored it to *The Fascinating Girl*, and Aubrey continued to self-publish it.

In 1995 Ellen Fein and Sherrie Schneider's highly popular *The Rules: Time-Tested Secrets for Capturing the Heart of Mr. Right* borrowed so heavily from Andelin's material that her family members teased her about it. *The Rules*, a dating manual, instructed women how to behave to get a marriage proposal in almost the same way that Andelin's *Fascinating Girl* did. In fact, the similarity between the two books was remarkable. For instance, a woman seeking marriage must allow the man to be in control. "In a relationship, the man must take charge. . . . We're not making this up—biologically, he's the aggressor." Like the Fascinating Girl, a *Rules* girl never chased a man. Rather, she waited for him to pursue her. *Rules* girls acted girly. The authors advised their readers to flirt and be coy when a suitor tried to kiss them. "This will turn him into a tiger" they promised. Intellect and ability didn't attract men, said Fein and Schneider. A woman should play down these aspects of her personality and instead wear feminine, sexy clothes, and act ladylike and mysterious. They instructed women to wear tight jeans, short skirts, and low-cut blouses in bright colors. They also told them to stop wearing their hair in short styles and grow it long. In order to get a man to propose marriage, a girl had to master the feminine manner. When talking to a man, they advised women to keep their conversations short, cheerful, and flirtatious.

Gestures should always be soft and feminine.[32] Women looking for Mr. Right should never tell a man what to do. The authors cautioned, "You don't own him. Don't fix him. You will end up emasculating him and he will come to see you as a domineering shrew." The dating gurus Fein and Schneider, like Andelin, told women that besides developing the feminine manner, they should not talk too much. They said that most men found talkative women annoying. One man, they said, stopped calling a woman he was interested in simply because she would not stop talking. Men, they claimed, didn't want to be bored with the details of a woman's day, or listen to them complain about their aches and pains. Men were not attracted to women who were negative, unhappy, or who told long-winded stories.[33] Fein and Schneider denied knowing anything about Andelin or her work. Yet their book was so similar to *The Fascinating Girl* it was uncanny. Andelin made little of the alleged use of her material. As she said earlier of Roseanne Barr and others, she was happy that people were still getting her precious message to those who would listen. She insisted, "My success has ignited others. I'm not jealous because someone is preaching what I'm preaching . . . you ignite people and they ignite others, like a forest fire."[34]

Unconcerned that her ideas were making fortunes for popular writers, Andelin concentrated on writing a family history for her children. During this period, she vacillated between reviving her Fascinating Womanhood movement and leaving it for good. She returned to her idea of creating a video series. This time she wanted to offer streamlined video classes that could be distributed through leaders of churches, synagogues, and mosques. Again, the idea never panned out. While Helen wrote her history, Aubrey kept himself busy. Influenced by Promise Keepers, he produced a manuscript for another book, *Back to the Hearth: Herein Lies All Hope for America*. Helen believed the manuscript, a strident reassertion of Christian masculinity and a condemnation of feminists, was too harsh for popular consumption and urged him not to publish it.[35] Their daughter Ginny agreed, feeling it was too unkind. Aubrey took the advice. He had his original manuscript bound but never published the book.

In 1997 Helen hired a webmaster and inaugurated one of her most successful ideas to date: a website called "Marriage, the Fascinating Way." She posted her newsletter and answered fan mail online. Through the website, she maintained a lively business selling books and supplies and dispensing no-nonsense marriage advice at no cost to the thousands of women who continued to seek her out.[36] Hundreds of women joined the website's chat group, and some posted advertisements for pen pals. Andelin began to post back issues of *The Fascinating Womanhood Newsletter* so that women who hadn't subscribed could catch up. Brian suggested that his mother put the workbook online and allow women to download it for free. Fearing that she would forfeit her copyright, she decided against it. She continued to get success stories and letters of thanks, which she put up on the website. Among the letters and comments she received:

> Praise the Lord. I am so impressed by this website. Thank God for placing you on the www.

> Your F.W. book has helped me be a more sweetly submissive wife and a more gentle and soft spoken mother. . . . With great affection, North Carolina.

> Since I've dropped being so masculine in chores, finances, sports, sexual relations and so many ways, my husband has put up curtain rods, hung draperies, done yard work and taken me to dinner twice. He is aroused sexually more like when we were first married.

> Within six months John's business tripled. We ordered a new car, and we bought a large old home. . . . He remodeled the kitchen for me and hired a cleaning lady.

> Only God saved our marriage and I praise Him for putting F.W. into my hands.[37]

Andelin got requests from women all over the country who wanted to become authorized teachers. Most, however, taught without permission or held study groups with their friends and wrote to tell Andelin about it later. Although her life had just gotten much easier, Andelin continued to be plagued by thoughts of the millions of women she was not reaching.

After watching the April General Conference of the LDS Church on TV, she once again became distressed about the high divorce rate among Mormon couples. She wrote an impassioned letter to the president of the church, Gordon B. Hinckley, asking for a private meeting. She wrote to other LDS leaders as well, and sent copies of her book. Convinced she had the solution to divorce, she pled for a chance to meet with the president and be recognized. She could help save marriages if only they would listen to her, she said. Just as before, her letters were answered by aides who thanked her for her interest but made it clear that the church wasn't interested.

In 1997, the same year that Andelin launched her website, the American Enterprise Institute for Public Policy Research announced a victory for women's causes. Among younger women, the report said, the wage gap had been closed. Women were now earning 98 percent of men's wages. More women than men were enrolled in higher education, and they now constituted 59 percent of the labor force. In law, medicine, accounting, and dentistry— professions that had traditionally been dominated by men—nearly half of practitioners were women. And, said the study, women were less likely to be unemployed than men. "Women had effectively achieved equality," said the report's author, Paul Johnson. Although the Equal Rights Amendment had been defeated, he argued, the Equal Pay Act of 1963 and the Civil Rights Act of 1964, both of which had been passed thirty years earlier, were effectively working to guarantee equality for women.[38] Johnson's assertions were later disproved by newer statistics: in 2007 Shankar Vedantam wrote in the *Washington Post* that women working full time made only 77 percent of their male counterparts' salaries. Part of this was that, because of the social risks, women were more hesitant than men to ask for raises. Those who did usually asked for less than men—especially those women with male bosses. Women, said Vedantam, were still being discriminated against in the workforce.[39]

Early in 1999, when the Andelins were living in Arizona, Aubrey experienced excruciating pain in his stomach that lasted for several days. An advocate of home remedies and healthy food, Helen put her husband on a complicated detoxifying juice fast. He felt some relief after the fast, but soon his symptoms returned. Worried, Helen and Aubrey returned to Missouri to see their son Paul, a physician practicing in Monett. A physical examination revealed that his father was gravely ill, and Paul rushed him to the hospital in

Springfield, forty miles away, for medical tests. Aubrey was diagnosed with advanced-stage colon cancer. Within the week, he underwent major surgery to remove the cancer, but the doctors were not optimistic. His surgeon gave him just months to live. Helen and Aubrey returned to their Farmville cottage to wait. Based on their healthy diet and living habits, Helen could scarcely believe that her husband's condition was incurable. Aubrey, however, was more realistic. When he got home, he picked a suitable burial spot under a large oak tree on the Farmville property so that his children and grandchildren could visit his grave after he died. Aubrey was not afraid to die; in fact, he welcomed it. Calm and at peace, he believed that his time on earth was finished, and he was ready to meet his maker. "He had absolute faith in the next life," said Helen. While Aubrey lay dying on a makeshift bed in the living room, his wife cared for him around the clock. Overcome with grief, she beseeched her husband, "Why do you want to leave me? Aren't I important to you?" Aubrey, refusing medication, encouraged his wife to be strong. He told her that in time she would come to see that his death was the right thing at the right time. A few days before he died, he gave each of his children a final blessing. He had a lengthy conversation with his wife, which she transcribed. Near the end, the family held a vigil at Aubrey's bedside. They lit candles, played sacred music, and meditated. Helen later described this time before her husband's death as a time of tremendous spiritual outpouring, much like the Pentecost described in the New Testament. Andelin's fourteen-year-old granddaughter, Cherry, experienced a vision during the vigil, seeing personages from the spirit world in the cottage. Helen went into great detail about the vision in interviews; she believed that her relatives from "beyond the veil" had come to comfort her. On June 29, 1999, less than ninety days after his diagnosis, Aubrey Andelin died. Following his death, Paul obtained the necessary permission to bury his father's body at Farmville, and the grieving family laid him to rest. Of her husband, Helen said, "Aubrey had a temper. He was a difficult man. But, that's why he loved me, because I put up with him, and because I loved him for who he was."[40] Aubrey and Helen had been married for fifty-seven years. "My parents had a life-long romance," said daughter Ginny.[41]

The same year that Aubrey died, the author Laura Doyle published *The Surrendered Wife: A Practical Guide to Finding Intimacy, Passion, and Peace with a Man.* In her book, Doyle, like Andelin, told women that by giving up control, they would gain more power.[42] She urged them to yield, even when they didn't feel like it. Women, she instructed, had to stop criticizing and correcting their husbands, or risk becoming like his mother. Mirroring Andelin, she urged unhappy women not to blame their husbands, but look to their own behavior. She advised, "It is up to you and you alone." Women, she taught, needed to allow their husbands to be themselves without any instruction or criticism. "Don't teach, improve, or correct," she counseled. She believed that most men who behaved badly were probably great guys who were forced to constantly defend themselves against the unwarranted criticism of their wives. Like Andelin, she said that men, if treated properly, would become the kind of husband a woman always dreamed of. A surrendered wife never gave her husband disapproving looks or unsolicited suggestions, or gasped at his bad driving. Doyle said that if a husband took the wrong freeway exit, a wife should never correct him—even if it meant going past the state line. About a husband who cheated she said, "It may have been his inappropriate reaction to years of emasculation and criticism from his wife." She assured women that a marriage could heal from a husband's infidelity once the wife began surrendering. Like Andelin, Doyle taught that the man was the natural leader, and that he should control the family finances. When a woman let go of handling the money, Doyle said, she freed herself from the worries that come with being the family banker. A man who paid his own bills and directed the income felt more like a man. Doyle agreed with Andelin in saying that it was counterproductive for a woman to have strong opinions. She said that when faced with a decision, a wife should simply say to her husband, "Whatever you think." Giving her husband the chance to make the decisions showed that she trusted him. Finally, Doyle instructed women to let their husbands take them on a "no-control" date. On the date, the husband made all the decisions—where to go, what to do, what his wife would wear, and what she would eat for dinner. This exercise, said Doyle, would give a woman the opportunity to practice "trusting him to be in charge for a change." Doyle, like Andelin, encouraged women to "abandon the myth of equality."[43]

The author Danielle Crittenden also took Andelin's lead. In her book *What Our Mothers Didn't Tell Us: Why Happiness Eludes the Modern Woman,* she criticized "outdated feminist attitudes" that advised young women to put off marriage and children in favor of careers. She believed that adopting feminist ideas did not lead women to happier lives, but instead left them lonely, stressed, and yearning for fulfillment. Women who put their careers above all else, she warned, often ended up lamenting the fact that they couldn't find a suitable man to marry and were too old to have children. For these women, the cost of putting off marriage until it was too late was simply not worth it. "Lifelong independence can be its own kind of prison," she said. Rather than having it all as their mothers had taught them, successful career women often felt confused and insecure. "The problem that has no name" that Betty Friedan had articulated in 1963 applied not to housewives, said Crittenden, but to successful female executives. Marriage, on the other hand, was liberating. Crittenden agreed with Andelin in saying that *all* women, no matter how independent, or how successful they appeared in their chosen careers, were in truth, happier and more fulfilled when they were in a loving relationship where they felt cherished.

In 2000 Andelin decided to take a break from her website. She was too tired and too grieved over Aubrey's death to go on. She told readers that she was leaving due to her husband's death, saying that she was lost without him. She and Aubrey had been so devoted to each other that they became antisocial and hadn't made friends outside the marriage. For Helen, losing Aubrey was like losing a leg. Still in mourning, Andelin suffered stress and anxiety attacks. One of her daughters suggested she see a psychiatrist. She took the advice, and the doctor advised that the best thing she could do for her situation was get back to her work and start writing another book. She did, and the result was *Scriptural Review of Fascinating Womanhood*. Based on a literal interpretation of the Bible, Andelin used scriptures to support the entire text of the 1990 edition of *Fascinating Womanhood*. She also found scriptures to buttress her views on subjects as varied as weight control and positivity. Andelin obtained a copyright for the booklet and published it herself. She also began work on two more books: *The Womanly Art of Thrift*, a book about budgeting, and *The Domestic Goddess*, about homemaking. Andelin also created outlines for an advice book, *Dear Helen*, and for *Wisdom of the Ages*, a compilation of quotes and poems she had collected through the years; however, she was never able to finish these books.

That year, 2000, she received a letter from a gay man thanking her for writing *Fascinating Womanhood*. He told her that FW teachings had allowed him to develop his feminine side and had helped save his relationship with his partner. Incensed at the "misuse" of her book, Andelin wrote a scathing letter calling the man to repentance for his "unspeakable" sins. Later she regretted her harsh reply, saying, "I wish I wouldn't have written it. At the time, it made me sick to my stomach and I was filled with anger." She now viewed homosexuals as troubled people who needed understanding.[44]

After eight months away, Andelin returned to her website. She gave permission for women to teach classes without authorization, and encouraged them to find partners to support one another in their studies of *Fascinating Womanhood*. She seemed out of touch as she once again took up the tired subject of feminism. In response to a letter condemning FW and saying that the fate of unrecognized and under-appreciated homemakers was depression and sometimes suicide, Andelin wrote, "If anyone is committing suicide it's men who are married to feminists." Skeptical of higher education, she said of college students, "It is easy to see why some women become involved with the views of feminism. The words *rights* and *freedom* and *equality* sound so fair and square." Students, she believed, were especially attracted to feminism if they had mothers who hated housework and men. They were easy targets for feminism. One reader who agreed with Andelin described attending a women's college where, she observed, feminism "ran rampant," and she was "surrounded by man haters." At first, she agreed with the feminists. Then, as she learned more about them, she began to see them as confused, stupid, and even insane. Andelin's website got its share of critics. "I am utterly repulsed by the ignorance and banality of your thoughtless website," said one reader. "I think that a century of knowledge and progress has gone by without your noticing." Andelin answered her detractors with warnings of unhappiness. Women who rejected their God-given roles were destined to live lives of misery and loneliness, she said.[45]

By 2002 Andelin had become a recluse. She maintained her vegetarianism, shunning milk and eggs and consuming mostly fruits, vegetables, nuts, and sprouted seeds.[46] Andelin became interested in reruns of the television show *The Scarecrow and Mrs. King*. She believed the two main characters, Amanda and Lee, were the closest thing to a Fascinating Woman and Man of Steel and Velvet that she knew of. She advertised the show on her website and encouraged her readers to watch it. She wrote letters to the TV station hoping to get the legal rights to the production so that she could make video clips of the show and sell them to her followers as examples of how to live the principles of *Fascinating Womanhood*. As one might guess, she never succeeded in getting the rights to the series, but she continued to use examples from the show in her newsletter. Although she lived close to her children and grandchildren, Andelin was still unhappy at Farmville. Lonely without Aubrey, she tried to keep her spirits up by working on her website and answering mail. One follower wrote, "I praise our great Creator for your book. Thank you! . . . If only everyone knew!" Andelin continued her dire warnings to women who didn't follow her advice. She wrote, "As FW flourishes world-wide, I predict a rude awakening. . . . Men will no longer put up with a self-interested, slovenly homemaker who neglects his masculine need, tramples on his pride, and makes his life a living hell. . . . A woman will either improve or [be] deserted."[47] She continued to hold women responsible for their troubled marriages.

That year, Andelin announced the creation of online classes. She reversed her earlier decision and allowed her workbook to be available electronically to students who wanted to download and print it themselves. In her efforts to keep Fascinating Womanhood alive, she searched for ways to rebuild her teaching program and make it as vibrant as it was in the seventies. Hoping to create interest among her online readers, she outlined a new program. For a six-dollar fee and the completion of an FW study group, one could become an authorized teacher. After completing the requirements to become authorized, teachers could then become certified. In order to be certified, a woman had to teach three in-home classes, pass a written test, provide a passport-sized photo, and be interviewed by Andelin over the telephone. Only after being certified was a teacher eligible to teach in church education or outreach programs. Her readers, however, didn't care about being authorized or certified. Nor did they want to pay fees and take tests. The women who wanted to teach Fascinating Womanhood ordered teaching materials online and did so without permission. Andelin's dreams of rebuilding a teaching force fell by the wayside. Although she had big ideas, Andelin, now in her eighties, had no way to accomplish them; she no longer had an organization. Not willing to give up, she tried to revive Womanhood Day by encouraging her readers to notify local TV and radio stations. Her efforts fell flat, as most of her readers didn't know what Womanhood Day was. Despite her failures, she continued to get letters of appreciation from her readers.

In 2004 the popular radio personality and socially conservative relationship advisor Laura Schlessinger continued to capitalize on the return to traditional roles that Helen Andelin had been preaching for her entire career. Selling millions of copies of her advice books, including the best-selling marriage manual, *Proper Care and Feeding of Husbands,* Schlessinger became so popular that her radio program was featured on over 450 radio stations. Trim, strident, and devoutly religious, "Dr. Laura," a marriage and family counselor, sermonized her opinion that women and men had God-given gender-specific roles. She said, "In the real world of humans, women have a unique urge toward bonding and nesting and nurturing. Men have a unique urge toward protecting, providing, and conquering."[48] Schlessinger didn't blame husbands for unhappy marriages. Like Andelin, she held the women responsible. "Far from being oppressed in their marriages, most wives are the oppressors," she said.[49] Women, she said, were responsible for the bad attitudes, negativity, and poor behavior of their husbands, not the men themselves. She agreed with Andelin's belief that a woman's proper behavior could result in dramatic changes in her husband. Schlessinger wrote, "Men are indeed simple. . . . If you change certain aspects of your interaction, like magic you will see changes in them, too."[50] Like Andelin, she encouraged women to stop complaining and criticizing their husbands, to wear feminine clothes, and to greet their husbands at the door with a kiss, a good meal, and a back rub. She also encouraged wives to be sexually available. Schlessinger called a woman's lack of effort in satisfying her husband's sexual needs "gender abuse." Like her predecessor, she encouraged women not to talk about their problems. Troubled wives should talk to their girlfriends instead. The reward for such womanly behavior was appreciation, affection, approval, and love. In fact, she said, men, if treated properly, would love the source of their newfound happiness "almost as loyally as dogs."[51] Although years apart in their public careers, Schlessinger shared deep ideological connections to Andelin. Using key aspects of the Fascinating Womanhood philosophy, she offered updated versions of popular romantic advice that Andelin had made famous a generation earlier.

By 2005 fewer than 25 percent of U.S. households consisted of a man, a woman, and children. Most homes were single-parent households. In what the authors Barbara Ehrenreich and Deirdre English, in their book *The Hearts of Men: American Dreams and the Flight from Commitment*, called the "opt-out revolution," women left the workforce in droves to stay home, have children, and concentrate on their marriages. Single women also left their jobs to get married and have babies. Many of these women were highly educated, successful career women. They believed that success was not in the boardroom; it was at home.[52] In a *Los Angeles Times* article, *The Return of the Happy Housewife*, Charlotte Allen reported that two University of Virginia sociologists concluded that women who stayed home didn't suffer from Friedan's "problem that has no name." In fact, 52 percent of stay-at-home wives said that they were "very happy," compared to just 41 percent of wives in the workforce. The more traditional a marriage was, "the higher the percentage of happy wives." Even wives who identified themselves as feminists reported that they were happier with marriages in which they could stay home with their children. "Increasing numbers of married women . . . have been quietly dropping out of the labor force in favor of more traditional arrangements," said Allen. In 1988, 59 percent of married women with children under twelve months worked outside the home. In 1994 the number was 55 percent.[53] Meghan O'Rourke, in her article *Desperate Feminist Wives*, agreed with Allen. Citing the same University of Virginia study, she concluded that, married working women were less happy than women who lived "as if Friedan never existed." O'Rourke said that this was because traditional marriages supported clearly defined male–female roles.[54] She added that women who came from a religious background, and were thus more likely to live in traditional marriages, were better at adjusting to problematic situations than their feminist sisters were.

If a 2006 episode of ABC's popular reality show *Wife Swap* is any example, these conclusions seem to be accurate. While only popular entertainment and not a scientific study, the show is instructive nonetheless. In this *Wife Swap* episode, a thirty-six-year-old Los Angeles Police Department detective, Lillian Fuentes, "swapped" places with the thirty-five-year-old Dawn Lawson, a devout Christian and self-confessed Domestic Goddess, for two long weeks. Each woman, trading homes and lifestyles, went to live with the other family in order to teach them about their respective ways of life. Lawson, a stay-at-home mother of three, who quoted both Andelin and the King James Bible, and also conducted FW study sessions in her home, asserted that the principles of *Fascinating Womanhood* were timeless. She credited FW teachings for the idyllic atmosphere of her home. "Domestic Goddess, my ass," declared Fuentes, as she contemplated the countless homemaking duties Lawson normally performed. A single mother who completed a rigorous routine of predawn pushups and belly crunches before work each morning and lived out of wedlock with her boyfriend, Fuentes could hardly believe anyone would choose to live as Lawson did. At the end of the swap period, both women happily returned to their previous lifestyles, with no desire to change their routines or ideas about male–female relationships. Lawson told TV interviewers that she was "marvelously happy" being a wife and mother. Fuentes, on the other hand, said that she was tired of juggling work and family, and that she was only moderately happy. While entertaining fare, the larger significance of the *Wife Swap* episode was that Andelin—still the subject of amusement for her outdated ideas—remained, for a considerable segment of the population, a powerful and enduring force in American popular culture. As a testament to her ongoing relevance, in May of 2005 Andelin was offered a generous contract by Bantam/Random House to reissue *Fascinating Womanhood* as a trade paperback. Inexperienced at making her own business decisions, and fearful of being taken advantage of, she didn't accept the offer at the time. That year she published her autobiography, *One Small Moment between Two Eternities*.

Too old to keep up her crusade, and convinced that FW needed a successful businessman to maintain it, Andelin enlisted her son Brian to help her revive the Fascinating Womanhood empire. Knowing that her followers wanted a woman leader, she instructed him to remain behind the scenes. Working together, Helen and Brian developed a plan to champion FW and restore it to its previous glory. They decided to set up a nonprofit organization, raise money, and take the message of Fascinating Womanhood to individual church ministers to get their support. With the backing of the ministers, they believed they could get the churches to sponsor FW classes all across the country, and eventually bring the movement back to its heyday. The ministers knew which couples were having trouble, and Helen felt that they would be happy to recommend *Fascinating Womanhood* in order to save those distressed marriages. In deference to his authority, Andelin felt that the minister must believe that FW was *his* program. Rather than having a female member of his congregation running it, Helen and Brian believed that the minister himself had to be responsible for choosing and overseeing the teachers and encouraging members of his flock to participate. Ministers would be motivated to adopt FW, said Andelin, because saving marriages would increase the number of churchgoers. By offering FW classes, the ministers could renew the wives' commitment to God, who would then encourage their husbands who were not attending to go to church. In order to accomplish their goals, Brian and Helen revived the idea to produce a series of videos. One video would serve as a promotional tool to sell the ministers on the idea, and the others would be supplementary materials for the classes. Andelin believed that the nonprofit organization could raise enough money to hire Hollywood actors to star in the videos. Brian would develop a pilot program in which selected churches could try out the plan. Helen was convinced that if she could get the attention of individual churches, FW would continue to grow and change lives.

To get their plan going, in 2003 Brian established a nonprofit organization called the Renaissance Society. The main goal of the organization, explained Helen, was to carry the message of FW worldwide. The mission statement of the Renaissance Society, however, did not mention Fascinating Womanhood. Brian, she explained, had a more far-reaching purpose, and didn't want to be limited to the promotion of FW. Instead, he sought to recapture traditional family roles by educating the public and promoting what he called the "divine destiny of women." Helen believed that with his talents for organization and self-promotion, her son would recruit a board of directors, secure a large support staff, and build a strong, well-functioning, worldwide organization. Meanwhile she believed she could build a large teaching force, much like a military organization. The Renaissance Society, she anticipated, would support itself through donations and the sale of books and supplies to churches. But Andelin would have to wait for the new organization to take off. Brian was busy. Besides being involved in two other nonprofit organizations, he was engaged in helping one of his brothers start a new business. When asked if Brian planned to work full-time promoting the goals of the Renaissance

Society after he finished his other projects; Andelin admitted that he was reluctant to make such a commitment. But, she believed, that when the right time came, he would step forward and "do his duty." After two years of waiting, Andelin became distraught that Fascinating Womanhood was not going forward. "There's so much to do and it's only me . . . If it could only be like it was in the '70s."[55] But it couldn't be like it was in the 1970s. Helen Andelin was broke. The nonprofit foundation was going nowhere. She couldn't afford a secretary, and she couldn't afford to print more workbooks and lesson outlines.

Despite the fact that Helen could not accomplish her goals for revitalizing Fascinating Womanhood, the movement was already an American institution and an international one. By 2005 *Fascinating Womanhood* had sold three million copies and had been translated into seven languages. It continued to sell around the world. Four hundred thousand women in fifteen countries had taken FW classes.[56] *Man of Steel and Velvet* had sold three hundred thousand copies, *The Fascinating Girl*, one hundred and sixteen thousand copies, and her final book, *All about Raising Children* had sold ten thousand copies. In February 2007 Andelin, at eighty-six, signed the biggest book contract of her career. After offering her a handsome advance, Bantam/Random House reissued *Fascinating Womanhood*. The days of whirlwind publicity tours and thousands of teachers were long gone, but the message lived on. In her article in *The Nation*, Katha Pollitt affirmed the relevance of Andelin and her message. Calling her "the Moses of the Movement," Pollitt, who supported women forgoing careers to instead stay home to raise children, praised Andelin for telling women they had the right to quit work. As the result of Andelin's teachings, she said, scores of educated young women were going back home.[57] Andelin was also still on the radar as far as her detractors went. An *Elle* magazine article entitled "The Not-So-Perfect Wife: Why Are Men Scared to Marry?" poked fun at Andelin and her "outdated" philosophy. Strong, capable women were exciting to men, said one male interviewee. When asked what he thought of fascinating women, he said, "How demeaning is it to men to assume that we need to be coddled and sucked up to like some demented infantile senior executive. . . . Don't make us go back to being big fat jerks, okay?"[58]

In 2006 Andelin placed all of her copyrights in the Renaissance Society. Although she had given the leadership of FW to her son, she continued to run things herself. Still in good physical health, she worked out at a local gym three days a week with a personal trainer and swam at the local YMCA. Andelin renewed her interest in politics. She and Brian created a website called National Overhaul to urge citizens to educate themselves about current issues and utilize their political power. Andelin called on America to clean up the media and return prayer and discipline to the public schools. She spoke out against deceitful business practices, corporate greed, and excessive taxes. Andelin believed that the majority of people upheld moral values and that only a small vocal minority had brought the nation to its current state of immorality. She cautioned, "We cannot let minority groups such as [those who advocate] abortion, same-sex marriage, and condoms on the school grounds win out because of our apathy."[59] Despite her enthusiastic proclamations, Andelin was slowing down. She had developed mild and intermittent dementia and sometimes did not know where she was or would forget the names of her grandchildren. She became unable to work on her writing projects. Helen began to prepare for her funeral. One day she visited the mortician in Monett. Lucid at the time, she interviewed him in detail about his procedures; she wanted to be certain he was going to do his very best to ensure she looked good for her funeral. She instructed her children that she didn't want a fancy casket—just a simple, unadorned pine box. Six months later, while walking on her farm, Andelin tripped and broke a bone in her pelvis. She couldn't move and had to have an ambulance take her to the hospital. After a brief stay, she returned home in a wheelchair and moved in with her daughter Ginny. From there, Andelin declined quickly. She knew the end was near. She didn't want to be a burden to her family, and she wanted to be with Aubrey in the next life. She asked her sons Paul and Brian to give her a blessing and ask God for a speedy death for her. The sons gave her the blessing, asking God to respect her wishes. Three weeks later, her prayers were answered. On June 7, 2009, Helen Andelin died in a back bedroom in her daughter's home. Ginny and Brian were by her side. She was eighty-nine years old. Andelin is survived by eight children, sixty-one grandchildren, one hundred and fifteen great-grandchildren, and one great-great grandchild. She is buried at the Farmville cemetery next to Aubrey.

In December 2012, Brian Andelin died of chronic lymphocytic leukemia. Six months earlier, he signed a contract with Bantam/Random House to print *Fascinating Womanhood* until 2020. *Fascinating Womanhood* came out in Polish in January 2012, and it is currently being translated into Croatian. All of Andelin's books are still available in the Unites States and can be purchased in bookstores and online. Although there are no more authorized teachers, some women still teach FW. Others meet in study groups in private homes and at churches to support each other in practicing the FW principles. Before her death, Andelin forged an unlikely friendship with Student Minister Jeffery Muhammad, of the Muhammad Mosque #48 in Dallas, Texas. Muhammad, the Dallas representative of the Honorable Minister Louis Farrakhan and the Nation of Islam (NOI), became acquainted with Andelin over the telephone when he contacted her to purchase copies of *Fascinating Womanhood* and *Man of Steel and Velvet* for the members of his congregation. Muhammad Mosque #48, one of 162 NOI mosques and study groups nationwide, is under the direction of the controversial black Muslim leader Louis Farrakhan. Farrakhan became the leader of the Nation of Islam in 1975. Known for his black supremacist views, Farrakhan has been called racist and anti-Semitic by his critics. The NOI is a black nationalist organization that promotes the spiritual, social, and economic welfare of African Americans by emphasizing personal morality, the welfare of the community, and the importance of the family. It is estimated that there are fifty thousand black Muslims in the United States. Black Muslims follow the Koran and the Bible's Old Testament and adhere to traditional male and female roles. These roles, they believe, are dictated by nature and by God.

While women are encouraged to stay home and care for their husbands and children, they are not forbidden to work. Men are responsible for leading and providing for the family. According to Jeffery Muhammad, the content of *Fascinating Womanhood* and *Man of Steel and Velvet,* which are used in the mosque's marriage and orientation classes, coincides with and supports the principles of the Nation of Islam, and are important resources for the members of his congregation. *Fascinating Womanhood* and *Man of Steel and Velvet* are on the recommended reading list at the mosque, and they are used in other NOI mosques as well. According to Muhammad, Louis Farrakhan himself has given a nod of approval to both books. Recently, Muhammad Mosque #48 sponsored a Healthy Relationship Initiative for married couples and used *FW* and *MSV* books for the project. Muhammad believes that the

Andelin's books should be studied and taught in classrooms throughout America. [60]

Shortly before his death, Brian talked at length about his plans for the future of Fascinating Womanhood. Although *Man of Steel and Velvet* was still selling in 2012, Brian said he planned to let it go out of print. He believed the book was outdated, and there were no plans to modernize it. He renamed the "Marriage, the Fascinating Way" website Fascinatingwomanhood.net. Since its inception in 1997, the website has had over 350,000 visitors. On the home page, underneath an obituary of Andelin, it says, "A dedicated new team is being assembled to carry on the message of Fascinating Womanhood." As of 2012, however, a team still had not been assembled, nor had the website been updated since his mother's death in 2009. Visitors to the site could still get back copies of the online newsletter and place orders for books and teaching materials, but emails have gone unanswered. The eight-week online class and the discussion board were both discontinued, but Brian said that plans to start a new FW chat room were underway. Because producing a monthly newsletter, including an advice column and success stories was too laborious, he planned to write a quarterly message instead. Brian, who said that he could often feel his mother's presence, admitted that many of his mother's ideas were unrealistic. He believed that the best thing for the future of FW was to let it die out and then start again with a fresh, modernized form. "Fascinating Womanhood had its time," he said. "It already started a revolution. . . . It had its influence." Brian's vision for the new, revitalized Fascinating Womanhood movement was a message that focused on teenage girls. Teenagers, he said, were the "new faces" of the movement. While not giving up his mother's marriage-oriented message, Brian wanted to implement a program that would teach young women "how to be feminine, admire men, and find suitable mates" before they started dating boys. A recent visit to a college campus only supported his mission. He said that seeing girls wearing jeans, carrying backpacks, and wearing no makeup was "tragic." Andelin said he had a fashion designer friend working on a line of clothing for college girls that would "emphasize womanhood." Brian planned to promote the clothing himself, and in doing so, reverse the trend of young women dressing so much "like men." This feminine attire, he hoped, would "remind them they are girls."

While Brian didn't have any plans to let *The Fascinating Girl* go out of print, he thought it was dated and too long to use in his new program. He planned to develop a "crisper, more abbreviated" version of the book that would be more attractive to young women. The book, he said, would be utilized in small mother–daughter study groups in which women would learn "what God expected of them." He said he would develop updated graphics and videos to support the study groups, and he intended to produce an online program as well. Brian said he had enlisted the help of one of his daughters to write the new book and workbook. He had not yet settled on a title. Brian also wanted to develop a series of YouTube video classes that would interest teenagers. He planned to accomplish his goals for FW by utilizing his nonprofit foundation and recruiting the ministers of individual churches to support him. At the time of his interview, Brian had not started work on any of his plans, but he said he would do so soon. He was looking for a grant writer to donate time to his project to help him get the necessary funding for the Renaissance Society, he said. Once the Renaissance Society was solvent, he said, he could pursue his objectives.

In the years following Helen's retreat from active leadership of her movement, feminism continued to evolve. Third-wave feminism, the name given to a new and heterogeneous brand of women's activism that emerged in the 1990s, is a movement that extends beyond the white, middle-class audience to which women's liberation spoke to four decades ago. It began as a response to the failures of the women's movement of the 1960s and '70s and the backlash of the 1980s. Third-wave feminism seeks to include women of color, poor and working-class women, straight women, and lesbian, bisexual, transgendered, and transsexual women; that is, it focuses on diversity. In its efforts to end stereotyping, third-wave feminism challenges all definitions of womanhood. Many third-wave "activists" prefer not to call themselves feminists. They believe that the term is too constricting. Instead of labeling themselves, they work for acceptance of all forms of women's experience. Like the earlier movements, third-wave feminism engages in sexual politics. Lesbian, transgendered, and transsexual women are among its beneficiaries. Third-wave feminism goes beyond national borders; it is a global movement. While the effort remains vibrant, it is mostly unrecognized in popular culture. Even as third-wave feminism presses forward, the values of the 1980s and 1990s prevail. Today, TV commercials and magazine ads show mostly white, middle-class, stay-at-home moms shopping for groceries, serving dinner to their families, vacuuming carpets, and cleaning toilet bowls. Women's magazines devote large sections to the subjects of marriage, motherhood, and the domestic arts. Women are marrying younger and having more children. Some modern women have rejected the militant crusades of their feminist mothers in favor of the kind of life advocated by Andelin and those who followed her. The feminist author Susan Faludi, in her book *Backlash: The Undeclared War against American Women*, argues that despite women's choice to return to more traditional roles, they are not better off. Women, she points out, represent two-thirds of all poor adults. They are still discriminated against in the workforce. Day care is almost as difficult to find today as it was in 1975, and women who work full time make only 77 percent of a man's salary. While there are more women than men graduating from college, women's educational achievements have not proved sufficient to close the wage gap: In jobs for new college graduates, men are hired first, and their starting salaries are higher than those of their female counterparts. Women are more likely than men to work in poor-paying "pink collar" jobs such as nursing, teaching, cleaning, secretarial work, childcare, and waitressing. Nevertheless, Andelin's ideas remain in the public mind.

While many of Andelin's notions about femininity seem to have gone by the wayside, some relationship experts still use her philosophies. In her 2009 advice manual, *Secrets about Men Every Woman Should Know: Find Out How They Really Feel about Women, Relationships, Love and Sex*, the popular author Barbara De Angelis uses a cavemen analogy. She says that men are emotionally distant and competitive because they can't help it; they "evolved" that way. In prehistoric times, she argues, men were the protectors and providers. Modern-day men, like their primeval ancestors, want to protect and provide but are unhappy because in today's world they seldom have the opportunity. Consequently, they suffer from what she calls the "Displaced Warrior" syndrome.[61] Women who understand a man's need to be in charge and do not compete with him for leadership, she says, have a good chance of making the relationship work. Like Andelin, De Angelis urges women, who she describes as nurturing, emotional, and searching for love, not to nag, correct, rescue, or mother their men. Family counselor and

TV talk show host Dr. Phil McGraw agrees. In his 2012 book *Love Smart: Find the One You Want—Fix the One You Got*, he teaches single women old-fashioned techniques for finding Mr. Right. If a woman follows his advice, McGraw promises that she will not only find her man but can "bag 'em, tag 'em, and take 'em home."[62] Like Andelin, McGraw identifies traditional differences between men and women. Man, he says, wants to be the leader. He is competitive and wants to be right. Like De Angelis, McGraw compares him to a caveman. Woman, on the other hand, is more nurturing and seeks love. McGraw says that a woman who wants to find a man and marry him must understand his masculine traits. She must also make herself appealing, develop character, and play hard to get. By changing her own behavior, says McGraw, a woman can actually "fix" a man and transform him into a hero. He urges women to lower their expectations. If they can get 80 percent of what they want in a man, giving up the other 20 percent is worth it. Like Andelin, McGraw doesn't speak to men. Instead, he tells women to make themselves into the kind of woman a man wants. Both De Angelis and McGraw support what Andelin said about men and women back in 1965.

Although it is likely that these modern-day relationship experts don't know who Helen Andelin is, they continue to be guided by the ideas that distinguished her. Its form has changed, but to large numbers of women the fascinating womanhood movement remains popular today, with the original book still selling in the United States and around the world. These days, a career in the home is no longer out of style. In fact, women who decide to "opt out" of the workforce in favor of staying home to raise children are a fast-growing segment of the population. In an online survey conducted in 2012 by ForbesWoman.com and TheBump.com, one thousand women from dual-income households answered questions about their employment decisions after having children. Sixty-four percent of the women who responded said they had careers outside the home, and thirty-three percent stayed home with their children. Eighty-four percent of the working women said that staying home was "a financial luxury they aspire to." One third said that they resented their partners for not earning enough to make that luxury possible. While the survey represents a very small group of women, it points to a developing trend among working mothers.[63] Increasing numbers of women see giving up their careers and returning home as an improvement over their current situation. In the 1960s and '70s, Andelin's fascinating womanhood movement provided an alternative to the ideas forwarded by the women's liberation movement. It offered a familiar and comforting message during times of political and social unrest. It was another choice for those women who couldn't identify with the ideals and leaders of the feminist movement. In the 1980s Fascinating Womanhood contributed to the backlash against the women's movement and the reassertion of family values. In the 1990s Andelin's ideas resurfaced in popular self-help and relationship manuals. Andelin's message that full-time homemaking is a worthwhile endeavor is again popular. In answer to her prayers for knowledge, Andelin believed she was led to "a hidden treasure." She took the information she found and made it into a message that has touched the lives of millions of women. Women of all races, religions, and socioeconomic groups have followed Andelin and her simple prescriptions for a happy marriage. Helen Andelin, wife, mother, author, spiritual seeker, and movement leader, has influenced an entire generation.

AFTERWORD

*B*rian Andelin died before he was able to realize his goals for revitalizing the Fascinating Womanhood empire. Upon Brian's death, control of the publishing and distribution rights for Helen and Aubrey's books, the management of the company, future royalties, and ownership of the FW website were passed to his children.

On December 8, 2012, the Andelin family, including Brian's seven children, gathered at the family farm in Pierce City for his funeral. He was buried near his father and mother in the family cemetery. After the service, Brian's children packed up the remaining inventory of their grandparents' books and other publications, along with boxes of files and the records for the publishing company, and moved them from Aubrey and Helen's home in Missouri to Salt Lake City. According to Helen's daughter, Dixie, Brian's children disagreed about what should happen with FW and she suspects that there was discord among them about its future. Since the funeral, Brian's children have not maintained contact with their uncles and aunts and none of Helen's children know the status of the FW business. "It's as though it doesn't exist anymore," said Dixie.

Dixie and her sister, Ginny, believe that Brian's children either don't know or can't agree on what to do with the FW business and so are avoiding doing anything at all. Dixie, who tried unsuccessfully to make contact with Brian's children shortly after they moved her parents' belongings to Utah, said that she and her siblings are "staying out of it" to avoid family tensions. Dixie said that she and Brian were not close and she had no knowledge of his plans to rewrite *The Fascinating Girl*, to let *Man of Steel and Velvet* go out of print, or to redirect his mother's marriage-oriented message to focus on teenagers. Dixie did not know of efforts by any of Brian's daughters to write a new book. She said Brian's claims that he was working on YouTube videos, a supporting workbook, and a line of feminine clothing were "only wishes." All indications are that Brian's Renaissance Society was never the working entity that Helen dreamed it would be. It was just a name.

Although she is sad about the uncertain fate of her mother's legacy, Dixie and her daughter Amanda (Bird) have decided to move forward with their own plans to continue Helen's life work. They are writing a sequel to *Fascinating Womanhood* and expect to release it in 2015 to coincide with the fifty-year anniversary of the publication of Helen's original book. They have also inaugurated a new FW website called "Fascinating Womanhood, A Guide to a Happier Marriage," which Dixie says is now the "official" website. She no longer has access to her mother's fascinatingwomanhood.net site because the passwords have been changed. The new website is still under construction, but attractively displays pictures of Helen, a letter to FW followers from Dixie welcoming them to the site, and an advertisement for an upcoming eight-week online Fascinating Womanhood course. Although the future of the FW business remains uncertain, Helen's daughters and granddaughter are determined to keep her legacy alive.

Notes

1. I was a teenager when Helen Andelin came to Phoenix on a book tour to promote *Fascinating Womanhood*. My mother, a Fascinating Womanhood teacher, took my older sister, several women friends, and me to the airport to meet her and get autographs. This description is my personal recollection, an impression that remains vivid to this day.

2. Helen B. Andelin, "Childhood," in "One Small Moment between Two Eternities," 2005, Helen B. Andelin Archive, Special Collections, J. Willard Marriott Library, University of Utah, Salt Lake City (hereafter cited as Andelin Archive). Andelin's memoir does not contain page numbers but is divided into titled sections. It is important to note that Andelin's memoir includes information inconsistent with some of her earlier accounts. Andelin wrote several accounts of her life. She printed and bound only "One Small Moment," for family distribution. The other five accounts are more like reports or journals—shorter, printed on letter-sized paper, and stapled together. Some of these earlier accounts, possibly drafts, were among her papers. Information from all of these versions is used in the present work.

3. Andelin, "My Mother" and "My Testimony," in "One Small Moment," Andelin Archive. Mormons do not believe in infant baptism and instead baptize children at age eight, "the age of accountability." A child's father or another close male member of the family usually performs the ordinance. Baptisms of this sort are no longer performed in temples but at local church buildings. They tend to be for close family only. A newly baptized person undergoes a public confirmation attended by the entire congregation.

4. Andelin, "Personal Growth" in "One Small Moment," Andelin Archive.

5. Most LDS children are fourteen when they receive a patriarchal blessing—a personal blessing given by a designated "patriarch" or elder, whose calling it is to provide this service for the religious community. The blessings, private affairs, are considered sacred. They are transcribed for the recipient to keep, and serve as a sort of spiritual blueprint for the rest of one's life.

6. Andelin, "My Testimony," in "One Small Moment," Andelin Archive.

7. Helen Andelin, "History of F.W.," 36, Andelin Archive. Note that in the bibliography of the present work, there are five distinct sources with similar names: "Brief Biography of Helen Berry Andelin," "Brief History of F.W.," "Brief History of Fascinating Womanhood," "Brief Profile of Helen Andelin and Fascinating Womanhood," and "History of F.W." These are early drafts that were later edited and used in Andelin's autobiography, "One Small Moment."

8. The Word of Wisdom comes from section 89 of the Doctrine and Covenants, one of the four books considered sacred scripture by Mormons. Andelin, "Fascinating Womanhood," in "One Small Moment," Andelin Archive.

9. Mormons believe the Word of Wisdom to be a commandment. Those who do not observe it are not allowed a temple recommend. However, the section on eating meat is usually given little attention, in light of the more dramatic warnings about the evils of alcohol, tobacco, and coffee. Eating meat during times of plenty would not be considered reason enough to deny a temple recommend to a member of the church. Helen Andelin, Recorded interviews with Helen Andelin in Pierce City, MO, 2000, transcripts in Andelin Archive.

10. Andelin, "My Career in the Home," in "One Small Moment," Andelin Archive.

11. Mormons believe that heaven consists of three kingdoms, with the celestial kingdom being the highest of the three. It is only there that families live together for eternity, dwelling in the presence of God. Andelin, "My Dream," in "One Small Moment," Andelin Archive.

12. Andelin, "My Testimony," in "One Small Moment," Andelin Archive.

13. Andelin, Recorded interviews, Pierce City, MO, 2002, Andelin Archive.

14. A bishopric consists of the bishop, the ward leader, and two counselors. Aubrey was a counselor. A ward is a geographic location of followers, much like a neighborhood parish.

15. Andelin, "Brief History of F.W.," 1, Andelin Archive.

16. Andelin, "Brief History of F.W.," 36, Andelin Archive.

17. Louis M. Grafe and Loyola Grafe, *The Secrets of Fascinating Womanhood, or The Art of Attracting Men: A Practical Course of Lessons in the Underlying Principles by Which Women Attract Men—Leading to the Proposal and Culminating in Marriage* (Saint Louis: The Psychology Press, 1922).

18. *The Pearl of Great Price* is the title of a compilation of revelations from God to Joseph Smith beginning in 1830. The revelations were canonized by the Mormon Church in 1888. The significance of Andelin's comparing, in "Brief History of F.W.," her discovery and scripture is significant because she is making the claim that the message she received from God was of equal importance to the revelations given to those LDS men believed to be prophets. Italics are Andelin's.

19. Andelin, Recorded interviews, Pierce City, MO, 2002, Andelin Archive.

20. Andelin, "Our Growing Children and AFSTP," in "One Small Moment," Andelin Archive.

21. Andelin, Recorded interviews, Pierce City, MO, 2002, Andelin Archive.

22. Andelin, "The Hidden Treasure," in "One Small Moment," Andelin Archive.

23. Betty Friedan, *The Feminine Mystique* (New York: W. W. Norton, 2008), 15.

24. Andelin, Recorded interviews, Pierce City, MO, 2001, Andelin Archive.

CHAPTER 2, THE IDEAL WOMAN (FROM A MAN'S POINT OF VIEW)

1. Helen Andelin, *Fascinating Womanhood: How the Ideal Woman Awakens a Man's Deepest Love and Tenderness* (New York: Bantam Dell, 2007), 2.

2. Helen Andelin, *The Fascinating Womanhood Newsletter,* June 1969, 2, Andelin Archive.

3. Carolyn Nolte-Watts, "Author Discovers New Pedestal for Women," *St. Petersburg Times*, April 8, 1975.

4. Joan Cook, "She Takes a Stand against Liberation," *New York Times*, September 28, 1970.

5. Helen Andelin, *Fascinating Womanhood* (Santa Barbara: Pacific Press Publishers 1990), 17, 18–19, 23.

6. See Barbara Welter, "The Cult of True Womanhood: 1820–1860," *American Quarterly* 18, no. 2 (Summer 1966), part 1.

7. Gen. 3:16.

8. Andelin, *Fascinating Womanhood* (Bantam Dell, 2007), 129.

9. Andelin, Letters to Teachers, March 1966, Andelin Archive.

10. Andelin, *The Fascinating Womanhood Newsletter*, Spring 1969, Andelin Archive.

11. Helen Andelin, "Fascinating Womanhood Publication for Women," July/August 1969, 3, Andelin Archive.

12. Col. 3:18.

13. Andelin, *The Fascinating Womanhood Newsletter*, October 1968, 2, Andelin Archive.

14. Sally Dallos and Rudi Dallos, *Couples, Sex and Power: The Politics of Desire* (Philadelphia: Open University Press, 1997), 14.

15. Nolte-Watts, "Author Discovers New Pedestal for Women," *St. Petersburg Times*, April 8, 1975.

16. Andelin, *The Fascinating Womanhood Newsletter*, October 1968, 8; Spring 1974, 10, Andelin Archive.

17. Rusty Brown, "'Obey' Is the Key Word in Her Marriage Vow," *Cleveland, Ohio Press*, April 3, 1975.

18. Helen Andelin, "Obstacles," in *The Fascinating Womanhood Newsletter* 8, no. 2 (March/April 1981).

19. Andelin, Recorded interviews, Pierce City, MO, 2001, Andelin Archive.

20. E. Merrill Root, "Feminine Woman: The Lady Is a Conservative," *American Opinion* (June 1971), 22.

21. Louise Farr, "Peddling the Pedestal: Helen Andelin's Fascinating Womanhood Course Preaches Male Supremacy and Promises to Put a 'Sparkle' Back into Marriage," *New Times*, October 17, 1975, 52.

22. Eph. 5:22–24.

23. Andelin, *The Fascinating Womanhood Newsletter*, March 1968, 3, Andelin Archive.

24. Marilyn Busch, "Marriage Not a Democracy," *Omaha World-Herald*, November 7, 1975.

25. Andelin, *The Fascinating Womanhood Newsletter*, Spring 1974, 3, Andelin Archive.

26. Andelin, *Fascinating Womanhood* (1965), 155.

27. Andelin, Recorded interviews, Pierce City, MO, 2001, Andelin Archive.

28. Andelin, *Fascinating Womanhood* (1965), 143, 163.

29. Andelin, *The Fascinating Womanhood Newsletter*, November 1969, 2, Andelin Archive.

30. Andelin, *Fascinating Womanhood* (1972), 162.

31. Andelin, *The Fascinating Womanhood Newsletter*, Winter 1971, 7, Andelin Archive. Emphasis is Andelin's.

32. Andelin, Recorded interviews, Pierce City, MO, 2001–2002, Andelin Archive.

33. Lori Ann Haubenstock, "The Andelins Give Fascinating Advice on Playing House," *Tampa Times*, January 27, 1978.

34. Elaine Viets, "What More Could a Woman Want?" *St. Louis Post-Dispatch*, July 20, 1975.

35. Andelin, *The Fascinating Womanhood Newsletter*, March/April 1979, Andelin Archive.

36. Matt. 18:3–4.

37. Sherrie Ricchiardi, "She Says Male Supremacy Is Key to Happy Marriage," *Des Moines Sunday Register*, November 16, 1975.

38. Andelin, *Fascinating Womanhood* (2007), 352.

39. Andelin, *The Fascinating Womanhood Newsletter*, September 1969, 9, Andelin Archive.

40. Aubrey Andelin, ed., *Fascinating Womanhood Success Stories* (Santa Barbara: Pacific Press Publishers, 1973), 157.

41. Andelin, *The Fascinating Womanhood Newsletter*, October 1969, Andelin Archive.

42. Andelin, *The Fascinating Womanhood Newsletter*, February 2, 1970, 11; March 1970, reprint from 1963.

43. Andelin, "Letter to Teachers," *The Fascinating Womanhood Newsletter, 1965–1996*, October 1965, Andelin Archive.

44. Andelin, *The Fascinating Womanhood Newsletter*, July/August 1969, Andelin Archive.

45. Andelin, Recorded interviews, Pierce City, MO, 2001, Andelin Archive.

46. Aubrey Andelin, *Success Stories*, 57.

47. Andelin, Correspondence, Andelin Archive.

48. Andelin, *The Fascinating Womanhood Newsletter*, July/August 1969, 3, Andelin Archive.

49. Andelin, Recorded interviews, Pierce City, MO, 2001–2002, Andelin Archive.

50. Andelin, "Brief History of Fascinating Womanhood," 2.

51. Andelin, Recorded interviews, Pierce City, MO, 2001, Andelin Archive.

52. Andelin, "How I Came to Write Fascinating Womanhood," in *The Fascinating Womanhood Newsletter*, February 1970, 2.

53. John Weeks, "Womanhood Can Be Fascinating," *Sun-Telegram* (San Bernardino, CA), October 11, 1974, C-1.

54. Andelin, Recorded interviews, Pierce City, MO, 2001, Andelin Archive.

55. Andelin, "My Own Marriage Success" and "My Great Need," in "One Small Moment," Andelin Archive.

56. Andelin, Recorded interviews, Pierce City, MO, 2001, 2002, Andelin Archive.

57. Verna Johnson to Helen Andelin, October 27, 1971, in Correspondence, Andelin Archive.

58. Andelin, "My Great Need," in "One Small Moment," Andelin Archive.

59. Phyllis W. Heald to Helen Andelin, July 16, 1964, in Correspondence, Andelin Archive.

60. Andelin, "My Great Need," in "One Small Moment," Andelin Archive.

61. Andelin, Recorded interviews, Pierce City, MO, 2001, Andelin Archive.

62. Andelin, *The Fascinating Womanhood Newsletter*, February 1970, 2, Andelin Archive.

63. Andelin, "My Great Need," in "One Small Moment," Andelin Archive.

64. Andelin, *The Fascinating Womanhood Newsletter,* March 1970, 1, Andelin Archive.
65. Andelin, Recorded interviews, Pierce City, MO, 2001, Andelin Archive. In later editions of her book, Andelin credited the works of Victor Hugo, William Thackeray, Norman Vincent Peale, and Marie N. Robinson.
66. Andelin, *The Fascinating Womanhood Newsletter,* Winter 1971, Andelin Archive.
67. Andelin, Recorded interviews, Pierce City, MO, January 2001, Andelin Archive.
68. Andelin, *Fascinating Womanhood* (2007), 353.
69. Helen C. Smith, "Liberation or Submission," *Atlanta Constitution,* April 15, 1975, 5-B.
70. *Marriage the Fascinating Way,* "The Flaws of Feminism," marriagethefascinatingway.net (accessed February 23, 2003). The new address for the Web site is www.fascinatingwomanhood.net.
71. Andelin, *The Fascinating Womanhood Newsletter,* July/August 1971, Andelin Archive.
72. "God Is Basis of Family, Says Founder of Course," *Arizona Daily Star* (Tucson, AZ), April 12, 1975.
73. Andelin, *The Fascinating Womanhood Newsletter,* Winter 1971, 8, Andelin Archive.
74. Andelin, *The Fascinating Womanhood Newsletter,* Fall 1971, 7, Andelin Archive.
75. Andelin, *The Fascinating Womanhood Newsletter,* Spring 1972, 9, Andelin Archive.
76. Andelin, Recorded interviews, Pierce City, MO, 2001, Andelin Archive.

CHAPTER 3, EVERYWOMAN'S HEAVEN ON EARTH

1. Marie N. Robinson, *The Power of Sexual Surrender* (Garden City, NY: Doubleday & Company, 1959), 81.
2. Joan McCoy, "You've Come a Long Way Baby? Is Woman's Place Still in the Home?" *Rocky Mountain News* (Denver, CO), February 9, 1971.
3. Andelin, *The Fascinating Womanhood Newsletter,* April 1969, 1, Andelin Archive.
4. Ellen Baker, "Author Offers Pathway to Marital Happiness," *Tulsa Daily World,* March 19, 1975.
5. Mary Lynn White, "Fewer Problems When Man Heads House," *Cincinnati Post,* June 21, 1971.
6. Andelin, "Insights," in *The Fascinating Womanhood Newsletter,* January 1978, Andelin Archive.
7. Andelin, *Fascinating Womanhood* (2007), 39.
8. Andelin, *Fascinating Womanhood* (2007), 71, 383.
9. Andelin, Recorded interviews, Phoenix, AZ, 2005, Andelin Archive.
10. Andelin, *The Fascinating Womanhood Newsletter,* October 1969, 3, Andelin Archive.
11. Linda Ryan, "Here's How to Win Hubby's Love and Devotion," *NW Omaha Sun,* November, 25, 1971.
12. Andelin, *The Fascinating Womanhood Newsletter,* September 1969, 10, Andelin Archive.
13. Aubrey P. Andelin, *Fascinating Womanhood Principles Applied to Sex* (Santa Barbara, CA: Pacific Press Publishers, 1973), 3.
14. Sherry Ricchiardi, "She Says Male Supremacy Is Key to Happy Marriage," *Des Moines Sunday Register,* November 16, 1975.

15. Aubrey Andelin, ed., *Fascinating Womanhood Success Stories* (Santa Barbara, CA: Pacific Press Publishers, 1973), 210.

16. Tim. 2:11, 12.

17. Peter 3:1

18. Joan Wolverton, "Helen Andelin: A Counter to 'Lib,'" *Seattle Times,* February 18, 1971.

19. Kathy Rethlake, "How to Keep Your Man Happy," *Evening Outlook* (Santa Monica), February 12, 1976, 29.

20. Tim. 5:8.

21. Andelin, *The Fascinating Womanhood Newsletter,* July/August 1970, 1, Andelin Archive.

22. Andelin, *Fascinating Womanhood* (2007), 229.

23. Phyllis McGinley, "College Education for the Housewife?" *Ladies Home Journal,* October 1962.

24. Prov. 31:27.

25. Andelin, *Fascinating Womanhood* (1972), 228.

26. Eleanor Doyle, "The Business of Being a Woman," *Sacramento Union,* May 14, 1975.

27. Helen Andelin, ed., "I Felt Like a Parasite," in "Fascinating Womanhood Publication for Women," Spring 1973, Andelin Archive.

28. Judith Sills, "The Surprising Key to a Happy Marriage," *Family Circle Magazine,* September 1, 2000.

29. Brown, Rusty. "'Obey' Is the Key Word in Her Marriage Vow," *Cleveland Ohio Press,* April 3, 1975.

30. Camille Cole Nuffer, *Down Happiness Road* (Salt Lake City: Deseret News Press, 1944). Camille Cole Nuffer was my grandmother. She did not know anything about Fascinating Womanhood, nor would she have agreed with it if she had.

31. Helen Andelin, "Letter to Teachers," 1966, *The Fascinating Womanhood Newsletter: 1965–1996,* and "When Women Fail at Homemaking," October 1971, *The Fascinating Womanhood Newsletter: 1965–1996,* Andelin Archive.

32. Andelin, *The Fascinating Womanhood Newsletter,* November 1968, 7; December 1968, 12, Andelin Archive.

33. Andelin, *Fascinating Womanhood* (1965), 228, 229.

34. Paul Johnson, *A History of the American People* (New York: HarperCollins, 1998), 974.

35. Andelin, Recorded interviews, Pierce City, MO, 2002, Andelin Archive.

36. Jong's phrase, taken from her 1972 "Seventeen Warnings in Search of a Feminist Poem," is quoted in Sherry Argov, *Why Men Love Bitches* (Avon, MA: Adams Media, 2002), 90.

37. Teacher application of Alwilda Braun, in *Teacher Applications, 1970–2005,* Andelin Archive.

38. Andelin, *The Fascinating Womanhood Newsletter,* December 1970, 2, Andelin Archive.

39. Andelin, "Questions and Answers," *The Fascinating Womanhood Newsletter* 3, no. 5. (September/October 1978). Note: The newsletter went from a monthly publication to a quarterly, then reverted to a monthly. At one point it had volume numbers; most of the time it did not.

40. Andelin, *The Fascinating Womanhood Newsletter*, Fall 1973, 9, Andelin Archive.
41. Lucille DeView, "Fascinate Men by Being Your Fascinating Self," *Detroit News*, May 5, 1975.
42. Andelin, *The Fascinating Womanhood Newsletter*, Spring 1972, 8, Andelin Archive.
43. Andelin, Recorded interviews, Pierce City, MO, 2001, Andelin Archive.
44. DeView, "Fascinate Men," 9.
45. Helen Andelin, "Marriage the Fascinating Way," http://www
.marriagethefascinatingway.net (accessed January 1997).
46. Andelin, *The Fascinating Womanhood Newsletter*, May/June 1978, Andelin Archive.
47. "Fascinating Womanhood: Phenomenon of Our Times," *The Men's Section* (Ann Arbor) 1, no. 1 (June 1972).
48. Carolyn Nolte-Watts, "Author Discovers New Pedestal for Women," *St. Petersburg Times*, October 1975.
49. Andelin, *The Fascinating Womanhood Newsletter*, March 1969, 3, Andelin Archive.
50. Frances Phinney, "Understanding Men Leads to Happier Marriage," *Everett Herald* (WA), October 30, 1968.
51. Andelin, "The Adjustable Wife," *The Fascinating Womanhood Newsletter*, Fall 1971, 3, Andelin Archive.
52. Dave Smith, "The Making of a Non-liberationist," *Los Angeles Times*, December 5, 1975.
53. Andelin, *The Fascinating Womanhood Newsletter*, May 1969, Andelin Archive.
54. Andelin, *The Fascinating Womanhood Newsletter*, April 1969, 4, Andelin Archive.
55. Andelin, Recorded interviews, Pierce City, MO, 2002, Andelin Archive.
56. Aubrey Andelin, *Success Stories*, 72.
57. Aubrey P. Andelin, *Fascinating Womanhood Principles Applied to Sex* (Santa Barbara, CA: Pacific Press Publishers, 1973), 29.
58. Andelin, Recorded interviews, Phoenix, 2005, Andelin Archive.
59. Andelin, *Fascinating Womanhood Principles*, 7.
60. Andelin, *Fascinating Womanhood Principles*, 8, 16.
61. Andelin, Recorded interviews, Phoenix, 2005, Andelin Archive.
62. Andelin, *Fascinating Womanhood Principles*, April 1969, 6, Andelin Archive.
63. Andelin, *Fascinating Womanhood Principles*, March 1971, 4, Andelin Archive.
64. Andelin, *Fascinating Womanhood Principles*, Winter 1972, 11, Andelin Archive.
65. Andelin, *Fascinating Womanhood Principles*, January 1976.
66. Andelin, *Fascinating Womanhood* (2007), 136.

CHAPTER 4, HEYDAY

1. Helen Andelin, Letters to Teachers, March 1966, Andelin Archive.
2. Alice Webb, recorded interview with author, July 2005.
3. Andelin, Recorded interviews, Pierce City, MO, 2002, Andelin Archive.
4. Jean Tyson, "Men's Role Not Superior: Liberationists Are Unhappy," *Atlanta Journal*, September 16, 1970.
5. Andelin, Recorded interviews, Phoenix, AZ, 2005, Andelin Archive.
6. Andelin, "The Man from New York," in "One Small Moment," Andelin Archive.

7. Andelin, Recorded interviews, Pierce City, MO, 2001, Andelin Archive.

8. Andelin, "The Man from New York," in "One Small Moment," Andelin Archive.

9. Andelin, Recorded interviews, Pierce City, MO, 2002, Andelin Archive.

10. Andelin, "My Career in the Home," in "One Small Moment," Andelin Archive. Italics are Andelin's.

11. Andelin, Recorded interviews, Pierce City, MO, 2001, Andelin Archive.

12. Andelin, *The Fascinating Womanhood Newsletter,* April 20, 1970, Andelin Archive.

13. Teacher application of Jaquie Davison, March 2, 1976, in *Teacher Applications, 1970–2005,* Andelin Archive; Louise Farr, "Peddling the Pedestal: Helen Andelin's Fascinating Womanhood Course Preaches Male Supremacy and Promises to Put a 'Sparkle' Back into Marriage," *New Times,* October 17, 1975, 52.

14. Jaquie Davison, *I Am a Housewife!—A Housewife Is the Most Important Person in the World* (New York: Guild Books, 1972).

15. Helen Andelin to President Richard Nixon, March 24, 1971, in Correspondence, Andelin Archive.

16. Andelin, *The Fascinating Womanhood Newsletter,* Spring 1970, Andelin Archive.

17. Andelin, Recorded interviews, Pierce City, MO, 2002, Andelin Archive.

18. Andelin, *The Fascinating Womanhood Newsletter,* Spring 1970, Andelin Archive.

19. Andelin, Recorded interviews, Phoenix, AZ, 2005, Andelin Archive.

20. Helen Andelin, *The Fascinating Girl* (Santa Barbara: Pacific Press Publishers, 1970), 178–79.

21. Andelin, *Fascinating Girl,* 263.

22. Andelin, Recorded interviews, Phoenix, 2005, Andelin Archive.

23. Andelin, "A Visit from an Angel," in "One Small Moment," Andelin Archive; Andelin, Recorded interviews, Phoenix, 2005, Andelin Archive.

24. "Demonstration Planned Sept. 30: Women's Liberation Foes Will Strike Back," *Los Angeles Times,* August 26, 1970.

25. Aubrey Andelin, *Man of Steel and Velvet: A Guide to Masculine Development* (Santa Barbara, CA: Pacific Press Publishers, 1972), 13.

26. "Marabel Morgan," *Ohio History Central: An Online Encyclopedia of Ohio History,* http://www.ohiohistorycentral.org/w/Marabel_Morgan (accessed April 22, 2007).

27. Marilyn Busch, "Author: Marriage Not a Democracy," *Omaha World-Herald,* November 7, 1975.

28. "The Sexes: Total Fascination," *Time Magazine,* March 19, 1975.

29. Karen Greene, "Fascinating Womanhood Author's Life Pattern," *Seattle-Times,* April 12, 1975.

30. Mary Leonard, "You Know What Your Man Wants, Girls, So Doll Up in Saran Wrap and, and, ZOWIE!!" *National Observer,* May 17, 1975.

31. Jean Tyson, "He's Fascinating, Too: Mrs. Andelin's Husband, Aubrey, Shows the Velvet," *Atlanta Journal,* October 7, 1975.

32. "Aubrey Andelin, An Advocate for Men," *South Bay Daily Breeze* (Torrence, CA), January 29, 1975, 12.

33. Barbara Hunting, "He Writes about Perfect Man," *Huntsville News* (AL), October 10, 1976.

34. Andelin, Recorded interviews, Phoenix, AZ, 2005, Andelin Archive.

35. Andelin, Recorded interviews, Pierce City, MO, 2001, and Phoenix, 2005, Andelin Archive.

36. Teacher application of Gilly Kuehn, 1979, in *Teacher Applications, 1970–2005,* Andelin Archive; Gilly Kuehn, recorded interview with author, Anaheim, CA, June 4, 2012.
37. Teacher application of Joan Kimble, 1975, in *Teacher Applications, 1970–2005,* Andelin Archive.
38. "How to Be Man's Ideal Woman," *Evening Herald* (Rock Hill, SC), June 25, 1975.
39. Teacher application of Saundria Garner, 1979, in *Teacher Applications 1970–2005,* Andelin Archive.
40. Teacher application of Grace Chavis, 1970, in *Teacher Applications 1970–2005,* Andelin Archive; telephone interview with author, June 6, 2012.
41. Teacher application of Jeannie Wright, May 1971, in *Teacher Applications 1970–2005,* Andelin Archive.
42. Andelin, Recorded interviews, Pierce City, MO, 2002, Andelin Archive.
43. Andelin to Thomas S. Monson, April 16, 1971, in Correspondence, Andelin Archive.
44. Andelin to Spencer W. Kimball, May 23, 1975, in Correspondence, Andelin Archive.
45. Virginia Lee Warren, "In This Day of Liberation, They Study How to Please Their Men," *New York Times Magazine,* June 28, 1975.
46. "Fascinating Womanhood: Phenomenon of Our Times," *The Men's Section* (Ann Arbor, MI), June 1972.

CHAPTER 5, ENEMIES

1. Reed Bradford, paraphrased in letter from Helen Andelin to Alvin R. Dyer, May 20, 1968, in Correspondence, Andelin Archive.
2. Andelin, "The Opposition," in "One Small Moment," Andelin Archive.
3. Andelin, Recorded interviews," Phoenix, 2005, Andelin Archive.
4. Andelin, "The Opposition," in "One Small Moment," Andelin Archive.
5. Andelin, Recorded interviews, Pierce City, MO, 2001, Andelin Archive.
6. Howard W. Hunter to Helen Andelin, April 10, 1968, in Correspondence, Andelin Archive.
7. Andelin, Recorded interviews, Pierce City, MO, 2002, Andelin Archive.
8. Helen Andelin to Alvin R. Dyer, May 20, 1968, in Correspondence, Andelin Archive.
9. See Marion Yeates, "Why Shouldn't Mormon Women Want *This* Priesthood?" in *Women and Authority: Re-Emerging Mormon Feminism*, ed. Maxine Hanks (Salt Lake City: Signature Books, 1992), 353–64, http://signaturebookslibrary.org/?=1162.
10. Andelin, "The Opposition," in "One Small Moment," Andelin Archive.
11. Joan Geiger, "Seattle Women Clash over Right to 'Slavery,' Freedom," *Seattle Times,* September 22, 1968.
12. Corrine Zager, "Wife No Longer Neglected," *North Central Outlook* (Seattle, WA), October 10, 1968.
13. Andelin, *The Fascinating Womanhood Newsletter,* April 20, 1970; Andelin to author, July 22, 2007.

14. Andelin, "FW News," *The Fascinating Womanhood Newsletter,* October 1970, 2.
15. Andelin, "Marriage the Fascinating Way," April 2000.
16. Andelin, *The Fascinating Womanhood Newsletter,* November 1970, 2.
17. Andelin, Recorded interviews, Pierce City, MO, 2002, Andelin Archive.
18. Helen Andelin to President Richard M. Nixon, September 5, 1970, in Correspondence, Andelin Archive.
19. Andelin, *The Fascinating Womanhood Newsletter,* April 1970.
20. Andelin, *The Fascinating Womanhood Newsletter,* April 20, 1970, 9, and January 1971, 4.
21. Gail Collins, *America's Women: Four Hundred Years of Dolls, Drudges, Helpmates and Heroines* (New York: William Morrow, 2003), 444.
22. Louise Farr, "Peddling the Pedestal: Helen Andelin's Fascinating Womanhood Course Preaches Male Supremacy and Promises to Put a 'Sparkle' Back into Marriage," *New Times,* October 17, 1975, 52.
23. Gilbert Y. Steiner, *Constitutional Inequality: The Political Fortunes of the Equal Rights Amendment* (Washington, D.C.: Brookings Institution, 1985), 60.
24. Andelin, Recorded interview, Pierce City, MO, 2002, Andelin Archive.
25. Farr, "Peddling the Pedestal," 52.
26. Andelin, Recorded interviews, Pierce City, MO, 2002, Andelin Archive.
27. Helen Benson, "New Revolution: A Means to End War of the Sexes," *Santa Barbara News-Press,* April 13, 1970.
28. "Protests against Women's Lib," *Goleta Valley Sun* (CA), April 15, 1970.
29. Andelin, *The Fascinating Womanhood Newsletter,* Spring 1971.
30. This is Andelin's recollection of events. While records indicate that an investigation was conducted by Porter in response to Andelin's persistent requests, neither Lee's commission of an official critique nor Andelin's account of Porter's report being sent to Church headquarters for presidential consideration can be substantiated.
31. Blaine Porter to Aubrey and Helen Andelin, April 22, 1971, Correspondence, Andelin Archive.
32. Jeff McClellan, "A Lingering Influence: Top 10 BYU Professors," *BYU Magazine,* September 16, 1999.
33. Aubrey Andelin to Finn Paulsen, November 13, 1973, Correspondence, Andelin Archive.
34. Janet Chusmir, "Anti-Lib Pair: 'Be an Angel and Stay Home,'" *Miami Herald,* May 4, 1971.
35. Andelin, *The Fascinating Womanhood Newsletter,* January 1970.
36. Doris Blake, "A Day of Femininity to Challenge Libs," *New York Daily News,* September 22, 1970.
37. "Demonstration Planned Sept. 30: Women's Liberation Foes Will Strike Back," *Los Angeles Times,* August 26, 1970.
38. Andelin, Recorded interviews, Pierce City, MO, 2001, Andelin Archive.
39. Walker A. Tomkins, "Santa Barbaran Challenges Leaders of the 'New Morality' on TV Shows," *Santa Barbara News-Press,* February 13, 1971.
40. Farr, "Peddling the Pedestal," 52.
41. William Masters and Virginia E. Johnson, "A Warning about Books that Teach Women to Pretend," *Redbook Magazine,* March 1976.

42. Helen C. Smith, "Marriage: Liberation or Submission?" *Atlanta Constitution*, April 15, 1975.

43. Andelin, *The Fascinating Womanhood Newsletter*, Winter 1972, 6.

44. Betty Friedan, *The Feminine Mystique* (New York: W. W. Norton, 2008), 252, 256, 293.

45. Benson, "New Revolution."

46. Patricia Sullivan, "Voice of Feminism's Second Wave," *Washington Post*, February 5, 2006.

47. Phyllis Schlafly, *The Power of the Positive Woman* (New Rochelle, NY: Arlington House Publishers, 1977), 21.

48. Barbara Ehrenreich, *The Hearts of Men: American Dreams and the Flight from Commitment* (Garden City, NY: Anchor Press/Doubleday, 1983), 148.

49. Andelin, *The Fascinating Womanhood Newsletter*, Fall 1974.

50. Andelin, "Letter to Teachers," June 1, 1977, *The Fascinating Womanhood Newsletter: 1965–1996*, Andelin Archive.

51. Andelin, Recorded interviews, Phoenix, AZ, 2005, Andelin Archive.

52. Farr, "Peddling the Pedestal," 52.

53. Andrew Kopkind, "America's New Right," *New Times*, September 30, 1977, 21–25.

54. Letter to Helen Andelin from Seminole, FL, 1974, Correspondence, Andelin Archive.

55. Andelin, *The Fascinating Womanhood Newsletter*, October 1970, 8, Andelin Archive.

56. Alice Neuffer, "Success Stories 1968–1971," Author's archive.

57. Andelin, Recorded interviews, Phoenix, AZ, 2005, Andelin Archive.

58. Andelin, Recorded interviews, Pierce City, MO, March 2001, Andelin Archive.

59. Sandra Pesman, "They Just Love Being Fascinating Women," *Chicago Daily News*, September 26, 1970.

60. Elaine Viets, "What More Could a Woman Want?" *St. Louis Post-Dispatch*, July 20, 1975.

61. Sally Ann Mass, "A Ministry of Womanhood," *The Press* (Loma Linda, CA), October 10, 1974.

62. Farr, "Peddling the Pedestal," 52.

63. Mormon presidents, believed to be prophets, serve as the head of the Church until death. When a president dies, the Council of Twelve Apostles meets to determine the new replacement. Mormons believe God himself chooses the new president and prophet. So strong is this conviction that members believe that to follow the prophet is to follow God himself and that God will not allow the prophet to lead the Church astray by his own weakness or sin.

64. Andelin, "The Opposition," in "One Small Moment," Andelin Archive.

65. Andelin, Recorded interviews, Phoenix, July 2005, Andelin Archive.

66. Andelin, "The Opposition," in "One Small Moment," Andelin Archive.

67. Andelin, Recorded interviews, Phoenix, AZ, 2005, Andelin Archive.

68. Andelin, "The Opposition," in "One Small Moment," Andelin Archive.

69. Andelin, "The Opposition," in "One Small Moment," Andelin Archive; Andelin, Recorded interviews, Pierce City, MO, 2001, Andelin Archive.

70. Aubrey Andelin to Elders Gordon B. Hinckley and Marvin J. Ashton, February 1977, Correspondence, in Andelin Archive.

71. Andelin, Recorded interviews, Pierce City, MO, 2000, Andelin Archive.

CHAPTER 6, FARMVILLE

1. Andelin, Recorded interviews, Pierce City, MO, 2001, Andelin Archive.
2. Andelin, Recorded interviews, Pierce City, MO, 2001, Andelin Archive.
3. Andelin, "Summary of 22 Years," in "One Small Moment," Andelin Archive; Andelin, Recorded interviews, Pierce City, MO, 2002, Andelin Archive.
4. Andelin, Recorded interviews, Pierce City, MO, 2002, Andelin Archive.
5. Andelin, "Letter to Teachers," April 10, 1979, *The Fascinating Womanhood Newsletter, 1965–1996,* Andelin Archive.
6. Andelin, Recorded interviews, Pierce City, MO, 2002, Andelin Archive.
7. The connection between evangelical religion and the Amway Corporation is made in Evelyn Pringle, "Amway, Republicans & That Old Time Religion," *Scoop Independent News,* December 14, 2004, www.scoop.co.nz/stories/HL0412/S00154 .htm.
8. Andelin, "Dreams and Interpretations That Were Dreamed by Helen Andelin in Reference to *Fascinating Womanhood* and *The Fascinating Girl,*" Andelin Archive.
9. Susan Faludi, *Backlash: The Undeclared War against American Women* (New York: Three Rivers Press, 2006).
10. Pringle, "Amway."
11. Phyllis Schlafly, *The Power of the Positive Woman* (New Rochelle, NY: Arlington House, 1977).
12. Andelin, *The Fascinating Womanhood Newsletter,* March/April 1979, Andelin Archive.
13. Andelin, "Women's Lib Leaders Admit, 'We Were Wrong about Marriage, Motherhood, Beauty and Men,'" *The Fascinating Womanhood Newsletter* 4, no. 2 (March/April 1979).
14. Elizabeth Rice Hanford, *Me? Obey Him?: The Obedient Wife and God's Way of Happiness and Blessings in the Home* (Murfreesboro, TN: Sword of the Lord Publishers, 1972), 88.
15. Hanford, *Me? Obey Him?,* 38, 64, 75.
16. Betty Friedan, *The Second Stage* (New York: Dell, 1991); Nan Robertson, "Betty Friedan Ushers in a 'Second Stage,'" *New York Times,* October 19, 1981, 1–4.
17. Robertson, "Betty Friedan," 3.
18. Patricia Sullivan, "Voice of Feminism's 'Second Wave,'" *Washington Post,* February 5, 2006, A01.
19. In her 2000 memoir *My Life So Far,* Friedan claimed that her husband, Carl, beat her. Later she clarified her statement, saying that they both used physical force against one another. See Patricia Sullivan, "Voice of Feminism's Second Wave," *Washington Post,* February 5, 2006, 2.
20. Barbara Berg, "The Quality Time Trap," *Ladies Home Journal,* July 1986, 76–81.
21. Marian Tremper, "How Not to Get Dumped on His Way up," *Cosmopolitan Magazine,* September 1986, 108–11.
22. Willard F. Harley, Jr., *His Needs, Her Needs: Building an Affair-Proof Marriage* (Grand Rapids, MI: Fleming H. Revel, 1986), 157.

23. Andelin, Recorded interviews, Pierce City, MO, 2002, Andelin Archive.

24. Nicolas Davidson, "The Myth of Feminism: Lies, Damned Lies and Statistics," *National Review*, May 19, 1989.

25. Linda Burton, Janet Dittmer, and Cheri Loveless, *What's a Smart Woman Like You Doing at Home?* (Vienna, VA: Mothers At Home Publishers, 1992), 11.

26. Burton, Dittmer, and Loveless, *What's a Smart Woman Like You Doing at Home?*, 12, 25.

27. Andelin, Recorded interviews, Pierce City, MO, 2002, and Phoenix, 2005, Andelin Archive.

28. P. B. Wilson, *Liberated through Submission: God's Design for Freedom in All Relationships* (Eugene, OR: Harvest House, 1990).

29. For more on this subject, see Rhys H. Williams, *Promise Keepers and the New Masculinity: Private Lives and Public Morality* (Lanham, MD: Lexington Books, 2001).

30. John Gray, *Men Are from Mars, Women Are from Venus: The Classic Guide to Understanding the Opposite Sex* (New York: HarperCollins, 1992) 43, 164.

31. Elisa Petrini, Senior Editor, Bantam Books, to Helen Andelin, July 26, 1994, in Correspondence, Andelin Archive.

32. Ellen Fein and Sherrie Schneider, *The Rules: Time-Tested Secrets for Capturing the Heart of Mr. Right* (New York: Warner Books, 1995), 9, 23, 127.

33. Fein and Schneider, *The Rules*, 20, 35.

34. Andelin, Recorded interviews, Pierce City, MO, 2001, Andelin Archive.

35. Andelin, Recorded interviews, Pierce City, MO, 2002, Andelin Archive. Copy of Aubrey Andelin's "Back to the Hearth" manuscript (1995), Andelin Archive.

36. Between 1997 and 2009, Andelin's website (marriagethefascinatingway.net) had more than 350,000 page hits. Note that this website then became www.fascinatingwomanhood.net, which claims 4,186 visitors.

37. Comments from visitors to www.marriagethefascinatingway.net in December 1997 and August 1999 (accessed January 2000).

38. Paul Johnson, *A History of the American People* (New York: HarperCollins, 1997), 975–76.

39. Shankar Vedantam, "Salary, Gender, and the Cost of Haggling," *Washington Post*, February 15, 2007.

40. Andelin, Recorded interviews, Phoenix, AZ, 2005, Andelin Archive.

41. Ginny Leavitt, recorded interview with author, Pierce City, MO, 2001.

42. Laura Doyle, *The Surrendered Wife: A Practical Guide to Finding Intimacy, Passion, and Peace with a Man* (New York: Simon & Schuster, 2001), 45.

43. Doyle, *Surrendered Wife*, 25, 29, 41, 46.

44. Andelin, Recorded interviews, Pierce City, MO, 2002, and Phoenix, AZ, 2005, Andelin Archive.

45. Andelin, "Marriage the Fascinating Way," March 2002, April 2002.

46. Andelin, Recorded interviews, Pierce City, MO, 2002, Andelin Archive.

47. Andelin, "Marriage the Fascinating Way," April 2000, February 2003.

48. Laura Schlessinger, *The Proper Care and Feeding of Husbands* (New York: HarperCollins, 2004), 27.

49. Schlessinger, *Care and Feeding*, 75.

50. Schlessinger, *Care and Feeding*, 5.

51. Schlessinger, *Care and Feeding*, 5, 21, 68, 75.
52. Barbara Ehrenreich and Deirdre English, *For Her Own Good: Two Centuries of the Experts' Advice to Women* (New York: Anchor Books, 2005), 357.
53. Charlotte Allen, "The Return of the Happy Housewife," *Los Angeles Times*, March 5, 2006.
54. Meghan O'Rourke, "Desperate Feminist Wives: Why Wanting Equality Makes Women Unhappy," *Slate,* http://www.slate.com/articles/news_and_politics/the _highbrow/2006/03/desperate_feminist_wives.html, March 6, 2006.
55. Andelin, Recorded interviews, Pierce City, MO, 2001, and Phoenix, 2005, Andelin Archive.
56. Andelin, "Marriage the Fascinating Way," November 2005.
57. Katha Pollitt, "Betty Friedan 1921–2006," *The Nation*, February 27, 2006.
58. Gil Swartz, "The Not-So-Perfect Wife: Why Are Men Scared to Marry?," *Elle Magazine*, October 2006.
59. Helen Andelin, *National Overhaul*, http://nationaloverhaul.com/main.htm (accessed February 7, 2011).
60. Jeffery Muhammad, Telephone interview with author, July 9, 2012.
61. Barbara De Angelis, *Secrets about Men Every Woman Should Know: Find Out How They Really Feel about Women, Relationships, Love and Sex* (New York: Random House, 2009).
62. Dr. Phil McGraw, *Love Smart: Find the One You Want—Fix the One You Got* (New York: Simon & Schuster, 2005).
63. Meghan Casserly, "Is 'Opting Out' the New American Dream for Working Women?" *ForbesWoman.com*, September 12, 2012, http://www.forbes.com/sites/ meghancasserly/2012/09/12/is-opting-out-the-new-american-dream-for-working -women.

Bibliography

ARCHIVAL SOURCES

Helen B. Andelin Archive, Special Collections, J. Willard Marriott Library, University of Utah

Allen, Gladys. "LDS and Liberated!," *Latter Day Saint Woman*, 9–13. nd.

Andelin, Helen B. "Brief Biography of Helen Berry Andelin." 1992.

———. "Brief History of F.W." nd.

———. "Brief History of Fascinating Womanhood." nd.

———. "Brief Profile of Helen Andelin and Fascinating Womanhood." nd.

———. Correspondence. 1966–Present. nd.

———. "Dreams and Interpretations That Were Dreamed by Helen Andelin in Reference to Fascinating Womanhood and the Fascinating Girl." nd.

———. "History of F.W." nd.

———. "Early Childhood." nd.

———, ed. "Fascinating Womanhood Publication for Women," 1973. Santa Barbara.

———. "Fascinating Womanhood Teacher's Lesson Guide," 1977, 1997.

———. "Fascinating Womanhood Workbook for Students, 1998."

———. Letters to Teachers. March 1966.

———. *One Small Moment between Two Eternities: Life's [Sic] History of Helen Andelin.* 2005.

———. Recorded Interviews in Pierce City Missouri and Phoenix, Arizona. 2000, 2001, 2003, 2005. Transcripts in Helen B. Andelin Archive.

———. *The Fascinating Womanhood Newsletter*, 1965–1997.

Forsyth, Dixie. "Recorded Interview, 2001."

"Teacher Applications, 1970–2005."

AUTHOR'S ARCHIVE

Andelin, Brian. Transcript of telephone conversations. Edited by Julie Neuffer. Atlanta, GA; Colombia, MO; and Washington, D.C., 2001, 2005, 2012.

Muhammad, Jeffery. Telephone interview with author. July 9, 2002. Transcript.

Neuffer, Alice. *Success Stories, 1965–1970.*

Neuffer, Julie D. *Summary of Teacher Applications, 1970–2005.* 2012.

Webb, Alice E. Recorded Interviews in Mesa, AZ, 2005. Audiotape.
Electronic Correspondence. *Papers of Helen B. Andelin*. Author's archive.

BOOKS

Andelin, Aubrey P. *Man of Steel and Velvet: A Guide to Masculine Development.*
Santa Barbara, CA: Pacific Press Publishers, 1972.
———, ed. *Fascinating Womanhood Success Stories.* Santa Barbara, CA: Pacific
Press Publishers, 1973.
———. *Fascinating Womanhood Principles Applied to Sex.* Santa Barbara, CA:
Pacific Press Publishers, n.d.
Andelin, Aubrey P., and Helen B. Andelin. "Ancestors of Aubrey Passey Andelin
and Helen Berry Andelin." Pierce City, MO, 1992.
Andelin, Helen B. *The Fascinating Girl.* Santa Barbara, CA: Pacific Press
Publishers, 1970.
———. *Fascinating Womanhood.* Santa Barbara, CA: Pacific Press Publishers, 1965.
———. *Fascinating Womanhood.* Santa Barbara, CA: Pacific Press Publishers, 1972.
———. *Fascinating Womanhood: How the Ideal Woman Awakens a Man's Deepest
Love and Tenderness.* New York: Bantam, 1990.
———. "Marriage, the Fascinating Way," 1997–2009. *Scriptural Review of Fascinat-
ing Womanhood.* Pierce City, MO: Pacific Press Publishers, 2000.
———. *The Secrets of Winning Men*, formerly *The Fascinating Girl.* Pierce City,
MO: Pacific Press Publishers, 1994.
Argov, S. *Why Men Love Bitches.* Avon, MA: Adams Media Corp., 2002.
Balmer, Randall. *American Fundamentalism: The Ideal of Femininity in Funda-
mentalism and Gender.* Edited by John Stratton Hawley. New York: Oxford
University Press, 1994.
Barry, John M. *The Great Influenza: The Epic Story of the Deadliest Plague in His-
tory.* New York: Penguin Books, 2005.
Brown, Ruth Murray. *For a "Christian America": A History of the Religious Right.*
Amherst, MA: Prometheus Books, 2002.
Burton, Linda, Janet Dittmer, and Cheri Loveless. *What's a Smart Woman Like You
Doing Home?* Rev. ed. Vienna, VA: Mothers At Home Publishers, 1992.
Collins, Gail. *America's Women: Four Hundred Years of Dolls, Drudges, Helpmates
and Heroines.* New York: William Morrow, 2003.
Conover, Pamela Johnston, and Virginia Gray. *Feminism and the New Right: Con-
flict over the American Family.* New York: Praeger, 1983.
Coontz, Stephanie. *The Way We Never Were: American Families and the Nostalgia
Trap.* New York: Basic Books, 1992.
Crittenden, Ann. *The Price of Motherhood: Why the Most Important Job in the
World Is Still the Least Valued.* 1st ed. New York: Metropolitan Books, 2001.
Crosby, Alfred W. *America's Forgotten Pandemic: The Influenza of 1918.* 2nd.
ed. New York: Cambridge University Press, 2003.
Dallos, Sally, and Rudi Dallos. *Couples, Sex and Power: The Politics of Desire.* Phil-
adelphia: Open University Press, 1997.

Davison, Jaquie. *Cancer Winner: How I Purged Myself of Melanoma*. Pierce City, MO: Pacific Press, 1977.

———. *I Am a Housewife!—A Housewife Is the Most Important Person in the World*. New York: Guild Books, 1972.

De Angelis, Barbara. *Secrets about Men Every Woman Should Know: Find Out How They Really Feel about Women, Relationships, Love and Sex*. New York: Random House, 2009.

Doyle, Laura. *The Surrendered Wife: A Practical Guide to Finding Intimacy, Passion, and Peace With a Man*. New York: Simon & Schuster, 2001.

Ehrenreich, Barbara. *The Hearts of Men: American Dreams and the Flight from Commitment*. Garden City, NY: Anchor, 1983.

Ehrenreich, Barbara, and Deirdre English. 1st ed. *For Her Own Good: 150 Years of the Experts' Advice to Women*. Garden City, NY: Anchor, 1978.

Faludi, Susan. *Backlash: The Undeclared War against American Women*. 15th anniv. ed. New York: Three Rivers Press, 2006.

Fein, Ellen, and Sherrie Schneider. *The Rules: Time-Tested Secrets for Capturing the Heart of Mr. Right*. New York: Warner Books, 1995.

Friedan, Betty. *The Feminine Mystique*. 20th anniv. ed. New York: Norton, 1983.

———. *The Feminine Mystique*. New York: Norton, 2008.

———. *The Second Stage*. New York: Dell, 1991.

Grafe, Louis M., and Loyola Grafe. *Fascinating Womanhood, or, the Art of Attracting Men: A Practical Course of Lessons in the Underlying Principles by Which Women Attract Men—Leading to the Proposal and Culminating in Marriage. In 8 Parts*. St. Louis, MO: Psychology Press, 1922.

Gray, John. *Mars and Venus Together Forever*. New York: HarperPerennial, 2005.

———. *Men Are from Mars, Women Are from Venus: The Classic Guide to Understanding the Opposite Sex*. New York: HarperCollins, 1992.

Griffith, R. Marie. *God's Daughters: Evangelical Women and the Power of Submission*. Berkeley: University of California Press, 1997.

Hanford Rice, Elizabeth. *Me? Obey Him?: The Obedient Wife and God's Way of Happiness and Blessings in the Home*. Murfreesboro, TN: Sword of the Lord Publishers, 1972.

Hanks, Maxine. *Women and Authority: Re-emerging Mormon Feminism*. Salt Lake City: Signature Books, 1992.

Harley, Willard F., Jr. *His Needs, Her Needs: Building an Affair-Proof Marriage*. Grand Rapids, MI: Fleming H. Revel, 1986.

Hatch, Nathan O. *The Democratization of American Christianity*. New Haven, CT: Yale University Press, 1989.

Hawley, J. S. *Fundamentalism and Gender*. New York: Oxford University Press, 1994.

Horowitz, Daniel. *Betty Friedan and the Making of the* Feminine Mystique: *The American Left, the Cold War, and Modern Feminism*. Amherst: University of Massachusetts Press, 1998.

Jackson, Kenneth T. *Crabgrass Frontier: The Suburbanization of the United States*. New York: Oxford University Press, 1985.

Johnson, Paul. *A History of the American People*. New York: HarperCollins, 1998.

Lerner, H. G. *The Dance of Anger: A Woman's Guide to Changing the Patterns of Intimate Relationships*. New York: Harper & Row, 1985.

Lienesch, Michael. *Redeeming America: Piety and Politics in the New Christian Right*. Chapel Hill: University of North Carolina Press, 1993.

Martin, William C. *With God on Our Side: The Rise of the Religious Right in America*. New York: Broadway Books, 2005.

McGirr, Lisa. *Suburban Warriors: The Origins of the New American Right, Politics and Society in Twentieth-Century America*. Princeton, NJ: Princeton University Press, 2001.

McGraw, Dr. Phil. *Love Smart: Find the One You Want—Fix the One You Got*. New York: Simon & Schuster, 2005.

Nuffer, Camille Cole. *Down Happiness Road*. Salt Lake City: Deseret News Press, 1944.

Peril, Lynn. *Pink Think: Becoming a Woman in Many Uneasy Lessons*. New York: W. W. Norton, 2002.

Pilzer, Paul Zane. *God Wants You to Be Rich: The Theology of Economics*. New York: Simon & Schuster, 1995.

Rhys, H. Williams. *Promise Keepers and the New Masculinity: Private Lives and Public Morality*. Lanham, MD: Lexington Books, 2001.

Robinson, Marie N. *The Power of Sexual Surrender*. Garden City, NY: Doubleday & Company, 1959.

Ruether, Rosemary Radford, and Rosemary Skinner Keller, eds. *Women and Religion in America*. 3 vols. San Francisco: Harper & Row, 1981–1986.

Schlafly, Phyllis. *The Power of the Positive Woman*. New Rochelle, NY: Arlington House Publishers, 1977.

Schlessinger, Laura. *The Proper Care and Feeding of Husbands*. 1st ed. New York: HarperCollins, 2004.

Steiner, Gilbert Y. *Constitutional Inequality: The Political Fortunes of the Equal Rights Amendment*. Washington, D.C.: Brookings Institution, 1985.

Warren, E., and A. W. Tyagi. *The Two-Income Trap: Why Middle-Class Mothers and Fathers Are Going Broke*. New York: Basic Books, 2003.

Watson, J. *How to Help Your Husband Make More Money So You Can Be a Stay-at-Home Mom*. New York: Warner Books, 2003.

Wilson, P. B. *Liberated through Submission: God's Design for Freedom in All Relationships*. Eugene, OR: Harvest House, 1990.

Woolf, Naomi. *The Beauty Myth: How Images of Beauty Are Used Against Women*. New York: Perennial, 2002.

ARTICLES

"Aubrey Andelin, An Advocate for Men." *South Bay Daily Breeze* (Torrence, CA), January 29, 1975.

"Anti-ERA Evangelist Wins Again." *Time*, July 3, 1978.

"'Childlikeness' Is Not Just Kid Stuff." *Arkansas Gazette*, March 25, 1975.

"Couple Team Up to Write Own 'Liberation' Books." *Fort Worth Star-Telegram,* October 28, 1975.

"Course Suggests Ways, Means of Making Marriages Happier." *Sunday World-Herald* (Omaha, NE), September 26, 1971.

"Demonstration Planned Sept. 30: Women's Liberation Foes Will Strike Back." *Los Angeles Times,* August 26, 1970.

"Fascinating Womanhood; Phenomenon of Our Times." *Men's Section,* June 1972.

"God Is Basis of Family Says Founder of Course." *Arizona Daily Star,* April 1975.

"How to Be Man's Ideal Woman." *Evening Herald* (Rock Hill, SC), June 25, 1975.

"Marriage: Liberation or Submission?" *Atlanta Constitution,* April 15, 1975.

"Protests against Women's Lib," *Goleta Valley Sun* (CA), April 15, 1970.

"The Sexes: Total Fascination." *Time Magazine,* March 19, 1975.

"The Start of an ERA." *Time Magazine,* January 6, 1975.

Baker, Ellen. "Author Offers Pathway to Marital Happiness." *Tulsa Daily World,* March 19, 1975.

Bauer, Cheryl. "Homemaking a Full-Time Job." *Forest Hills Journal* (Cincinnati, OH), January 9, 1979.

Benson, Helen. "New Revolution: A Means to End War of the Sexes." *Santa Barbara News-Press,* April 1970.

Berg, Barbara. "The Quality Time Trap." *Ladies Home Journal,* July 1986.

Blake, Doris. "A Day of Femininity to Challenge Libs." *New York Daily News,* September 22, 1970.

Brown, Rusty. "'Obey' is the Key Word in Her Marriage Vow." *Cleveland Ohio Press,* April 3, 1975.

Busch, Marilyn. "Marriage Not a Democracy." *Omaha World-Herald,* November 7, 1975.

Casserly, Meghan. "Is 'Opting Out' the New American Dream for Working Women?" ForbesWoman, September 12, 2012. http://www.forbes.com/sites/meghancasserly/2013/11/19/.

Chusmir, Janet. "Anti-Lib Pair: 'Be an Angel and Stay Home.'" *Miami Herald,* May 1971.

Cohen, Patricia. "Today, Some Feminists Hate the Word 'Choice.'" *New York Times,* January 15, 2006.

Cook, Joan. "She Takes a Stand Against Liberation." *New York Times,* September 28, 1970.

Davidson, Nicholas. "Lies, Damned Lies, and Statistics: The Myth of Feminism." *National Review,* May 19, 1989, 44–46.

DeView, Lucille. "Fascinate Men by Being Your Fascinating Self." *Detroit News,* May 5, 1975.

Doyle, Eleanor. "The Business of Being a Woman." *Sacramento Union,* May 1975.

Dresner, Zita Z. "Roseanne Barr: Goddess or She-Devil." *Journal of American Culture* 16, no. 2 (1993): 37–44.

Ehrenreich, Barbara. "The Wretched of the Hearth: The Undainty Feminism of Roseanne Barr." *New Republic* 202, no. 14 (April 1990): 28.

Farr, Louise. "Peddling the Pedestal: Helen Andelin's Fascinating Womanhood Course Preaches Male Supremacy and Promises to Put a 'Sparkle' Back into Marriage." *New Times*, October 17, 1975, 52.

Geiger, Joan. "Seattle Women Clash over Right to 'Slavery,' Freedom." *Seattle Times,* September 22, 1968.

Greene, Karen. "Fascinating Womanhood Author's Life Pattern." *Seattle Times,* April 12, 1975.

Heartfield, James. "There Is No Masculinity Crisis." *Genders* 35 (2002): 290–303.

Hunting, B. "He Writes about the Perfect Man." *Huntsville News* (Huntsville, AL), October 10, 1976.

Kimble, Joan. "How to Be a Man's Ideal Woman." *Los Angeles Evening Herald,* June 25, 1975.

Kopkind, Andrew. "America's New Right." *New Times*, September 30, 1977, 21–25.

Landers, Ann. "Men Vs. Women—and Vice Versa." *Reader's Digest,* March 1969, 59.

Leonard, Mary. "You Know What Your Man Wants, Girls, So Doll Up in Saran Wrap . . . and . . . and . . . Zowie!!" *National Observer*, May 17, 1975, 1–3.

Marley, David John. "Phyllis Schlafly's Battle against the ERA and Women in the Military." *Minerva: Quarterly Report on Women and the Military,* Summer 2000.

Mass, Sally Ann. "A Ministry of Womanhood." *The Press* (Loma Linda, CA), October 10, 1974.

Masters, William H., and Virginia E. Johnson. "A Warning about Books that Teach Women to Pretend." *Redbook Magazine*, March 1976, 68–74.

McClellan, Jeff. "A Lingering Influence: Top 10 BYU Professors." *BYU Magazine,* September 16, 1999.

McCoy, Joan. "You've Come a Long Way Baby? Is Woman's Place Still in the Home?" *Rocky Mountain News,* February 9, 1971.

McGinley, P. "College Education for the Housewife—A Waste?" *Ladies Home Journal*, October, 1962.

Murphy, Pat. "Local Teacher Raps Women's Lib, Backs 'Fascinating Woman' Idea." *Anaheim Bulletin* (CA), January 19, 1977.

Nolte-Watts, Carolyn. "Author Discovers New Pedestal for Women." *St. Petersburg Times* (FL), October, 1975.

Paynter, Susan. "Wives Shouldn't Work." *Seattle Post-Intelligencer,* September 16, 1968.

Pesmen, Sandra. "They Just Love Being Fascinating Women." *Chicago Daily News,* September 26, 1970.

Phinney, Frances. "Understanding Men Leads to Happier Marriage." *Everett Herald* (WA), October 1968.

Pringle, Evelyn. "Amway, Republicans & That Old Time Religion." *Scoop Independent News*, December 14, 2004, http://www.scoop.co.nz/stories/HL0412/S00154.htm.

Pollitt, Katha. "Betty Friedan, 1921–2006." *Nation,* February 27, 2006.

Quinn, Sally. "Marabel Morgan: Total Woman or Total Fool?" *St. Petersburg Times* (FL), February 12, 1987.

Rethlake, Kathy. "How to Keep Your Man Happy." *Santa Monica Evening Outlook*, February 12, 1976.

Ricchiardi, Sherry. "She Says Male Supremacy Is Key to Happy Marriage." *Des Moines Sunday Register*, November 16, 1975.

Risinger, Elaine. "'Fascinating' Class Aids Marriages." *West Orange Suburban Group* (Orange, CA), March 23–24, 1977.

Robertson, Nan. "Betty Friedan Ushers in a 'Second Stage.'" *New York Times*, October 19, 1981, 1–4.

Root, E. Merrill. "Feminine Woman: The Lady Is a Conservative." *American Opinion,* June 1971.

Ryan, Linda. "Here's How to Win Hubby's Love and Devotion." *Northwest Omaha Sun,* November 25, 1971.

Sabo, Pat. "Stormy Marriage Changes to Happy Home Life." *Mesa Tribune* (AZ), June 14, 1969.

Schwartz, Gil. "The Not-So-Perfect Wife." *Elle*, October 2006, 158–60.

Sills, Judith. "The Surprising Key to a Happy Marriage." *Family Circle Magazine*, September 2000.

Smith, Dave. "The Making of a Nonliberationist: Fascinating Woman and the Big Old Meanie." *Los Angeles Times*, December 5, 1975.

Smith, Elaine, and Sheila Kritchman. "Happy Wives Are Helpless Wives?" *North Central Outlook* (Seattle, WA), September 26, 1968.

Smith, Helen C. "Marriage Can Be Fascinating Business." *Natches Democrat*, October 1975.

Stallings, Stephanie. "She's Fascinated with Ideal Womanhood." *News and Observer* (Raleigh, NC), November 4, 1975.

Strozier, G. "Make Him Feel Like a Man." *Detroit Free Press*, April 10, 1975.

Syfers, Judy. "Why I Want a Wife." On *CWLU herstory project* website. 1971. http://www.cwluherstory.org/why-i-want-a-wife.html (accessed February 11, 2014).

Sullivan, Patricia. "Voice of Feminism's 'Second Wave.'" *Washington Post*, February 5, 2006, A01.

Tompkins, Walker A. "Santa Barbaran Challenges Leaders of the 'New Morality' on TV Shows." *Santa Barbara News-Press*, February 13, 1971.

Tremper, Marian, "How Not to Get Dumped on His Way Up." *Cosmopolitan Magazine*, September 1986.

Tyson, Jean. "Men's Role Not Superior: Liberationists Are Unhappy." *Atlanta Journal,* September 16, 1970.

———. "He's Fascinating, Too: Mrs. Andelin's Husband, Aubrey, Shows the Velvet." *Atlanta Journal*, October 7, 1975.

Vedantam, Shankar. "Salary, Gender and the Cost of Haggling." *Washington Post*, February 15, 2007.

Viets, Elaine. "What More Could a Man Want?" *St. Louis Post-Dispatch*, July 20, 1975.

Warren, Virginia Lee. "In This Day of Liberation, They Study How to Please Their Men." *New York Times Magazine*, June 28, 1975.

Weeks, John. "Womanhood Can Be Fascinating." *Sun-Telegram* (San Bernardino, CA), October 11, 1974.

Welter, Barbara. "The Cult of True Womanhood: 1820–1860." *American Quarterly* 18 (Summer 1966): 151–74.

White, Mary Lynn. "Fewer Problems When Man Heads House." *Cincinnati Post*, June 21, 1971.

Wolverton, Joan. "Helen Andelin: A Counter to 'Lib.'" *Seattle Times*, February 18, 1971.

Yeates, Marian. "Why Shouldn't Mormon Women Want *This* Priesthood?" In *Women and Authority: Re-Emerging Mormon Feminism*, ed. Maxine Hanks. Salt Lake City: Signature Books, 1992, 353–64. http://signaturebookslibrary.org/?p=840 (accessed February 10, 2014).

Zager, Corrine. "Wife No Longer Neglected." *North Central Outlook* (Seattle, WA), October 10, 1968.

Index